I0483689

Principles Of Decorative Design

BY

Christopher Dresser,
Ph.D., F.L.S., F.E.B.S., etc.;

Author of "The Art of Decorative Design," "Unity in Variety,"
etc.

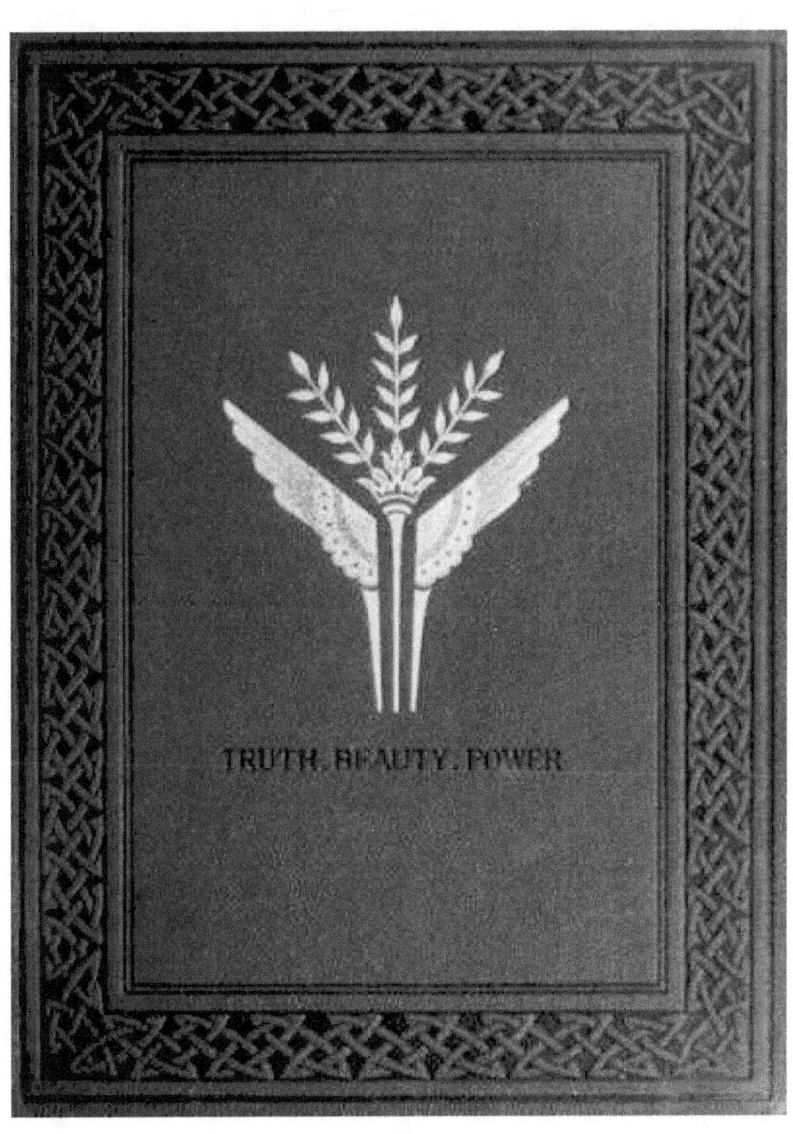

TRUTH. BEAUTY. POWER

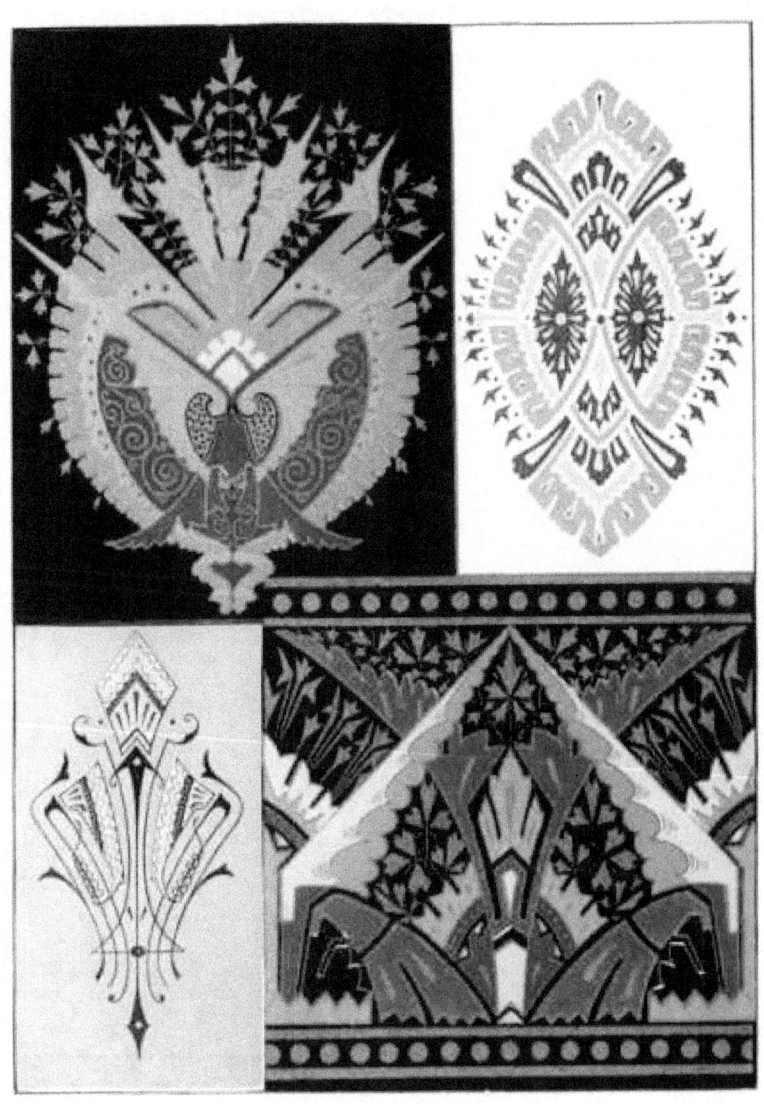

PREFACE.

Y object in writing this work has been that of aiding in the art-education of those who seek a knowledge of ornament as applied to our industrial manufactures.

I have not attempted the production of a pretty book, but have aimed at giving what knowledge I possess upon the subjects treated of, in a simple and intelligible manner. I have attempted simply to instruct.

The substance of the present work was first published as a series of lessons in the *Technical Educator*. These lessons are now collected into a work, and have been carefully revised; a few new illustrations have been inserted, and a final chapter added.

As the substance of this work was written as a series of lessons for the *Technical Educator*, I need not say that the book is addressed to working men, for the whole of the lessons in that publication have been prepared especially for those noble fellows who, through want of early opportunity, have been without the advantages of education, but who have the praiseworthy courage to educate themselves in later life, when the value of knowledge has become apparent to them.

That the lessons as given in the *Technical Educator* have not been written wholly in vain I already know, for shortly before I had completed this revision of them, I had the opportunity of visiting a provincial town hall which I had heard was being decorated, and was pleasingly surprised to see decoration of considerable merit, and evidences that much of what I saw had resulted from a consideration of my articles in the *Technical Educator*. The artist engaged upon the work, although having suffered the disadvantage of apprenticeship to a butcher, has established himself as a decorator while still a young man; and from the manifestation of ability which he has already given, I hope for a brighter future for one who, as a working man, must have studied hard. If these lessons as now collected into a work should lead to the development of the art-germs which doubtless lie dormant in other working men, the object which I have sought to attain in writing and collecting these together will have been accomplished.

Tower Cressy, Notting Hill,
London, W.

Principles of Design.

CHAPTER I.

DIVISION I.

There are many handicrafts in which a knowledge of the true principles of ornamentation is almost essential to success, and there are few in which a knowledge of decorative laws cannot be utilised. The man who can form a bowl or a vase well is an artist, and so is the man who can make a beautiful chair or table. These are truths; but the converse of these facts is also true; for if a man be not an artist he cannot form an elegant bowl, nor make a beautiful chair.

At the very outset we must recognise the fact that the beautiful has a commercial or money value. We may even say that art can lend to an object a value greater than that of the material of which it consists, even when the object be formed of precious matter, as of rare marbles, scarce woods, or silver or gold.

This being the case, it follows that the workman who can endow his productions with those qualities or beauties which give value to his works, must be more useful to his employer than the man who produces objects devoid of such beauty, and his time must be of higher value than that of his less skilful companion. If a man, who has been born and brought up as a "son of toil," has that laudable ambition which causes him to seek to rise above his fellows by fairly becoming their superior, I would say to him that I know of no means of his so readily doing so, as by his acquainting himself with the laws of beauty, and studying till he learns to perceive the difference between the beautiful and the ugly, the graceful and the deformed, the refined and the coarse. To perceive delicate beauties is not by any means an easy task to those who have not devoted themselves to the consideration of the beautiful for a long period of time, and of this be assured, that what now appears to you to be beautiful, you may shortly regard as less so, and what now fails to attract you, may ultimately become charming to your eye. In your study of the beautiful, do not be led away by the false judgment of ignorant persons who may suppose themselves possessed of good taste. It is common to assume that women have better taste than men, and some women seem to consider themselves the possessors of even authoritative taste from which there can be no appeal. They may be right, only we must be pardoned for not accepting such authority, for should there be any over-estimation of the accuracy of this good taste, serious loss of progress in art-judgment might result.

It may be taken as an invariable truth that knowledge, and knowledge alone, can enable us to form an accurate judgment respecting the beauty or want of beauty of an object, and he who has the greater knowledge of art can judge best of the ornamental qualities of an object. He who would judge rightly of art-works must have knowledge. Let him who would judge of beauty apply himself, then, to earnest study, for thereby he shall have wisdom, and by his wise reasonings he will be led to perceive beauty, and thus have opened to him a new source of pleasure.

Art-knowledge is of value to the individual and to the country at large. To the individual it is riches and wealth, and to the nation it saves impoverishment. Take, for example, clay as a natural material: in the hands of one man this material becomes flower-pots, worth eighteen-pence a "cast" (a number varying from sixty to twelve according to size); in the hands of another it becomes a tazza, or a vase, worth five pounds, or perhaps fifty. It is the art which gives the value, and not the material. To the nation it saves impoverishment.

A wise policy induces a country to draw to itself all the wealth that it can, without parting with more of its natural material than is absolutely necessary. If for every pound of clay that a nation parts with, it can draw to itself that amount of gold which we value at five pounds sterling, it is obviously better thus to part with but little material and yet secure wealth, than it is to part with the material at a low rate either in its native condition, or worked into coarse vessels, thereby rendering a great impoverishment of the native resources of the country necessary in order to its wealth.

Men of the lowest degree of intelligence can dig clay, iron, or copper, or quarry stone; but these materials, if bearing the impress of mind, are ennobled and rendered valuable, and the more strongly the material is marked with this ennobling impress the more valuable it becomes.

I must qualify my last statement, for there are possible cases in which the impress of mind may degrade rather than exalt, and take from rather than enhance, the value of a material. To ennoble, the mind must be noble; if debased, it can only debase. Let the mind be refined and pure, and the more fully it impresses itself upon a material, the more lovely does the material become, for thereby it has received the impress of refinement and purity; but if the mind be debased and impure, the more does the matter to which its nature is transmitted become degraded. Let me have a simple mass of clay as a candle-holder rather than the earthen candlestick which only presents such a form as is the natural outgoing of a degraded mind.

There is another reason why the material of which beautiful objects are formed should be of little intrinsic value besides that arising out of a consideration of the exhaustion of the country, and this will lead us to see that it is desirable in all cases to form beautiful objects as far as possible of an inexpensive material. Clay, wood, iron, stone, are materials which may be fashioned into beautiful forms, but beware of silver, and of gold, and of precious stones. The most fragile material often endures for a long period of time, while the almost incorrosible silver and gold rarely escape the ruthless hand of the destroyer. "Beautiful though gold and silver are, and worthy, even though they were the commonest of things, to be fashioned into the most exquisite devices, their money value makes them a perilous material for works of art. How many of the choicest relics of antiquity are lost to us, because they tempted the thief to steal them, and then to hide his theft by melting them! How many unique designs in gold and silver have the vicissitudes of war reduced in fierce haste into money-changers' nuggets! Where are Benvenuto Cellini's vases, Lorenzo Ghiberti's cups, or the silver lamps of Ghirlandajo? Gone almost as completely as Aaron's golden pot of manna, of which, for another reason than that which kept St. Paul silent, 'we cannot now speak particularly.' Nor is it only because this is a world 'where thieves break through and steal' that the fine gold becomes dim and the silver perishes. This, too, is a world where 'love is strong as death;' and what has not love—love of family, love of brother, love of child, love of lover—prompted man and woman to do with the costliest things, when they could be exchanged as mere bullion for the lives of those who were beloved?"[1] Workmen! it is fortunate for us that the best vehicles for art are the least costly materials.

Having made these general remarks, I may explain to my readers what I am about to attempt in the little work which I have now commenced. My primary aim will be to bring about refinement of mind in all who may accompany me through my studies, so that they may individually be enabled to judge correctly of the nature of any decorated object, and enjoy its beauties—should it present any—and detect its faults, if such be present. This refinement I shall attempt to bring about by presenting to the mind considerations which it must digest and assimilate, so that its new formations, if I may thus speak, may be of knowledge. We shall carefully consider certain general principles, which are either common to all fine arts or govern the production or arrangement of ornamental forms: then we shall notice the laws which regulate the combination of colours, and the application of colours to objects; after which we shall review our various art-manufactures, and consider art as associated with the manufacturing industries. We shall thus be led to consider furniture, earthenware, table and window glass, wall decorations, carpets, floor cloths, window-hangings, dress fabrics, works in silver and gold, hardware, and whatever is a combination of art and manufacture. I shall address myself,

---

[1] From a lecture by the late Professor George Wilson, of Edinburgh.

then, to the carpenter, the cabinet-maker, potter, glass-blower, paper-stainer, weaver and dyer, silversmith, blacksmith, gas-finisher, designer, and all who are in any way engaged in the production of art-objects.

But before we commence our regular work, let me say that without laborious study no satisfactory progress can be made. Labour is the means whereby we raise ourselves above our fellows; labour is the means by which we arrive at affluence. Think not that there is a royal road to success—the road is through toil. Deceive not yourself with the idea that you were born a genius—that you were born an artist. If you are endowed with a love for art, remember that it is by labour alone that you can get such knowledge as will enable you to present your art-ideas in a manner acceptable to refined and educated people. Be content, then, to labour. In the case of an individual, success appears to me to depend upon the time which he devotes to the study of that which he desires to master. One man works six hours a day; another works eighteen. One has three days in one; and what is the natural result? Simply this—that the one who works the eighteen hours progresses with three times the rapidity of the one who only works six hours. It is true that individuals differ in mental capacity, but my experience has led me to believe that those who work the hardest almost invariably succeed the best.

While I write, I have in my mind's eye one or two on whom Nature appeared to have lavishly bestowed art-gifts; yet these have made but little progress in life. I see, as it were, before me others who were less gifted by Nature, but who industriously persevered in their studies, and were content to labour for success; and these have achieved positions which the natural genius has failed even to approach. Workmen! I am a worker, and a believer in the efficacy of work.

We will commence our systematic course by observing that good ornament—good decorations of any character, have qualities which appeal to the educated, but are silent to the ignorant, and that these qualities make utterance of interesting facts; but before we can rightly understand what I may term the hidden utterance of ornament, we must inquire into the general revelation which the ornament of any particular people, or of any historic age, makes to us, and also the utterances of individual forms.

As an illustration of my meaning, let us take the ornament produced by the Egyptians. In order to see this it may be necessary that we visit a museum—say the British Museum—where we search out the mummy-cases; but as most provincial museums boast one or more mummy-cases, we are almost certain to find in the leading country towns illustrations that will serve our present purpose. On a mummy-case you may find a singular ornament, which is a conventional drawing of the Egyptian lotus, or blue water-lily [2] (see Figs. 1, 2, 3), and in all probability you will find this ornamental device repeated over and over again on the one mummy-case. Notice this peculiarity of the drawing of the lotus—a peculiarity common to Egyptian ornaments—that there is a severity, a rigidity of line, a sort of sternness about

---

[2] This can be seen growing in the water-tanks in the Kew Gardens conservatories, and in the Crystal Palace at Sydenham.

it. This rigidity or severity of drawing is a great peculiarity or characteristic of Egyptian drawing. But mark! with this severity there is always coupled an amount of dignity, and in some cases this dignity is very apparent. Length of line, firmness of drawing, severity of form, and subtlety of curve are the great characteristics of Egyptian ornamentation.

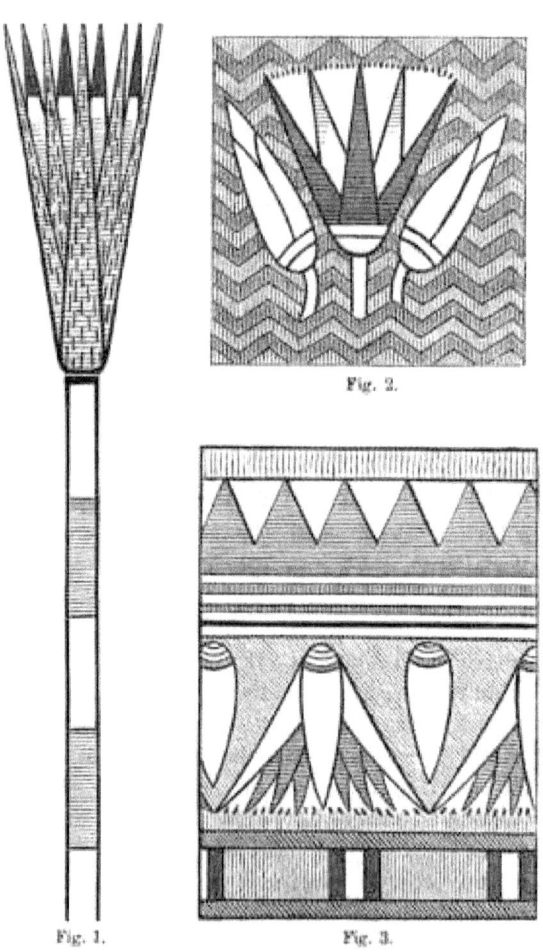

Fig. 1.

Fig. 2.

Fig. 3.

What does all this express? It expresses the character of the people who created the ornaments. The ornaments of the ancient Egyptians were all ordered by the priesthood, amongst whom the learning of this people was stored. The priests were the dictators to the people not only of religion, but of the forms which their ornaments were to assume. Mark, then, the expression of the severity of character and dignified bearing of the priesthood: in the very drawing of a simple flower we have presented to us the character of the men who brought about its production. But this is only what we are in the constant habit of witnessing. A man of knowledge writes with power and force; while the man of wavering opinions writes timidly and with feebleness. The force of the one character (which character has been made forcible by knowledge) and the weakness of the other is manifested by his written words. So it is with ornaments: power or feebleness of character is manifest by the forms produced.

The Egyptians were a severe people; they were hard task-masters. When a great work had to be performed, a number of slaves were selected for the work, and a portion of food allotted to each, which was to last till the work was completed; and if the work was not finished when the food was consumed, the slaves perished. We do not wonder at the severity of Egyptian drawing. But the Egyptians were a noble people—noble in knowledge of the arts, noble in the erection of vast and massive buildings, noble in the greatness of their power. Hence we have nobility of drawing—power and dignity mingled with severity in every ornamental form which they produced.

We have thus noticed the general utterance or expression of Egyptian drawing; but what specific communication does this particular lotus make? Most of the ornaments of the Egyptians—whether the adornments of sarcophagi, of water-vessels, or mere charms to be worn pendent from the neck—were symbols of some truth or dogma inculcated by the priests. Hence Egyptian ornament is said to be symbolic.

The fertility of the Nile valley was chiefly due to the river annually overflowing its banks. In spreading over the land, the water carried with it a quantity of rich alluvial earth, which gave fecundity to the country on which it was deposited. When the water which had overspread the surrounding land had nearly subsided, the corn which was to produce the harvest was set by being cast upon the retiring water, through which it sank into the rich alluvial earth. The water being now well-nigh within the river-banks, the first flower that sprang up was the lotus. This flower was to the Egyptians the harbinger of coming plenty, for it symbolised the springing forth of the wheat. It was the first flower of spring, or their primrose (first rose). The priesthood, perceiving the interest with which this flower was viewed, and the watchfulness manifested for its appearance, taught that in it abode a god, and that it must be worshipped. The acknowledgment of this flower as a fit and primary object of worship caused it to be delineated on the mummy-cases, and sarcophagi, and on all sacred edifices.

We shall have frequent occasion, while considering decorative art, to notice symbolic forms; but we must not forget the fact that all good ornaments make utterance. Let us in all cases, when beholding them, give ear to their teachings!

Egyptian ornament is so full of forms which have interesting significance that I cannot forbear giving one other illustration; and of this I am sure, that not only does a knowledge of the intention of each form employed in a decorative scheme cause the beholder to receive a special amount of pleasure when viewing it, but also that without such knowledge no one can rightly judge of the nature of any ornamental work.

There is a device in Egyptian ornament which the most casual observer cannot have failed to notice; it is what is termed the "winged globe," and consists of a small ball or globe, immediately at the sides of which are two asps, and from which extend two wings, each wing being in length about five to eight times that of the diameter of the ball (Fig. 4). The drawing of this device is very grand. The force with which the wings are delineated well represents the powerful character of the protection which the kingdom of Egypt afforded, and which was symbolised by the extended and overshadowing pinions.

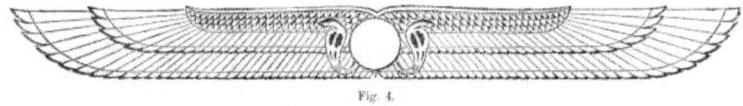

Fig. 4.

I know of few instances where forms of an ornamental character have been combined in a manner either more quaint or more interesting than in the example before us. The composition presents a charm that few ornaments do, and is worthy of careful consideration. But this ornament derives a very special and unusual interest when we consider its purpose, the blow which was once aimed at it, and the shock which its producers must have received, upon finding it powerless to act as they had taught, if not believed, it would.

The priesthood instructed the people that this was the symbol of protection, and that it so effectually appealed to the preserving spirits that no evil could enter where it was portrayed. With the view of giving a secure protection to the inmates of Egyptian dwellings, this device, or symbol of protection, was ordered to be placed on the lintel (the post over the door) of every building of the Egyptians, whether residence or temple.

It was to nullify this symbol, and to show the vain character of the Egyptian gods, that Moses was commanded to have the blood of the lamb slain at the passover placed upon the lintel, in the very position of this winged globe. It was also enjoined as a further duty that the blood be sprinkled on the door-post; but this was merely a new duty, tending further to show that even in position, as well as in nature, this winged globe was powerless to secure protection. This device, then, is of special interest, both as a symbolic ornament and as throwing light on Scripture history.

Besides the two ornamental forms mentioned—*i.e.*, the lotus and the winged globe—we might notice many others also of great interest, but our space will not enable us to do so; further information may, however, be got from the South Kensington Museum library,[3] where several interesting works on Egyptian ornament may be seen;—from the "Grammar of Ornament" by Mr. Owen Jones,—the works on Egypt by Sir Gardiner Wilkinson; and, especially,—by a visit to the Egyptian Court of the Crystal Palace at Sydenham, and by a

---

[3] Any person can have admission to the South Kensington Museum Art library and its Educational library, for a week, by payment of sixpence.

careful perusal of the hand-book to that court.[4] Much might also be said respecting Egyptian architecture, but on this we can say little here; yet, as the columns of the temples are of a very ornamental character, we may notice that in most cases they were formed of a bundle of papyrus[5] stems bound together by thongs or straps—the heads of the plant forming the capital of the column, and the stems the shaft (Fig. 5). In some cases the lotus was substituted for the papyrus; and in other instances the palm-leaf was used in a similar way; these modifications can be seen in the Egyptian Court at Sydenham with great advantage, and many varieties of form resulting from the use of the one plant, as of the papyrus, may also there be observed.

We have here an opportunity of noticing how the mode of building, however simple or primitive in character, first employed by a nation may become embodied in its ultimate architecture; for, undoubtedly, the rude houses first erected in Egypt were formed largely of bundles of the papyrus, which were gathered from the river-side—for wood was rare in Egypt—and, ultimately, when buildings were formed of stone, an attempt was made at imitating in the new material the form which the old reeds presented. But mark, the

---

[4] A hand-book to each of the historic courts erected in the Sydenham Palace was prepared at the time the courts were built. These are still to be got in the Literary department, in the north-east gallery of the building. They are all worthy of careful study.

[5] The papyrus was the plant from which Egyptian paper was made. It was also the bulrush of the Scriptures, in which the infant Moses was found.

imitation was no gross copy of the original work, but a well-considered and perfectly idealised work, substituting for the bundle of reeds a work having the true architectural qualities of a noble-looking and useful column. We must now pass from the ornament of the Egyptians to that of the Greeks, and here we meet with decorative forms having a different object and different aim from those already considered.

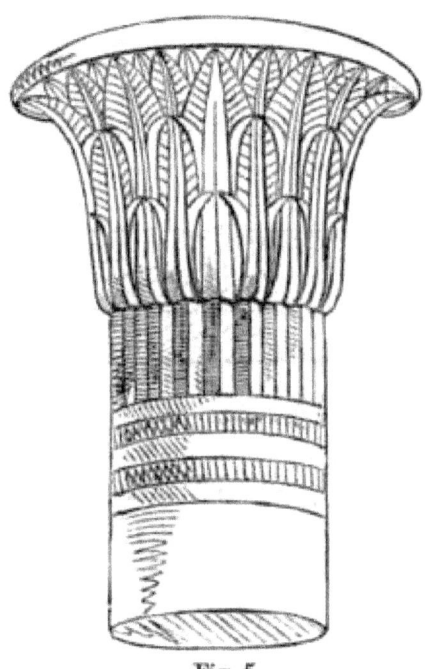

Fig. 5.

Egyptian ornament was symbolical in character. Its individual forms had specific meanings—the purport of each shape being taught by the priests—but we find no such thing as symbolism in Greek decoration. The Greeks were a refined people, who sought not to express their power by their art-works so much as their refinement. Before the mental eye they always had a perfect ideal, and their most earnest efforts were made at the realisation of the perfections of the mental conception of absolute refinement. In one respect the Greeks resembled the Egyptians, for they rarely created new forms. When once a form became sacred to the Egyptians, it could not be altered; but with the Greeks, while bound by no such law, the love of old forms was great; yet the Greeks did not seek simply to reproduce what they had before created, but laboured hard to improve and refine what they had before done; and even through succeeding centuries they worked at the refinement of simple forms and ornamental compositions, which have become characteristic of them as a people.

The general expression of Greek art is that of refinement, and the manner in which the delicately cultivated taste of some of the Greeks is expressed by their ornaments is astonishing. One decorative device, which we term the Greek Anthemion, may be regarded as their principal ornament—(the original ornamental composition by one of my pupils, Fig. 6, consists primarily of three anthemions)—and the variety of refined forms in which it appears is most interesting.

But it must not be thought that the Greek ornaments and architectural forms present nothing but refinement made manifest in form, for this is not the case. Great as is the refinement of some of these forms, we yet notice that they speak of more than the perfected taste of their producers, for they reveal to us this fact—that their creators had great knowledge of natural forces and the laws by which natural forces are governed. This becomes apparent in a marked degree when we inquire into the manner in which they arranged the proportion of the various parts of their works to the whole, and especially by a consideration of the subtle nature of the curves which they employed both in architectural members and in decorative forms; but into this we must not now inquire. Yet, by way of throwing some faint light upon the manner in which knowledge is embodied in Greek forms, I may refer to the Doric column, such as was employed in the Parthenon at Athens[6] (Fig. 7). The idea presented by this column is that of energetic upward growth which has come in contact with some superposed mass, the weight of which presses upon the column from above, while the energy of the upward growth causes the column to appear fully equal to the task of supporting the superincumbent structure. Mark this—that by pressure from above, or weight, the shaft of the column is distended, or bent out, about one-third of the distance from its base to its apex (just where this distension would occur, were the column formed of a slightly plastic material), and yet this distension of the shaft is not such as to give any idea of weakness, for the column appears to rise with the energy of such vigorous life as to be more than able to bear the weight which it has to sustain.

Mark also the singularly delicate curve of the capital of the column, which appears as a slightly plastic cushion intervening between the shaft and the superincumbent mass which it has to support. The delicacy and refinement of form presented by this capital is perhaps greater than that of any other with which we are acquainted.

---

[6] A capital, and portion of the shaft, of one of these columns are to be seen in the British Museum Sculpture room, and a cast of the same at the Crystal Palace, Sydenham. This Doric column is employed in the Greek Court of the Crystal Palace.

The same principle of life and energy coming in contact with resistance or pressure from above is constantly met with in the enrichments of Greek cornices and mouldings; but having called attention to the fact, I must leave the student to observe, and think upon, these interesting subjects for himself. Let me, however, say that there are few classic buildings in England which will aid the learner in his researches; there is but little poetry in our architectural buildings, and but little refinement in the forms of the parts, especially in our classic buildings; and, added to this, Greek art without Greek colouring is dead, being almost as the marble statue to the living form. For the purposes of my readers, the Greek Court at the Crystal Palace will be the best example for study.

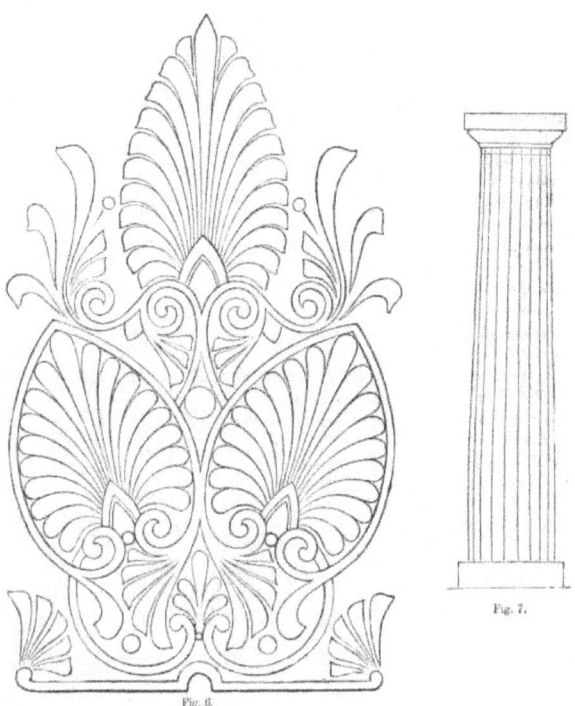

Fig. 6.

Fig. 7.

I might now review Roman ornament, and show that in the hour of pride the materials of which the Roman works were formed were considered, rather than the shapes which they assumed; and how we thus get little worthy of praise from the all-conquering Romans—how the sunny climate and religious superstitions of the East called forth the gorgeous and beautiful developments of art which have existed, or still exist, with the Persians, Indians, Turks, Moors, Chinese, and Japanese; but I have not space to do so; yet all the forms of ornament which these people have created are worthy of the most careful and exhaustive consideration, as they present art-qualities of the highest kind. I know of no ornament more intricately beautiful and mingled than the Persian—no geometrical strapwork, or systems of interlacing lines, so rich as those of the Moors (the Alhambraic)—no fabrics so gorgeous as those of India—none so quaintly harmonious as those of China; and Japan can supply the world with the most beautiful domestic articles that we can anywhere procure.

We must pass on, however, to what we may term Christian art, or that development of ornament which had its rise with the Christian religion, and has associated itself in a special manner with Christianity.

Neither the Egyptians nor early Greeks appear to have used the arch structurally in their buildings; the Romans, however, had the round arch as a primary structural element. This round arch was also used by the Byzantines, and amongst their ornaments we find those combinations of circles, or parts of circles, which so constantly recur in later times in Gothic architecture and Gothic ornament. Norman buildings, again, show us the round arch, and present us with such intersected arcs as would naturally suggest the pointed arch of later times, with which came the full development of Gothic or Christian architecture and ornamentation. There was a very fine and marvellously clever development of decorative art, enthusiastically worked at by the Christian monks of the seventh and eighth centuries, called Celtic, of which we have many beautiful examples in Professor Westwood's great work on early illuminated manuscripts; but what is generally understood by Christian or Gothic art had its finest development about the thirteenth century.

Gothic ornament, like the Egyptian, is essentially symbolic. Its forms have in many instances specific significance. Thus the common equilateral triangle is in some cases used to symbolise the Holy Trinity; so are the two entwined triangles. But there are many other symbols employed in Gothic ornament which set forth the mystery of the Unity of the Trinity. Thus in Fig. 8 we have three interlaced circles, which beautifully express the eternal Unity of the Holy Trinity, for the circle alone symbolises eternity, being without beginning and without end, and the three parts point to the Three Persons of the Godhead. A very curious and clever symbol of the Trinity is portrayed in Fig. 9, where three faces are so combined as to form an ornamental figure.

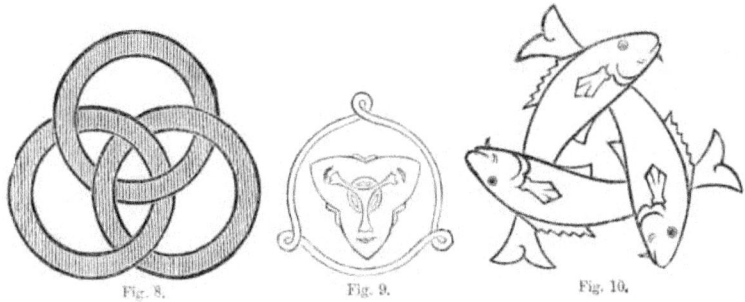

Fig. 8.   Fig. 9.   Fig. 10.

Baptism under the immediate sanction of the Divine Trinity was represented by three fishes placed together in the manner of a triangle (Fig. 10); but so numerous were Christian symbols after the ninth century, that to enumerate them merely would occupy much space. Every trefoil symbolised the Holy Trinity, every quatrefoil the four evangelists, every cross the Crucifixion, or the martyrdom of some saint. And into Gothic ornamentation the chalice, the crown of thorns, the dice, the sop, the hammer and nails, the flagellum, and other symbols of our Lord's passion have entered. But, besides these, we have more purely architectural forms making gentle utterance: the church spire points heavenwards, and the long lines of the clustered columns of the cathedral direct the thoughts upwards to heaven and to God.

Gothic ornament, having passed from its purity towards undue elaboration, began to lose its hold on the people for whom it was created, and the form of religion with which it had long been associated had become old, when the great overthrow of old traditions and usages occurred, commonly called the Reformation. With the reformation of religion came a revival of classic learning, and a general diffusion of knowledge, and thus the immediate necessity for art-symbols was passing away, it being especially to an unlettered people that an extended system of symbolism appeals. With this revival of classic learning came the investigation of classic remains—the exploration of Greek and Roman ruins; and while this was going on, a dislike to whatever had been associated with the old form of religion had sprung up, which dislike turned to hate as the struggle advanced, till the feeling against Gothic architecture and ornament became so strong that anything was preferred to it. Now arose Renaissance architecture and ornament (revival work), which was based on the Roman remains, but was yet remoulded, or formed anew; so that the ornament of the Renaissance is not Roman ornament, but a new decorative scheme, of the same genus as that of the Roman. Here, however, all my sympathies end. I confess that all Renaissance ornament, whether developed under the soft sky of Italy (Italian ornament), in more northerly France (French Renaissance), or on our own soil (Elizabethan, or English Renaissance), fails to awaken any feeling of sympathy in my breast; and that it, on the contrary, chills and repels me. I enjoy the power and vigour of Egyptian ornament, the refinement of the Greek, the gorgeousness of the Alhambraic, the richness of the Persian and Indian, the quaintness of the Chinese and Japanese, the simple honesty and boldness of the Gothic; but with the coarse Assyrian, the haughty Roman, and the cold Renaissance, I have no kindred feeling—no sympathy. They strike notes which have no chords in my nature: hence from them I instinctively fly. I must be pardoned for this my feeling by those who differ from me in judgment, but my continued studies of these styles only separate me further from them in feeling.

It will be said that in my writings I mingle together ornament and architecture, and that my sphere is ornament, and not building. I cannot separate the two. The material at command, the religion of the people, and the climate have, to a great extent, determined the character of the architecture of all ages and nations; but they have, to the same extent, determined the nature of the ornamentation of the edifices raised. Ornament always has arisen out of architecture, or been a mere reflex of the art-principles of the building decorated. We cannot rightly consider ornament without architecture; but I will promise to take no further notice of architecture than is absolutely necessary to the proper understanding of our subject.

DIVISION II.

In my previous remarks I have attempted to set forth some of the first principles of ornament, and to call attention to the purport or intention of certain of the leading historic styles, and the manner in which they make utterance to us of the faith or sentiments of their producers.

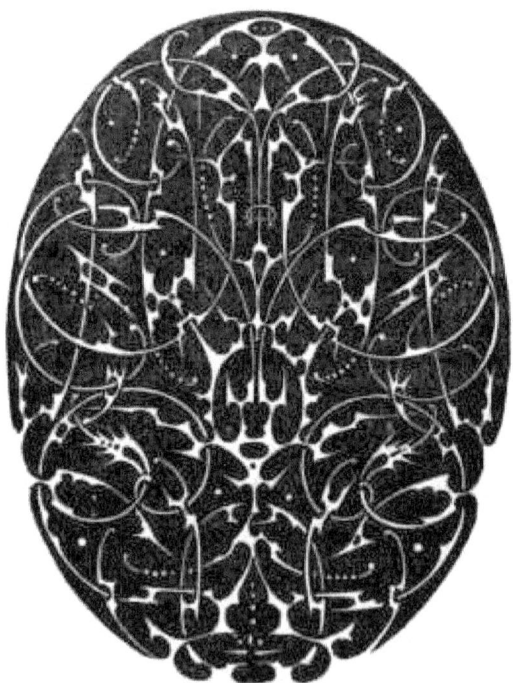

Fig. 11.

But there are other utterances of ornament, and other general expressions which decorative forms convey to the mind. Thus sharp, angular, or spiny forms are more or less exciting (Fig. 11); while bold and broad forms are soothing, or tend to give repose.

Sharp or angular forms, where combined in ornament, act upon the senses much as racy and pointed sayings do. Thus "cut" or angular glass, spinose metal-work, as the pointed foliage of some wrought-iron gates, and other works in which there is a prevalence of angles and points, so act upon the mind as to stimulate it, and thus produce an effect opposite to repose; while "breadth" of form and "largeness" of treatment induce tranquillity and meditation.

Nothing can be more important to the ornamentist than the scientific study of art. The metaphysical inquiry into cause and effect, as relating to decorative ideas, is very important— indeed, all-important—to the true decorator. He must constantly ask himself what effect such and such forms have upon the mind—which effects are soothing, which cheerful, which melancholy, which rich, which ethereal, which gorgeous, which solid, which graceful, which lovable, and so on; and in order to do this he must separate the various elements of ornamental composition, and consider these apart, so as to be sure that he is not mistaken as to what affects the mind in any particular manner, and he must then combine these elements in various proportions, and consider the effects of the various combinations on his own mind and that of others, and thus he will discover what will enable him to so act on the senses as to induce effects such as he may desire to produce.

Are we to decorate a dining-room, let the decoration give the sense of richness; a drawing-room, let it give cheerfulness; a library, let it give worth; a bed-room, repose; but glitter must never occur in large quantities, for that which excites can only be sparingly indulged in—if too freely employed, it gives the sense of vulgarity.

In this chapter I have to speak primarily of *Truth*, *Beauty*, and *Power*. Long since I was so fully impressed with the idea that true art-principles are so perfectly manifested by these three words, that I embodied them in an ornamental device which I painted on my study door, so that all who entered might learn the principles which I sought to manifest in my works.

There can be morality or immorality in art, the utterance of truth or of falsehood; and by his art the ornamentist may exalt or debase a nation.

Truth.—How noble, how beautiful; how righteous to utter it; and how debasing is falsehood; yet we see falsehood preferred to truth—that which debases to that which exalts, in art as well as morals; and I fear that there is almost as much that is false, degrading, and untrue in my beautiful art as there is of the noble, righteous, and exalting, although art should only be practised by ennobling hands. It is this grovelling art, this so-called ornamentation, which tends to debase rather than exalt, to degrade rather than make noble, to foster a lie rather than utter truth, which brings about the abasement of our calling, and causes our art to fail in many instances in laying hold of, and clinging to, the affections of the noble and the great. Ornamentation is in the highest sense of the word a Fine Art; there is no art more noble, none more exalted. It can cheer the sorrowing; it can soothe the troubled; it can enhance the joys of those who make merry; it can inculcate the doctrine of truth; it can refine, elevate, purify, and point onward and upward to heaven and to God. It is a fine art, for it embodies and expresses the feelings of the soul of man—that inward spirit which was breathed by the Creator into the lifeless clay as the image of his life—however noble, pure, or holy.

This being the case, those who ignore decoration cast aside a source of refinement, and deprive themselves of what may induce their elevation in virtue and morals. Such a neglect on the part of those who can afford luxuries would be highly censurable, were it not that the professors of the art are for the most part false pretenders, knowing not what they practise, and men ignorant of the power which they hold in their hands. The true artist is a rare creature; he is often unknown, frequently misunderstood, or not understood at all, and is not unfrequently lost to a people that prefer shallowness to deep meaning, falsehood to truth, and glitter to repose.

We now see the utter folly of appealing simply to what is called "taste" in matters of art, and the uselessness of yielding to the caprice (falsely called taste) of the uneducated in such matters, especially as this so-called taste is often of the most vulgar and debased order. We also see the absurdity of persons who employ a true artist interfering with his judgment and ideas. The true artist is a noble teacher; shall he be told, then, what morals he shall inculcate, and what lofty truths he shall embody in his works, or omit from them? Do we tell the preacher what he shall say, and ask him to withhold whatever is refining and elevating? We do not, and in art we must leave the professors free to teach, and hold them responsible for their teachings.

If I thought that I had now convinced my reader that decorative art does not consist merely in the placing together of forms, however beautiful they may be individually or collectively; nor in rendering objects simply what is called pretty; but that it is a power for good or evil; that it is what will elevate or debase—that which cannot be neutral in its tendency—I would advance to consider its principles; but I cannot teach, nor can I be understood, unless the reader *feels* that he who practises art wields a vast power, for the rightful use of which he must be held responsible.

All graining of wood is false, inasmuch as it attempts to deceive; the effort being made at causing one material to look like another which it is not. All "marbling" is false also: a floor-cloth made in imitation of carpet or matting is false; a Brussels carpet that imitates a Turkey carpet is false; so is a jug that imitates wicker-work, a printed fabric that imitates one which is woven, a gas-lamp that imitates an oil-lamp. These are all untruths in expression, and are, besides, vulgar absurdities which are the more lamentable, as the imitation is always less beautiful than the thing imitated; and as each material has the power of expressing beauty truthfully, thus the want of truth brings its own punishment. A deal door is beautiful, but it will not keep clean; let it then be varnished. It is now preserved, and its own characteristic features are enhanced by the varnish, so that its individuality is emphasised, and no untruth told. A floor-cloth can present a pattern with true and beautiful curves—how absurd, then, to try and imitate the dotty effect of a carpet; and the Brussels carpet can express truer curves than the Turkey carpet, then why imitate the latter in the finer material? But perhaps the most senseless of all these absurdities is the making an earthen jug in imitation of wicker-work when if so formed it would be useless as a water-vessel. I can imagine a fool in his simplicity priding himself on such a bright thought as the production of a vessel of this kind, but I cannot imagine any rightly constituted mind producing or commending such an idea. Let the expression of our art ever be truthful.

Beauty.—I will say little on this head, for decorative forms must be beautiful. Shapes which are not beautiful are rarely decorative. I will not now attempt to express what character forms should have in order that they be considered beautiful, but will content myself by saying that they must be truthful in expression, and graceful, delicate, and refined in contour, manifesting no coarseness, vulgarity, or obtrusiveness. My views of the beautiful must be gathered from the series of chapters which will follow, but this I may here say, that the beautiful manifests no want, no shortcoming. A composition that is beautiful must have no parts which could be taken from it and yet leave the remainder equally good or better. The perfectly beautiful is that which admits of no improvement. The beautiful is lovable, and, as that which is lovable, takes hold of the affections and clings to them, binding itself firmer and firmer to them as time rolls on. If an object is really beautiful we do not tire of it; fashion does not induce us to change it; the merely new does not displace it. It becomes as an old friend, more loved as its good qualities are better understood.

Power.—We now come to consider an art-element or principle of great importance, for if absent from any composition, feebleness or weakness is the result, the manifestation of which is not pleasant. With what power do the plants burst from the earth in spring! With what power do the buds develop into branches! The powerful orator is a man to be admired, the powerful thinker a man we esteem. Even the simple power, or brute force, of animals we involuntarily approve—the powerful tiger and the powerful horse call forth our commendation, for power is antagonistic to weakness. Power also manifests earnestness; power means energy; power implies a conqueror. Our compositions, then, must be powerful.

But besides all this, we, the professors of decorative art, must manifest power in our works, for we are teachers sent forth to instruct, and ennoble, and elevate our fellow-creatures. We shall not be believed if we do not utter our truths with power; let truth, then, be uttered with power, and in the form of beauty.[7]

There are other principles governing the production and application of ornament which we must now notice, the first of which is *utility*, for the first aim of the designer of any

---

[7] I have given in this chapter an original sketch (Fig. 12), in which I have sought to embody chiefly the one idea of power, energy, force, or vigour; and in order to do this, I have employed such lines as we see in the bursting buds of spring, when the energy of growth is at its maximum, and especially such as are to be seen in the spring growth of a luxuriant tropical vegetation; I have also availed myself of those forms to be seen in certain bones of birds which are associated with the organs of flight, and which give us an impression of great strength, as well as those observable in the powerful propelling fins of certain species of fish.

article must be to render the object which he produces useful. I may go further, and say that an article must be made not only useful, but as perfectly suited to the purpose for which it is intended as it can be. It matters not how beautiful the object is intended to be, it must first be formed as though it were a mere work of utility, and after it has been carefully created with this end in view it may then be rendered as beautiful as you please.

There are special reasons why our works should be useful as well as beautiful, for if an object, however beautiful it may be in shape, however richly covered with beautiful ornaments, or however harmoniously coloured, be unpleasant to use, it will ultimately be set aside, and that which is more convenient for use will replace it, even if the latter be without beauty. As an illustration of this fact, let us suppose the balustrade railings of a staircase very beautiful, and yet furnished with such projections as render it almost impossible that we walk up or down the stairs without tearing the dress, or injuring the person, and how soon will our admiration of the beautiful railing disappear, and even be replaced by hate! In like manner let the handle of a door, or the head of a poker, be so formed as to hurt the hand, and the simple round knob, or round head, will be preferred to it, however ornamentally or beautifully formed.

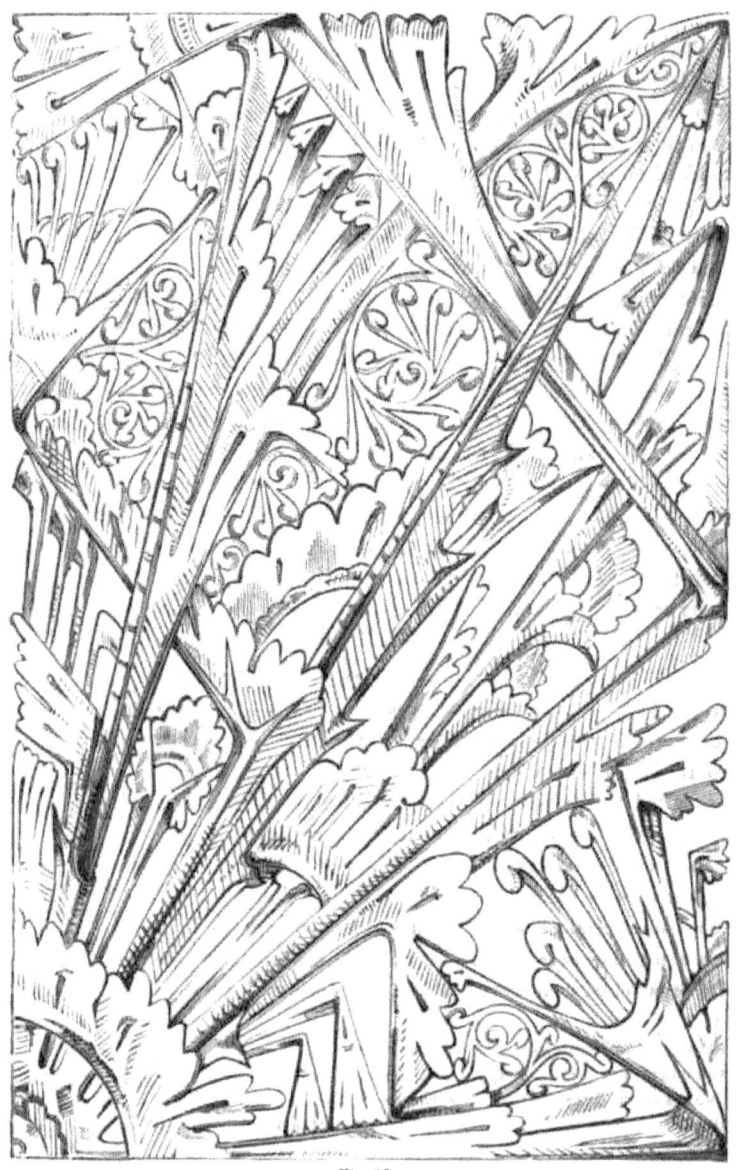

Fig. 12.

In relation to this subject, Professor George Wilson has said: "The conviction seems ineradicable from some minds, that a beautiful thing cannot be a useful thing, and that the more you increase the beauty of the necessary furniture or the implements of every-day life the more you lessen their utility. Make the Queen's sceptre as beautiful as you please, but don't try to beautify a poker, especially in cold weather. My lady's vinaigrette carve and gild as you will, but leave untouched my pewter ink-bottle. Put fine furniture, if you choose, into my drawing-room; but I am a plain man, and like useful things in my parlour, and so on. Good folks of this sort seem to labour under the impression that the secret desire of art is to rob them of all comfort. Its unconfessed but actual aim, they believe, is to realise the faith of their childhood, when it was understood that a monarch always wore his crown, held an orb in one hand and a sceptre in the other, and a literal interpretation was put upon Shakespeare's words,

'Uneasy lies the head that wears a crown.'

Were art to prosper, farewell to fire-proof, shapeless slippers, which bask like salamanders unharmed in the hottest blaze. An æsthetic pair, modelled upon Cinderella's foot, and covered with snow-white embroidery, must take their place, and dispense chilblains and frost-bite to miserable toes. Farewell to shooting-coats out a little at the elbows, to patched dressing-gowns, and hair-cloth sofas. Nothing but full-dress, varnished boots, spider-legged chairs, white satin chair-covers, alabaster ink-bottles, velvet door-mats, and scrapers of silver or gold. It is astonishing how many people think that a thing cannot be comfortable if it is beautiful. . . . If there be one truth which the Author of all has taught us in his works more clearly than another, it is the perfect compatibility of the highest utility with the greatest beauty. I offer you one example. All are familiar with the beautiful shell of the nautilus. Give the nautilus itself to a mathematician, and he will show you that one secret of its gracefulness lies in its following in its volute or whorl a particular geometrical curve with rigid precision. Pass it from the mathematician to the natural philosopher, and he will show you how the simple superposition of a great number of very thin transparent plates, and the close approximation of a multitude of very fine engraved lines, are the cause of its exquisite pearly lustre. Pass it from the natural philosopher to the engineer, and he will show you that this fairy shell is a most perfect practical machine, at once a sailing vessel and a diving-bell, in which its living possessor had, centuries before Archimedes, applied to utilitarian ends the law of specific gravity, and centuries before Halley had dived in his bell to the bottom of the sea. Pass it from the engineer to the anatomist, and he will show you how, without marring its beauty, it is occupied during its lifetime with a most orderly system of rowing and sailing tackle, chambers for food, pumps to keep blood circulating, ventilating apparatus, and hands to control all, so that it is a model ship with a model mariner on board. Pass it lastly from the anatomist to the chemist, and he will show you that every part of the shell and the creature is compounded of elements, the relative weights of which follow in each individual nautilus the same numerically identical ratio.

"Such is the nautilus, a thing so graceful, that when we look at it we are content to say with Keats—

'A thing of beauty is a joy for ever;'

and yet a thing so thoroughly utilitarian, and fulfilling with the utmost perfection the purely practical aim of its construction, that our shipbuilders would be only too thankful if, though sacrificing all beauty, they could make their vessels fulfil their business ends half so well."

Viewing our subject in another light, and with special reference to architecture, we notice that unless a building is fitted for the purpose intended, or, in other words, answers utilitarian ends, it cannot be esteemed as it otherwise might be, even though it be of great æsthetic beauty. In respect to this subject, Mr. Owen Jones has said: "The nave and aisles of a Gothic church become absurd when filled with pews for Protestant worship, where all are required to see and hear. The columns of the nave which impede sight and sound, the aisles for processions which no longer exist, rood screens, and deep chancels for the concealment of mysteries, now no longer such, are all so many useless reproductions which must be thrown aside." Further, "As architecture, so all works of the decorative arts, *should possess fitness*, proportion, harmony; the result of all which is repose." Sir M. Digby Wyatt has said: "Infinite variety and unerring fitness govern all forms in Nature." Vitruvius, that "The perfection of all works depends on their fitness to answer the end proposed, and on principles resulting from a consideration of Nature itself." Sir Charles L. Eastlake, that "In every case in Nature where fitness or utility can be traced, the characteristic quality, or *relative* beauty, is found to be identical with that of fitness." A. W. Pugin (the father): "How many objects of ordinary use are rendered monstrous and ridiculous simply because the artist, instead of seeking the most convenient form, and then decorating it, has embodied some extravagance to conceal the real purpose for which the article has been made." And with the view of pointing out how fitness for, or adaptation to, the end proposed is manifested in the structure and disposition upon the earth of plants, I have written in a little work now out of print: "The trees which grow highest upon the mountains, and the plants which grow upon the unsheltered plain, have usually long, narrow, and rigid leaves, which, owing to their form, are enabled to bear the fury of the tempest, to which they are exposed, without injury. This is seen in the ease of the species of fir which grow at great altitudes, where the leaves are more like needles than leaves such as commonly occur; and also in the species of heath which grow upon exposed moors: in both cases the plants are, owing to the form of the leaf, enabled to defy the blast, while those with broad leaves would be shattered and destroyed.

"Not only is the form of leaf such as fits these plants to dwell in such inhospitable regions, but other circumstances also tend to this result. The stems are in both cases woody and flexible, so that while they bend to the wind they resist its destroying influence by their strength and elasticity. In relation to the stem of the papyrus," which is a plant constantly met with in Egyptian ornaments, "the late Sir W. J. Hooker mentions an interesting fact which manifests adaptation to its position. This plant grows in water, and attaches itself to the margins of rivers and streams, by sending forth roots and evolving long underground stems in the alluvium of the sides of the waters. Owing to its position it is exposed to the influences of the current, which it has to withstand, and this it does, not only by having its stems of a triangular form—a shape well adapted for withstanding pressure—but also by having them so placed in relation to the direction of the stream, that one angle always meets the current, and thus separates the waters as does the bow of a modern steam-ship."

I might multiply illustrations of this principle of *fitness*, or *adaptation to purpose*, as manifested in plants, to an almost indefinite extent; but when all had been said we should yet have but the simple truth before us, that the chief end which we should have in creating any object, is that of rendering it perfectly fitted to answer the proposed end. If those works which are beautiful were but invariably useful, as they should be; if those objects which are most beautiful were also the most convenient—and there is no reason why they should not be so—how the beautiful would become loved and sought after! Cost would be of little moment, the price would not be complained of, if beautiful objects were works of perfect utility. But, alas! it is far otherwise: that which is useful is often ugly, and that which is beautiful is often inconvenient to use. This very fact has given rise to the highly absurd fashion of having a second poker in a drawing-room set of fire-irons. The one poker is ornamental, possibly, but it is to be looked at; the other is for use, and as it is not to be looked at, it is hidden away in some corner, or close within the fender. I do not wonder at the second poker being required; for nineteen out of every twenty pokers of an ornamental (?) character which I have seen during the last few years would hurt the hand so insufferably if they were used to break a lump of coal with, that it would be almost impossible to employ them constantly for such a purpose. But why not abolish the detestable thing altogether? If the poker is to be retained as an ornament, place it on the table or chimney-piece of your drawing-room, and not down on the hearth, where it is at such a distance from the eye that its beauties cannot be discovered. It is no use saying it would be out of place in such a position. If to poke the fire with, its place is within the fender; if it is an ornament, it should be placed where it can be best seen—in a glass case, if worthy of protection.

I hope that sufficient has now been said upon this all-important necessity, that, if an object is to be beautiful it should also be useful, to cause us to consider it as a primary principle of design that all objects which we create *must* be useful. To this as a first law we shall constantly have to refer. When we construct a chair we shall ask, is it useful? is it strong? is it properly put together? could it be stronger without using more, or another, material? and then we should consider whether it is beautiful. When we design a bottle we shall inquire, is it useful? is it all that a bottle should be? could it be more useful? and then, is it beautiful? When we create a gas-branch we shall ask, does it fulfil all requirements, and perfectly answer the end for which it is intended? and then, is it beautiful? And in relation to patterns merely we shall also have to make similar inquiries. Thus, if drawing a carpet design, we shall inquire, is this form of ornament suitable to a woven fabric? is it suitable to the particular fabric for which it is intended? is the particular treatment of the ornament which we have adopted the best possible when we bear in mind that the carpet has to be walked over, as it is to act in relation to our furniture as a background does to a picture, and is to be viewed at some distance from the eye? and then, is it beautiful? Such inquiries we shall put respecting any object the formation of which we may suggest: hence, in all our inquiries, I shall, as I love art, consider utility before beauty, in order that my art may be fostered and not despised.

There are many subjects yet not named in these pages which we ought to consider, but I must content myself by merely mentioning them, and you must be willing to think of them, and consider them with such care as their importance may demand. Some of them, however, we shall refer to when considering the various manufactures.

A principle of great importance in respect to design is, that *the material of which an object is formed should be used in a manner consistent with its own nature, and in that particular way in which it can be most easily "worked."*

Another principle of equal importance with that just set forth, is this: that *when an object is about to be formed, that material (or those materials) which is (or are) most appropriate to its formation should be sought and employed.* These two propositions are of very great importance, and the principles which they set forth should never be lost sight of by the designer. They involve the first principles of successful designing, for if ignored the work produced cannot be satisfactory.

Curves will be found to be beautiful just as they are subtle in character; those which are most subtle in character being most beautiful.

The arc is the least beautiful of curves (I do not here speak of a circle, but of the line, as a line, which bounds the circle); being struck from one centre its origin is instantly detected, while the mind requires that a line, the contemplation of which shall be pleasurable, must be in advance of its knowledge, and call into activity its powers of inquiry. The elliptic curve, or curve bounding the ellipse, is more beautiful than the arc, for its origin is not so strikingly apparent, being formed from two centres. The curve of the egg is more beautiful still, being formed from three centres.[8] As the number of centres necessary to the formation of a curve increases, the difficulty of detecting its origin also becomes greater, and the variety which the curve presents is also proportionally great; the variety being obviously greater as the number of the centres from which it is struck is increased.

Proportion, like the curve, must be of a subtle nature.

A surface must never be divided for the purpose of decoration into halves. The proportion of 1 to 1 is bad. As proportion increases in subtlety it also increases in beauty. The proportion of 2 to 1 is little better; the proportion of 3 to 8, or of 5 to 8, or of 5 to 13, is, however, good, the last named being the best of those which I have adduced; for the pleasure derived from the contemplation of proportion increases with the difficulty of detecting it. This principle is true in relation to the division of a mass into primary segments, and of primary segments into secondary forms, as well as in relation to the grouping together of parts of various sizes; hence it is worthy of special note.

A principle of order must prevail in every ornamental composition.

---

[8] The ellipse and egg-shape here spoken of are not those which are struck by compasses in any way, for the curves of such figures are merely combined arcs, but such as are struck with string, or a "tramel."

Confusion is the result of accident, while order results from thought and care. The operation of mind cannot well be set forth in the absence of this principle; at least, the presence of a principle of order renders the operation of mind at once manifest.

The orderly repetition of parts frequently aids in the production of ornamental effects.

The kaleidoscope affords a wonderful example of what repetition will do. The mere fragments of glass which we view in this instrument would altogether fail to please were they not repeated with regularity. Of themselves repetition and order can do much. (Figs. 13 and 14.)

Alternation is a principle of primary importance in certain ornamental compositions.

In the case of a flower (as the buttercup, or chickweed, for example) the coloured leaves do not fall over the green leaves (the petals do not fall over the sepals), but between them— they alternate with them. This principle is not only manifested in plants, but also in many ornaments produced in the best periods of art (Fig. 15).

If plants are employed as ornaments they must not be treated imitatively, but must be conventionally treated, or rendered into ornaments (Fig. 16).

A monkey can imitate, man can create.

These are the chief principles which we shall have to notice, as involved in the production of ornamental designs.

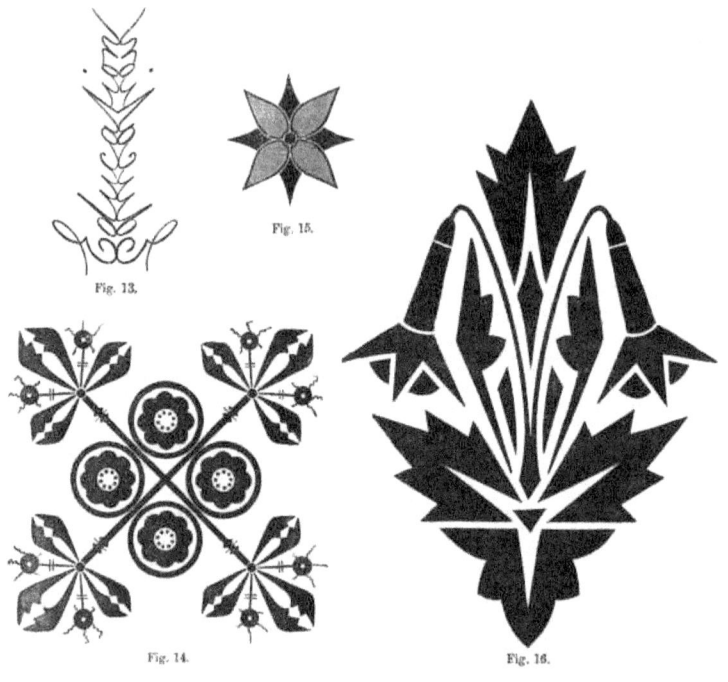

Fig. 13.

Fig. 15.

Fig. 14.

Fig. 16.

DIVISION III.

Some other principles of a less noble character than those which we have already noticed as entering into ornament yet remain to be mentioned. Man will be amused as well as instructed; he must be pleased as well as ennobled by what he sees. I hold it as a first principle that ornamentation, as a true fine art, can administer to man in all his varying moods, and under all phases of feeling. Decoration, if properly understood, would at once be seen to be a high art in the truest sense of the word, as it can teach, elevate, refine, induce lofty aspirations, and allay sorrows; but we have now to notice it as a fine art, administering to man in his various moods, rather than as the handmaid to religion or morals.

Humour seems to be as much an attribute of our nature as love, and, like it, varies in intensity with different individuals. There are few in whom there is not a certain amount of humour, and in some this one quality predominates over all others. It not unfrequently happens that men who are great thinkers are also great humorists—great talent and great humour being often combined in the one individual.

The feeling for humour is ministered to in ornament by the grotesque, and the grotesque occurs in the works of almost all ages and all peoples. The ancient Egyptians employed it, so did the Assyrians, the Greeks, and the Romans; but none of these nations used it to the extent of the artists of the Celtic, Byzantine, and "Gothic" periods. Hideous "evil spirits" were portrayed on the outside of almost every Christian edifice at one time, and much of the Celtic ornament produced by the early monks consisted of an anastomosis, or network, of grotesque creatures.

The old Irish crosses were enriched with this kind of ornamentation,[9] and some of the decorative embellishments of these works are of extraordinary interest; but those who have access to the beautiful work of Professor Westwood on Celtic manuscripts will there see this grotesque form of ornament to perfection. As regards the Eastern nations, while nearly all have employed the grotesque as an element of decorative art, the Chinese and Japanese have employed it

---

[9] Casts of one or two of these can be seen in the central transept of the Crystal Palace at Sydenham.

most largely, and for it they manifest a most decided partiality. The drawings of dragons, celestial lions (always spotted), mythical birds, beasts, fishes, insects, and other supposed inhabitants of the Elysian plains, which these people produce, are most interesting and extraordinary.

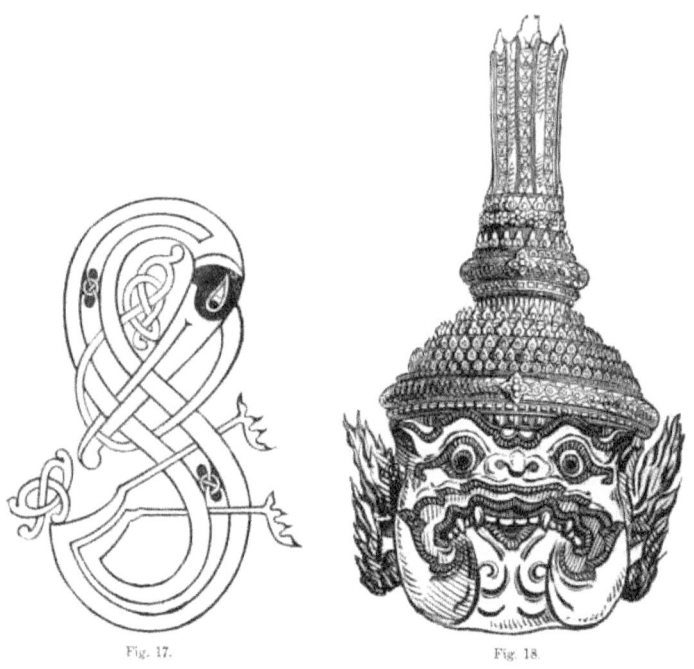

Fig. 17.   Fig. 18.

Without in any way going into a history of the grotesque, let us look at the characteristic forms which it has assumed, and what is necessary to its successful production. We have said that the grotesque in ornament is the analogue of humour in literature. This is the case; but the grotesque may represent the truly horrible or repellent, and be simply repulsive. This form is so seldom required in ornamentation that I shall not dwell upon it, and when required it should always be associated with power; for if the horrible is feeble it cannot be corrective, but only revolting, like a miserable deformed animal.

I think it may be taken as a principle, that the further the grotesque is removed from an imitation of a natural object the better it is, provided that it be energetic and vigorous— lifelike. Nothing is worse than a feeble joke, unless it be a feeble grotesque. The amusing must appear to be earnest.

In connection with this subject I give here a series of grotesques, with the view of illustrating my meaning, and I would fain give more, but space will not permit me to do so.

The initial letter S, formed of a bird, is a characteristic Celtic grotesque (Fig. 17). It is quaint and interesting, and is sufficiently unlike a living creature to avoid giving any sense of pain to the beholder, while it is yet in a most unnatural position. It is, in truth, rather an ornament than a copy of a living creature, yet it is so suggestive as to call forth the thought of a bird. It should be noticed, in connection with this figure, that the interstices between certain portions of the creature are filled by a knot. This is well—the whole thing; being an ornament, and not a naturalistic representation.

Fig. 18 is a Siamese grotesque head, and a fine sample it is of the curious form of ornament which it represents. Mark, it is in no way a copy of a human head, but is a true ornament, with its parts so arranged as to call up the idea of a face, and nothing more. Notice the volutes forming the chin; the grotesque, yet highly ornamental, lines forming the mouth and the upper boundary of the forehead, and the flambeauant ears; the whole thing is worthy of the most careful study.

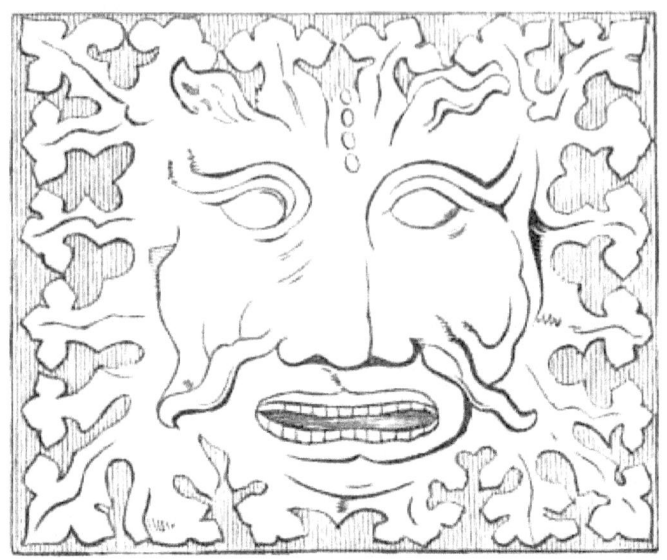

Fig. 19.

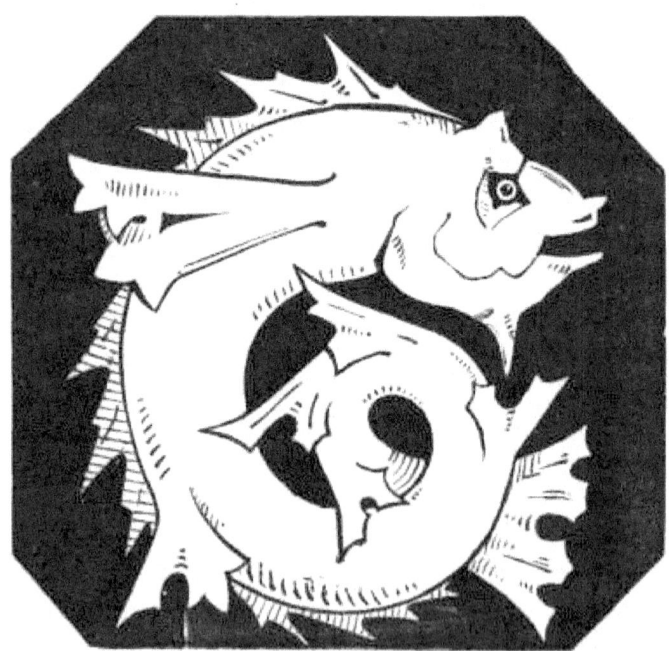

Fig. 20.

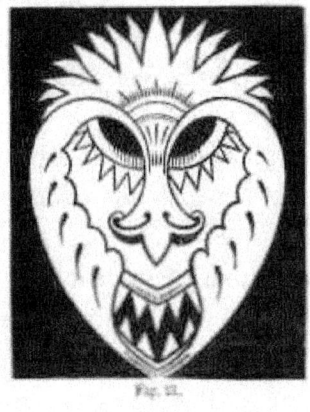

Fig. 19.

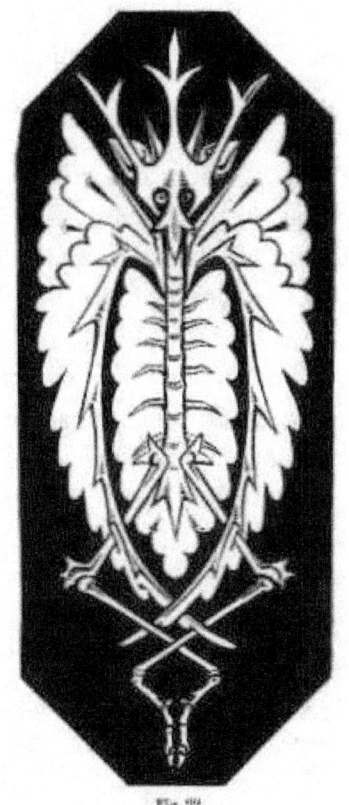

Fig. 20.

Fig. 19 is a Gothic foliated face; but here we have features which are much too naturalistic. We have, indeed, only a hideous human face with a marginal excrescence of leafage. This is a type to be avoided; it is not droll, nor quaint; but is simply unpleasant to look upon.

Fig. 20 is a fish, with the feeling of the grotesques of the Middle Ages. It is a good type, being truly ornamental, and yet sufficiently suggestive.

In order that I convey to the reader a fuller idea of my views respecting the grotesque than I otherwise could, I have sketched one or two original illustrations—Fig. 21 being suggestive of a face, Fig. 22 of a skeleton (old bogey), and Fig. 23 of an impossible animal. They are intentionally far from imitative. If naturalistic some would awaken a sense of pain, as they are contorted into curious positions, whereas that which induces no thought of feeling induces no sense of pain.

Of all grotesques with which I am acquainted, the dragons of the Chinese and Japanese are those which represent a combination of power, vigour, energy, and passion most fully. This is to be accounted for by the fact that these peoples are believers in dragons. When the sun or moon is eclipsed they believe that the luminous orb has been swallowed by some fierce monster, which they give form to in the dragon, and upon the occurrence of such a phenomenon they, with cans and kettles, make rough music, and thus cause the monster to disgorge the luminary, the brilliancy of which it would otherwise have for ever extinguished. I can understand a believer in dragons drawing these monsters with the power and spirit that the Chinese and Japanese do; but I can scarcely imagine that a disbeliever could do so—a man's very nature must be saturated with a belief in their existence and mischievous power, in order that he embody in his delineation such expression of the assumed character of this imaginary creature as do the Chinese and Japanese.

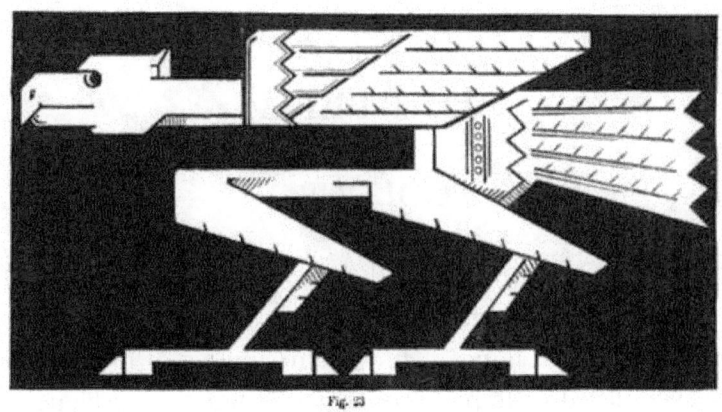

Fig. 23

Although I am not now considering the structure of objects, I may say that the grotesque should frequently be used where we meet with naturalistic imitations. We not unfrequently see a figure, naturally imitated, placed as a support to a superincumbent weight—a female figure as an architectural pillar bearing the weight of the entablature above, men crouched in the most painful positions supporting the bowl of some colossal fountain. Naturalistic figures in such positions are simply revolting, however perfect as works of sculpture. If weight has to be supported by that which has a resemblance to a living creature of any kind, the semblance should only be suggested; and the more unreal and woodeny (if I may make such a word) the support, if possessing the quaintness and humour of a true grotesque, the better.

It is not the business of the ornamentist to produce that which shall induce the feeling of continued pain, unless there is some exceptional reason for his so doing, and such a reason is of rare occurrence.

CHAPTER II.

COLOUR.

Having considered some of the chief principles involved in the production of decorative design so far as "expression" goes, we come to notice that constant adjunct of form which has ever played an important part in all decorative schemes—namely, colour.

Form can exist independently of colour, but it never has had any important development without the chromatic adjunct. From a consideration of history, we should be led to conclude that form alone is incapable of yielding such enrichments as satisfy; for no national system of decoration has ever existed in the absence of colour. Mere outline-form may be good, but it is not satisfying; mere light and shade may be pleasing, but it is not all that we require. With form our very nature seems to demand colour; and it is only when we get well-proportioned forms which are graceful, or noble, or vigorous, in combination with colours harmoniously arranged, that we are satisfied.

Possibly this feeling results from our contact with nature. The flowers appear in a thousand hues, and the hills are of ever-varying tints. What a barren world ours would appear, were the ground, the hills, the trees and the flowers, the sky and the waters all of one colour! Form we should have, and that in its richest variety; light and shade we should have, with ever-varying intensity and change; but colour would be gone.

There would be no green to cheer, no blue to soothe, no red to excite; and, indeed, there would be a deadness, although the world be full of life, so appalling that we can scarcely conceive of it, and cannot *feel* it.

Colour alone seems to have greater charms than form alone. A sunset is entrancing when the sky glows with radiant hues; the blue is almost lost in red, the yellow is as a sea of transparent gold, and the whole presents a variety and blending of tints which charm, and soothe, and lull to reverie; and yet all form is indistinct and obscure. If so charming when separate from form, what is colour when properly combined with beautiful shapes? It is difficult, indeed, for many of those for whom I write to answer this question, even by a mental conception, save by reference to nature; for I could scarcely point to a single building in England which would be in any way a satisfactory illustration of what may be done by the combination of forms and colours. There is a beauty in Art which we in England do not even know of: it does not exist around us, it is little talked of, rarely thought about, and never seen. A decorator is called in to beautify a house, and yet not one in fifty of the so-called decorators know even the first principles of their art, and would not believe were they told of the power of the art which they employ. They place on the walls a few sickly tints—so pale that their want of harmony is not very apparent. The colours of the wall become the colours of the cornice and of the doors, because they know not how to produce a harmony of hues; and the result is a house which may be clean, but which is in every other respect an offence against good taste. I do not wonder that persons here in England do not care to have their houses "decorated," nor do I wonder at their not appreciating the "decorations" when they are done. Colour, lovely colour, of itself would make our rooms charming.

There are few objects to which colour may not be applied, and many articles which are now colourless might be coloured with advantage. Our reasons for applying colour to objects are twofold, and here, in fact, we see its true use. 1st. Colour lends to objects a new charm—a charm which they would not possess if without it; and, 2nd, Colour assists in the separation of objects and parts of objects, and thus gives assistance to form. These, then, are the two objects of colour. Mark, first, it is to bestow on objects a charm, such as they could not have in its absence. In the hands of the man of knowledge it will do so—it will make an object lovely or lovable, but the mere application of colour will not do this. Colour may be so applied to objects as to render them infinitely more ugly than they were without it. I have seen many a bowl so coloured at our potteries as to be much less satisfactory when coloured than when white—the colouring having marred, rather than improved, its general effect. Here, again, it is knowledge that we want. Knowledge will enable us to transmute base materials into works of marvellous beauty, worth their weight in gold. Knowledge, then, is the true philosopher's stone; for, we may almost say, if possessed by the artist it does enable him to transmute the baser metals into gold. But a little knowledge will not do this. In order that we produce true beauty, we require much knowledge, and this can only be got by constant and diligent labour, as I have before said; but the end to be gained is worth the plodding toil. Believe me, there is a pleasure in seeing your works develop as things of beauty, delighting all who see them—not the illiterate only, but also the educated thinker—such as words fail to express. Although there is no royal road to art-power, and although the road is long, and lies through much toil and many difficulties, yet as you proceed there is pleasure in feeling that one obstacle after another is cleared from your path, and at the end there is inexpressible satisfaction. The second object of colour is that of assisting in the separation of form. If objects are placed near to one another, and these objects are all of the same colour, the beholder will have much more difficulty in seeing the boundaries or terminations of each than he would were they variously coloured; he would have to come nearer to them in order to see the limits of each, were all coloured in the same manner, than he would were they variously coloured; thus colour assists in the separation of form. This quality which colour has of separating forms is often lost sight of, and much confusion thereby results. If it is worth while to produce a decorative form, it is worth while to render it visible; and yet, how much ornament, and even good ornament, is lost to the eye through not being rendered manifest by colour! Colour is the means by which we render form apparent.

Colours, when placed together, can only please and satisfy the educated when combined harmoniously, or according to the laws of harmony. What, then, are the laws which govern the arrangement of colours? and how are they to be applied? We shall endeavour to answer these questions by making a series of statements in axiomatic form, and then we shall enlarge upon these propositions.

GENERAL CONSIDERATIONS.

1. Regarded from an art point of view, there are but three colours—*i.e.*, blue, red, and yellow.

2. Blue, red, and yellow have been termed *primary* colours; they cannot be formed by the admixture of any other colours.

3. All colours, other than blue, red, and yellow, result from the admixture of the primary colours.

4. By the admixture of blue and red, purple is formed; by the admixture of red and yellow, orange is formed; and by the admixture of yellow and blue, green is formed.

5. Colours resulting from the admixture of two primary colours are termed *secondary*: hence purple, orange, and green are secondary colours.

6. By the admixture of two secondary colours a *tertiary* colour is formed: thus, purple and orange produce russet (the red tertiary); orange and green produce citrine (the yellow tertiary); and green and purple, olive (the blue tertiary); russet, citrine, and olive are the three tertiary colours.

CONTRAST.

7. When a light colour is juxtaposed to a dark colour, the light colour appears lighter than it is, and the dark colour darker.[10]

8. When colours are juxtaposed, they become influenced as to their hue. Thus, when red and green are placed side by side, the red appears redder than it actually is, and the green greener; and when blue and black are juxtaposed, the blue manifests but little alteration, while the black assumes an orange tint or becomes "rusty."

9. No one colour can be viewed by the eye without another being created. Thus, if red is viewed, the eye creates for itself green, and this green is cast upon whatever is near. If it views green, red is in like manner created and cast upon adjacent objects; thus, if red and green are juxtaposed, each creates the other in the eye, and the red created by the green is cast upon the red, and the green created by the red is cast upon the green; and the red and the green become improved by being juxtaposed. The eye also demands the presence of the three primary colours, either in their purity or in combination and if these are not present, whatever is deficient will be created in the eye, and this induced colour will be cast upon whatever is near. Thus, when we view blue, orange, which is a mixture of red and yellow, is created in the eye, and this colour is cast

---

[10] If a dark grey tint be mixed upon a white slab it will appear dark in contrast with the white, but if a small portion of this same grey is applied to black paper it will appear almost white.

upon whatever is near; if black is in juxtaposition with the blue, this orange is cast upon it, and gives to it an orange tint, thus causing it to look "rusty."

10. In like manner, if we look upon red, green is formed in the eye, and is cast upon adjacent colours; or, if we look upon yellow, purple is formed.

HARMONY.

11. Harmony results from an agreeable contrast.

12. Colours which perfectly harmonise improve one another to the utmost.

13. In order to perfect harmony, the three colours are necessary, either in their purity or in combination.

14. Red and green combine to yield a harmony. Red is a primary colour, and green, which is a secondary colour, consists of blue and yellow—the other two primary colours. Blue and orange also produce a harmony, and yellow and purple, for in each ease the three primary colours are present.

15. It has been found that the primary colours in perfect purity produce exact harmonies in the proportions of eight parts of blue, 5 of red, and 3 of yellow; that the secondary colours harmonise in the proportions of 13 of purple, 11 of green, and 8 of orange; and that the tertiary colours harmonise in the proportions of olive 24, russet 21, and citrine 19.

16. There are, however, subtleties of harmony which it is difficult to understand.

17. The rarest harmonies frequently lie close on the verge of discord.

18. Harmony of colour is, in many respects, analogous to harmony of musical sounds.

QUALITIES OF COLOURS.

19. Blue is a cold colour, and appears to recede from the eye.

20. Red is a warm colour, and is exciting; it remains stationary as to distance.

21. Yellow is the colour most nearly allied to light; it appears to advance towards the spectator.

22. At twilight blue appears much lighter than it is, red much darker, and yellow slightly darker. By ordinary gaslight blue becomes darker, red brighter, and yellow lighter. By this artificial light a pure yellow appears lighter than white itself, when viewed in contrast with certain other colours.

23. By certain combinations colour may make glad or depress, convey the idea of purity, richness, or poverty, or may affect the mind in any desired manner, as does music.

TEACHINGS OF EXPERIENCE.

24. When a colour is placed on a gold ground, it should be outlined with a darker shade of its own colour.

25. When a gold ornament falls on a coloured ground, it should be outlined with black.

26. When an ornament falls on a ground which is in direct harmony with it, it must be outlined with a lighter tint of its own colour. Thus, when a red ornament falls on a green ground, the ornament must be outlined with a lighter red.

27. When the ornament and the ground are in two tints of the same colour, if the ornament is darker than the ground, it will require outlining with a still darker tint of the same colour; but if lighter than the ground no outline will be required.

ANALYTICAL TABLES OF COLOUR.

When commencing my studies both in science and art, I found great advantage from reducing all facts to a tabular form so far as possible, and this mode of study I would recommend to others. To me this method appears to have great advantages, for by it we see at a glance what otherwise is difficult to understand; if carefully done, it becomes an analysis of work; and by preparing these tabular arrangements of facts the subject becomes impressed on the mind, and the relation of one fact to another, or of one part of a scheme to another, is seen.

The following analytical tables will illustrate many of the facts stated in our propositions. The figures which follow the colours represent the proportions in which they harmonise:—

Primary Colours.			Secondary Colours.			Tertiary Colours.		
Blue	.	8	Purple	.	13	Olive	.	24
Red	.	5	Green	.	11	Russet	.	21
Yellow	.	3	Orange	.	8	Citrine	.	19

Primary Colours.		Secondary Colours.		Tertiary Colours.	
Red . 5 } Yellow . 3 }	Orange . . . 8				
Blue . 8 } Yellow . 3 }	Green . . . 11	} Citrine, or Yellow Tertiary	19		
Blue . 8 } Red . 5 }	Purple . . . 13				
Red . 5 } Yellow . 3 }	Orange . . . 8	} Russet, or Red Tertiary .	21		
Blue . 8 } Yellow . 3 }	Green . . . 11				
Blue . 8 } Red . 5 }	Purple . . . 13	} Olive, or Blue Tertiary .	24		

This latter table shows at a glance how each of the secondary and tertiary colours is formed, and the proportions in which they harmonise. It also shows why the three tertiary colours are called respectively the yellow tertiary, the red tertiary, and the blue tertiary, for into each tertiary two equivalents[11] of one primary enter, and one equivalent of each of the other primaries. Thus, in citrine we find two equivalents of yellow, and one each of red and blue; hence it is the yellow tertiary. In russet we find two equivalents of red, and one each of blue and of yellow; and in olive two of blue, and one each of red and yellow. Hence they are respectively the red and blue tertiaries.

---

[11] An equivalent of blue is 8, of red 5, of yellow 3.

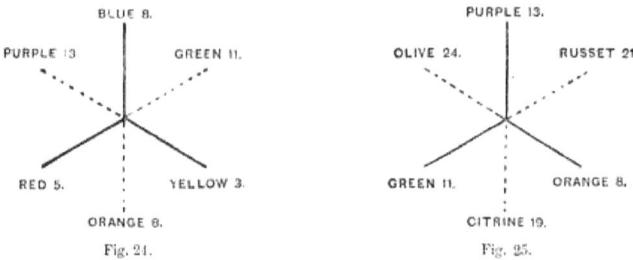

BLUE 8.

PURPLE 13.　　　　GREEN 11.

RED 5.　　　　YELLOW 3.

ORANGE 8.

Fig. 24.

PURPLE 13.

OLIVE 24.　　　　RUSSET 21.

GREEN 11.　　　　ORANGE 8.

CITRINE 19.

Fig. 25.

Figs 24 and 25 are diagrams of harmony. I have connected in the centre, by three similar lines, the colours which form a harmony; thus, blue, red, and yellow harmonise when placed together. Purple, green, and orange also harmonise (I have connected them by dotted lines in the first of the two diagrams). But when two colours are to produce a harmony, the one will be a primary colour, and the other a secondary formed of the other two primary colours (for the presence of the three primary colours is necessary to a harmony), or the one will be a secondary, and the other a tertiary colour formed of the two remaining secondary colours. Such harmonies I have placed opposite to each other; thus blue, a primary, harmonises with orange, a secondary; yellow with purple; and red with green; and the secondary colour is placed between the two primary colours of which it is formed; thus, orange is formed of red and yellow, between which it stands; green, of blue and yellow; and purple, of blue and red. In the second of the two diagrams we see that purple, green, and orange produce a harmony, so do olive, russet, and citrine. We also see that purple and citrine harmonise, and green and russet, and orange and olive.

Continuing this diagrammatic form of illustration, we may set forth the quantities in which the various colours harmonise: thus:—

Blue.
○ ○ ○ ○
○ ○ ○ ○

Red.
○ ○ ○ ○
○

Yellow.
○ ○ ○

Blue.
○ ○ ○ ○
○ ○ ○ ○

harmonises with

Orange.
○ ○ ○ ○
○ ○ ○ ○

Red.
○ ○ ○ ○
○

harmonises with

Green.
○ ○ ○ ○
○ ○ ○ ○
○ ○ ○

Yellow.
○ ○ ○

harmonises with

Purple.
○ ○ ○ ○
○ ○ ○ ○
○ ○ ○ ○
○

Purple.
○ ○ ○ ○
○ ○ ○ ○
○ ○ ○ ○
○

harmonises with

Citrine.
○ ○ ○ ○
○ ○ ○ ○
○ ○ ○ ○
○ ○ ○ ○
○ ○ ○

Green.
○ ○ ○ ○
○ ○ ○ ○
○ ○ ○

harmonises with

Russet.
○ ○ ○ ○
○ ○ ○ ○
○ ○ ○ ○
○ ○ ○ ○
○ ○ ○ ○
○

Orange.
○ ○ ○ ○
○ ○ ○ ○

harmonises with

Olive.
○ ○ ○ ○
○ ○ ○ ○
○ ○ ○ ○
○ ○ ○ ○
○ ○ ○ ○
○ ○ ○ ○

To those who are about to practise ornamentation, it is very important that they have in the mind's eye a tolerably accurate idea of the relative quantities of the various colours necessary to harmony, even where the colours are considered as existing in a state of absolute purity. We have rarely, however, to use the brightest blues, reds, and yellows which pigments furnish, and even these are but poor representatives of the potent colours of light as seen in the rainbow, and with the agency of the prism; nevertheless, a knowledge of the quantities in which these pure colours harmonise is very desirable. The proportions in which we have stated that colours perfectly harmonise, and in which the primary colours combine to form the secondaries, and the secondaries the tertiaries, are given in respect to the colours of light, and not of pigments or paints, which, as we have just said, are more or less base representatives of the pure colours of light. Yet certain pigments may, for our purpose, be regarded as representing pure colours. Thus, the purest real ultramarine we will regard as blue (cobalt is rather green, that is, it has a little yellow in it, and the French and German ultramarines are generally rather purple, or have a little red in them, yet the best of these latter is a tolerably pure colour), the purest French carmine as red (common carmine is frequently rather crimson, that is, has blue in it; vermilion is much too yellow), and lemon-chrome as yellow (the chrome selected must be without any green shade, and without any orange shade, however slight); and these pigments will be found to represent the colours of the prism as nearly as any that can be found. I would recommend the learner to get a small quantity of these colours in their powder form, substituting the best pale German ultramarine for real ultramarine, as the latter is of high price,[12] and to fill the various circles of our diagrams,

---

[12] Real ultramarine is sold at £8 per ounce. The best imitation, or German ultramarine, is procurable at any oil-

which represent the primary colours, with these pigments, mixing them with a little dissolved gum arabic and water— just ufficient to prevent the colours from rubbing off the paper. The secondary colours will be fairly represented by pale-green lake, often called drop-green, by orange-chrome— that of about the colour of a ripe, rather deep-coloured, orange-rind—and the purple by the admixture of pale German ultramarine and crimson-lake, in about equal proportions, with a little white to bring it to the same depth as the green. I cannot name any pigments which would well represent the tertiary colours. Citrine is about the colour of candied *lemon*-peel; olive about the colour of candied citron-peel, and russet is often seen on the skin of certain apples called "russet apples," in the form of a slight roughness; but this russet is in many cases not quite sufficiently red to represent the colour bearing the same name. Iron rust is rather too yellow. This colour should bear the same relation to red that the candied lemon-peel does to yellow.

If the student will try carefully to realise these colours, and will fill up the circles in our diagrams with them, he will thereby be much assisted in his studies; but it will be still better if he prepare fresh diagrams on a larger scale, and use squares instead of circles. I should recommend, and that I do strongly, that the student work out all the diagrams which I have suggested on a tolerably large scale, using the colours where I have used words. I should also advise him to do an

---

shop at about 3s. to 4s. per pound. The best carmine should be procurable at 6s. per ounce, but artists' colourmen often charge £1 1s., owing to the small demand for this pigment. The best chrome yellow (chrome yellow is kept in many shades) is about 1s. 6d. per pound.

ornament, say in red on a gold ground, and outline this red ornament with a deeper red; to do a gold ornament on a coloured ground, and outline it with black; and indeed to carefully work out an ornamental illustration of our propositions, Nos. 24, 25, 26, and 27, and to keep these before him till he is so impressed by them as to *feel* the principle which they set forth. This should be done on a large scale in all our designing-rooms and art-workshops.

As we shall have to refer to colours by naming pigments, and as I am constantly asked what pigments I employ, I shall enumerate the paints in my colour-box; but I shall place a dagger against those which I have in my private box, and which I do not supply in my offices; but these I seldom use. Of yellows I have king's yellow (not a permanent colour), very pale chrome, lemon-chrome (about the colour of a ripe lemon), middle-chrome (half-way between the lemon and orange-chrome), orange-chrome (about the colour of the rind of a ripe orange), yellow-lake, Indian yellow. Of reds— vermilion, carmine, crimson-lake. Of blues—[13]cobalt, German ultramarine, both deep and pale, Antwerp blue, indigo. Of greens—emerald, green-lake, pale and deep. Of browns—raw Turkey umber, vandyke, Venetian red, purple-brown, brown-lake. Besides these I have what is called

---

[13] Of all mediums in which colours can be mixed, paraffine is the safest; it is without chemical affinities, and is therefore well calculated to preserve pigments in their original condition.

celestial blue, which is a very pure and intense turquoise, vegetable black, flake white, and gold bronze.[14]

There are certain facts connected with the mixing of colours which must never be lost sight of; thus, while the colours of light co-mingle without any deterioration, or loss of brilliancy, pigments or paints will not do so, but by admixture tend to destroy one another. This takes place only to a small extent when but two primary colours are combined; but if any of the third primary enters into the composition of a tint, a decided deterioration, or loss of intensity, occurs.

For this reason we employ many pigments, so as to avoid as far as possible the mixing of colours. But there is another reason why the great admixture of colours is undesirable. Colours are chemical agents, and in some cases the various pigments act chemically on one another. Of all colours yellows suffer most by admixture with other colours: but this is accounted for by their delicacy and purity. For this reason I use a greater variety of yellow pigments than of red or blue.

Were it possible to procure three pigments devoid of chemical affinities, and each of the same physical constitution, as of equal degrees of transparency or opacity, one truly representing the blue of light, another the red, and another the yellow, we should need no others, for of these we could

---

[14] Some of these colours are not of a permanent character and could not be used in work intended to be lasting. I use them for patterns for our manufactures, where when the drawing is once copied in a fabric it is destroyed. Some of the brightest colours are unfortunately the most fleeting.

form all other colours; but as no pigments come even near to the fulfilment of these conditions, we have to employ roundabout and clumsy methods of arriving at desired results.

There is one statement which I have made that, perhaps, needs a little elucidation, although the careful student may have seen the reason of my assertion. I said that purple harmonised with citrine, green with russet, and orange with olive. I might have expressed it (and many would have done so) thus:—The complement of citrine is purple, the complement of russet is green, and the complement of olive is orange. A colour which is complementary to any other is that which, with it, completes the presence of the three primary colours: thus green is the complement of red, and red of green, for each, together with the colour to which it is the complement, completes the presence of the three colours. But in order to a harmony, the complement must be made up in certain proportions. Let us now refer to our second diagrammatic table, and we there see that citrine is formed of two equivalents of yellow and only one equivalent of red and of blue. Now, in order to a harmony, each primary should be present in two equivalents, as one is present in this quantity— *i.e.*, the yellow. One equivalent of blue and one of red (both of which are wanting in the citrine) form purple; hence purple is the complement of citrine, or the colour that with it produces a harmony. In russet one equivalent of blue and one of yellow are wanting, and these in combination are green— green, then, is the complement of russet. And in olive one equivalent of red and one of yellow are wanting—red and yellow form orange, hence orange is the complement of olive.

I have spoken of all colours as of full intensity and purity, but we have to deal also with other conditions. All colours may be darkened by black, when *shades* are produced; or reduced by white, when *tints* are produced. Besides these alterations in intensity, a portion of one colour may be added to another. Thus, if a small portion of blue be mingled with red, the red becomes a crimson or blue-red; or if a small portion of yellow be added to the red, the latter becomes a scarlet or yellow-red. In like manner, when yellow is in excess in a green, we have a yellow-green; or when blue is in excess, a blue-green; and so with the other colours. Such alterations produce *hues* of colour.

We now come to the subtleties of harmony. Thus, if we have a yellow-red or scarlet—a red with yellow in it—the green that will harmonise with it will be a blue-green; or if we have a blue-red or crimson—a red with blue in it—the green that will harmonise with it will be a yellow-green. This is obvious, for the following reasons:—Let us suppose a red represented by the equivalent number, five, with one part of blue added to it, thus causing it to be a blue-red or crimson. Were the red pure, there should be eleven parts of green as a complement to the five of red, of which green eight parts would be blue and three yellow; but the blue-red occurs in six parts, one of which is blue—there are, then, but seven parts of blue remaining in the equivalent quantity to combine with the three of yellow, one being already used; hence the green formed is a yellow-green, one of the equivalents of blue necessary to the formation of a true green being already in combination with the red, and thus absent from the green.

The same reasoning will apply to the scarlet-red and blue-green, and, indeed, to all similar cases; but to take the case of the crimson-red and yellow-green, as just given, and carry it a stage further, we might add two parts (out of the eight) of blue to the red, and make it more blue, and then form the complementary green of six parts of blue and three of yellow, and thus make it more yellow. Or we may go further still, and add to the red six of the eight parts of blue, when the admixture would appear as a red-purple rather than as a blue-red, in which case the complementary green—or, rather, green-yellow—would consist of two parts of blue and three of yellow. These facts are diagrammatically expressed in the following:—

Red. O O O O O } Blue. O } Crimson harmonises with	Yellow- { Green- {	O O O O O O O O O	Yellow Blue.
	Or,		

Red. O O O O O } Blue-
Blue. O O } Crimson harmonises with
	Very {
	Yellow {
	Green. {
		O O O
		O O O O O O
			Yellow.
			Blue.

	Or,		
Red. O O O O O } Red- Blue. O O O O O O } Purple harmonises with	Green- { Yellow. {	O O O O O	Yellow. Blue.

In all these cases it will be seen that we have eight parts of blue, five of red, and three of yellow, only the mode of combination varies. This variation may occur to any extent, provided the totals of each be always the equivalent proportions.

These remarks will apply equally to hues of colour, shades, and tints, and to shades and tints of hues.

Care, and a little practice, will enable the learner to arrange colours into a number of degrees of depth, or shades, as they are generally called. (We do not here use the term as signifying pure colours darkened with black.) Ten shades of each colour differing obviously in degree of depth can readily be arranged by the experienced, the ten shades being equidistant from each other as regards depth—that is, shade 3 will be as much darker than shade 2 as shade 2 is darker than shade 1, and so on throughout the whole. Purple is a colour intermediate between blue and red. Imagine ten hues between the purple and the red, and ten more between the purple and the blue: thus we should have purple, then a slightly red purple, then a rather redder purple, then a purple still redder, and so on till we get purple-reds, and finally the pure red; and the same variations of hue at the blue side also. Imagine, further, the green having ten hues extending towards the blue, and ten more stretching towards the yellow; and the orange having ten hues towards the red, and ten towards the yellow—in all cases I count the colour from which we start as one of the ten, thus:—

Blue									Purple									Red
0	9	8	7	6	5	4	3	2	1	2	3	4	5	6	7	8	9	0

—and we shall have 54 colours and hues of colour. Of each of these 54 colours and hues imagine 10 degrees of depth, and we get 540 colours, hues, tints, and shades, all differing from one another to an obvious degree.

Mark this fact, that any colour, tint, hue, or shade of such a diagram has its complement in one other of the colours, tints, hues, or shades of the diagram, and that only two of this series of 540 are complementary to each other; thus, if you fix on any one colour of the 540, there is but one colour in the whole that is complementary to it, and it is complementary to but this one other colour.

The student will do well to try and make a colour-diagram of this kind, of a simple character, say such as the following, only using pigments for my numbers; but in doing so he must exercise the utmost care, in order that he secure some degree of accuracy of tint or shade, and if he can call to his aid an experienced colourist it will be of great assistance to him.

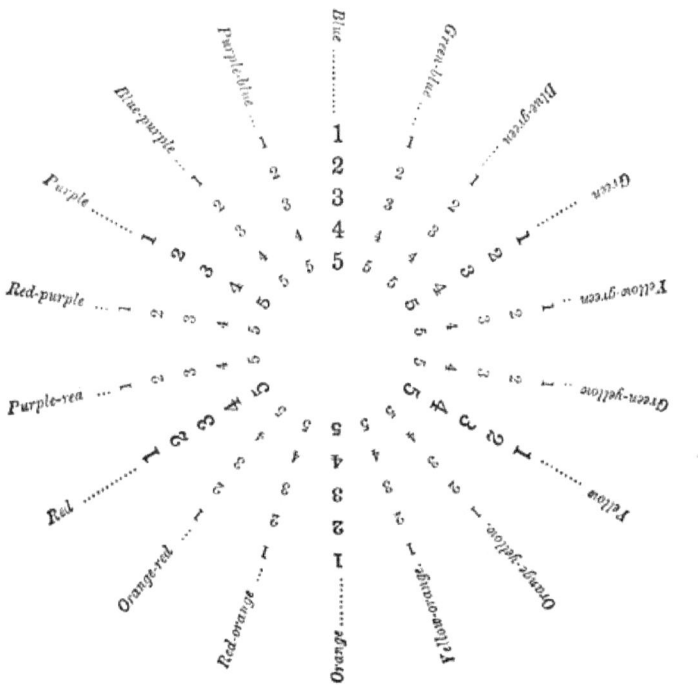

This table is highly valuable, as it gives ninety harmonies, if carefully prepared in colour; and the preparation of such a table is the very best practice that a student can possibly have.

Let us for a moment consider this table, and suppose that we want to find the complement to some particular colour, as the third shade of red. We find the complement of this in the third shade of green opposite. If we want the complement of the second shade of orange-yellow, we find it in the second shade of blue-purple opposite, and so on. Thus we have a means of at once judging of the harmony of colours.

It must ever be borne in mind that pigments mixed in the proportions given will not yield results such as would occur when the coloured rays of light are combined; thus three parts, either by weight or measure, of chrome yellow when combined with eight parts of ultramarine would not form a colour representing the secondary green, nor would the result be more satisfactory were other pigments combined in the proportions given. What we have said in respect to the proportions in which colours combine to form new colours applies only to the coloured rays of light.

It must now be noticed that while colours harmonise in the proportions stated, the areas occupied by the different colours may vary if there be a corresponding alteration in intensity. Thus eight of blue and eight of orange form a perfect harmony when both colours are of prismatic intensity; but we shall still have a perfect harmony if the orange is diluted to one-half its strength with white, and thus formed into a tint, provided there be sixteen parts of this orange of half strength to the eight parts of blue of full strength.

The orange might be further diluted to one-third of its full power, but then twenty-four parts would be necessary to a perfect harmony with eight parts of prismatic blue; or to one-fourth of its strength, when thirty-two parts would be necessary to the harmony.

It is not desirable that I occupy space with diagrams of these quantities, but the industrious student will prepare them for himself, and will strive to realise a true half-tint, quarter-tint, etc., which is not a very easy thing to do. By practice, however, it will readily be accomplished, and anything achieved is a new power gained.

What I have said respecting the harmony of blue with tints of orange will apply in all similar cases. Thus red will harmonise with tints of green, provided the area of the tint be increased as the intensity is decreased; and so will yellow harmonise with tints of purple under similar conditions.

But we may reverse the conditions, and lower the primary to a tint retaining the secondary in its intensity. Thus blue, if reduced to a half-tint, will harmonise with orange of prismatic intensity in the proportion of sixteen of blue to eight of orange; or, if reduced to a quarter-tint, in the proportion of thirty-two of blue to eight of orange. Red, if reduced to a half-tint, will harmonise in the proportion of ten red to eleven of green; and yellow as a half-tint in the proportion of six yellow to thirteen of purple.

The same remarks might be made respecting the harmony of shades of colour with colours of prismatic intensity. Thus, if orange is diluted to a shade of half intensity with black, it will harmonise with pure blue in the proportion of sixteen of orange to eight of blue, and so on, just as in the case of tints; and this principle applies to the harmony of all hues of colour also.

To go one step further: we scarcely ever deal with pure colours or their shades or tints, or even come as near them as we can. With great intensity of colour we seem to require an ethereal character, such as we have in those of light; but our pigments are coarse and earthy—they are too real-looking, and are not ethereal—they may be said to be corporeal rather than spiritual in character. For this reason we have to avoid the use of our purest pigments in such quantities as render their poverty of nature manifest, and to use for large surfaces such tints as, through their subtlety of composition, interest and please. A tint the composition of which is not apparent is always preferable to one of more obvious formation. Thus we are led to use tints which are subtly formed, and such as please by their newness and bewilder by the intricacy of formation.

To do what I here mean it is not necessary that many pigments be mixed together in order to the formation of a tint. The effect of which I speak can frequently be got by two well-chosen pigments. Thus a fine series of low-toned shades can be produced by mixing together middle-chrome and brown-lake in various proportions, and in all of the shades thus formed the three primary colours will be represented, but in some yellow will predominate, and in others red; while in many it will not be easy to discover to what proportionate extent the three primary colours are present.

Let us suppose that we make a tint by adding white to cobalt blue. This blue contains a small amount of yellow, and is a slightly green blue. But to this tint we add a small amount of raw umber with the view of imparting a greyness[15] or atmospheric character. Raw umber is a neutral colour, leaning slightly to yellow—that is, it consists of red, blue, and yellow,

---

[15] Cobalt, raw umber, and white make a magnificent grey, both in oil-colours, in tempera (powder-colours mixed with gum-water), and in distemper (powder-colours mixed with size).

with a slight excess of the latter. In order that an orange harmonise with this grey-blue of a slightly yellow tone, the orange must be slightly inclined to red, so as to form the complement of the little green formed by the yellow in the blue. It may harmonise with the grey-blue as a pure tint if the area of the diluted and neutralised primary is sufficiently extended, or may itself be likewise reduced to a tint of the same depth, when both tints would have the same area.

I might go on multiplying cases of this character to almost any extent, but these I leave the student to work out for himself, and pass to notice that while it is desirable to use subtle tints (often called "broken tints") it is rarely expedient to make up the full harmony by a large area of a tertiary tone and a single positive colour. Thus, we might have a shade or a tint of citrine spreading over a large surface as a ground on which we wished to place a figure. This figure would harmonise in pure purple were it of a certain size, and yet if thus coloured it would give a somewhat common-place effect when finished, for the harmony would be too simple and obvious. It would be much better to have the nineteen parts of citrine reduced, say, to half intensity, when the area would be increased to thirty-eight, with the figure of eight parts of blue and five of red, than of thirteen parts of purple.

But it would be better still if there were the thirty-eight parts of reduced citrine, three parts of pure yellow, thirteen of purple, five of red, and eight of blue, together with white, black, or gold, or all three (these may be added without altering the conditions, as all act as neutrals), for here the harmony is of a more subtle character.

If we count up the equivalents of the colours employed in this scheme of harmony, we shall see that we have, in the citrine—

Yellow6 (two equivalents).
Blue8 (one equivalent).
Red5 (one equivalent).

In the purple—

Blue8 (one equivalent).
Red5 (one equivalent).

Of the pure colours—

Yellow3 (one equivalent).
Red5 (one equivalent).
Blue8 (one equivalent).

Thus we have three equivalents of each primary, which give a perfect harmony.

I must not say more respecting the laws of harmony, for in the space of a small work it is impossible to do so, but proceed to notice certain effects or properties of colours, which I have as yet only alluded to, or have passed altogether unnoticed.

I have said that black, white, and gold are neutral as regards colour. This is the case, although many would suppose that gold was a yellow. Gold will act as a yellow, but it is generally employed as a neutral in decorative work, and it is more of a neutral than a yellow, for both red and blue exist largely in it.

The pictorial artist frames his picture with gold because it, being a neutral, does not interfere with the tints of his work. It has the further advantage of being rich and costly in appearance, and thus of giving an impression of worth where it exists.

Black, white, and gold, being neutral, may be advantageously employed to separate colours where separation is necessary or desirable.

Yellow and purple harmonise, but yellow is a light colour and purple is dark. These colours not only harmonise, but also contrast as to depth, the one being light and the other dark. The limit of each colour, wherever these are used in juxtaposition, is therefore obvious.

It is not so with red and green, for these harmonise when of the same depth. This being the case, and red being a glowing colour, if a red object is placed on a green ground, or a green object on a red ground, the "figure" and ground will appear to "swim" together, and will produce a dazzling effect. Colour must assist form, and not confuse it. It will do this in the instance just named if the figure is outlined with black, white, or gold, and there will be no loss of harmony. But experience has shown that this effect can also be averted by outlining the figure with a lighter tint of its own colour. Thus, if the figure is red and the ground green, an outline of lighter red (pink) may be employed. (See Proposition 26).

A blue figure on a red ground (as ultramarine on carmine), or a red figure on a blue ground, will also produce this swimming and unsatisfactory effect, but this is again obviated by an outline of black, white, or gold.

Employing the outline thus must not be regarded as a means of merely rendering what was actually unpleasant endurable, for it does much more—it affords one of the richest means of effect. A carmine ground well covered with bold green ornament having a gold outline is, if well managed, truly gorgeous; and were the figure blue on the red ground, the lavish use of gold would render the employment of yellow unnecessary as the yellow formed in the eye and cast upon the gold would satisfy all requirements.

It is a curious fact that the eye will create any colour of which there is a deficiency. This it will do, but the colour so created is of little use to the composition unless white or gold is present; if, however, there be white or gold in the composition, the colour which is absent, or is insufficiently represented, will be formed in the eye and cast upon these neutrals, and the white or the gold, as the case may be, will assume the tint of the deficient or absent colour. (See Propositions 8 and 9)

While this occurs (and sometimes it occurs to a marked degree, as can be shown by experiment), it must not be supposed that a composition in which any element is wanting is as perfect as one which reveals no want. It is far otherwise; only Nature here comes to our assistance, and is content to help herself rather than endure our short-comings; but in the one case we give Nature the labour of completing the harmony; while in the other, all being prepared, we receive a sense of satisfaction and repose.

In Proposition 8 we showed that when blue and black are juxtaposed, the black becomes "rusty," or assumes an orange tint; and in Proposition 9 we gave the cause of this effect. Let a blue spot be placed on a black silk necktie, and however black the silk, it will yet appear rusty. This is a fact; but we sometimes desire to employ blue on black, and wish the black to look black, and not an orange-black. How can we do this? Obviously by substituting for the black a very dark blue, as indigo. The bright blue spot induces orange (the complement of blue) in the eye. This orange, when cast upon black, causes the latter to look "rusty;" but if we place in the black an amount of blue sufficient to neutralise the orange cast upon it, the effect will be that of a jet-black.

We have now considered those qualities of colour, and those laws of contrast and harmony, which may be said to be of the grosser sort; but we have scarcely touched on those considerations which pertain to special refinement or tenderness of effect. But let me close the part of my subject of which I have treated, by repeating a statement already made—a statement, let me say, which first led me to perceive really harmony of colour—that *those colours, and those particular hues of colour, which improve each other to the utmost, are those which perfectly harmonise.* (Consider this statement in connection with Propositions 8, 9, 10, and 14)

We come now to consider delicacies and refinements in colour effects, which, although dependent upon the skilful exercise of the laws enunciated, are yet of a character, the power to produce which only results from the consideration of the works of the masters of great art-nations; but of these effects I can say little beyond pointing out what should be studied.

This principle however I cannot pass without notice—namely, that the finest colour effects are those of a rich, mingled, bloomy character.

Imagine a luxuriant garden, the beds in which are filled with a thousand flowers, having all the colours of the rainbow, and imagine these arranged as closely together as will permit of their growth. When viewed from a distance the effect is soft and rich, and full and varied, and is all that is pleasant. This is Nature's colouring. It is our work humbly to strive at producing like beauty with her.

This leads me to notice that primary colours (and secondary colours, also, when of great intensity) should be used chiefly in small masses, together with gold, white, or black.

Visit the Indian Museum at Whitehall,[16] and consider the beautiful Indian shawls and scarves and table-covers; or, if unable to do so, look in the windows of our large drapers in the chief towns, and see the true Indian fabrics,[17] and observe the manner in which small portions of intense reds, blues, yellows, greens, and a score of tertiary tints, are combined with white and black and gold to produce a very miracle of bloom. I know of nothing in the way of colour combination so rich, so beautiful, so gorgeous, and yet so soft, as some of these Indian shawls.

It is curious that we never find a purely Indian work otherwise than in good taste as regards colour harmony. Indian works, in this respect—whether carpets, or shawls, or

---

[16] This museum is open free to the public.

[17] These will only be seen in very first-class shops.

85

dress materials, or lacquered boxes, or enamelled weapons—are almost perfect—perfect in harmony, perfect in richness, perfect in the softness of their general effect. How strangely these works contrast with ours, where an harmonious work in colours is scarcely ever seen.

By the co-mingling (not co-mixing) of colours in the manner just described, a rich and bloomy effect can be got, having the general tone of a tertiary colour of any desired hue. Thus, if a wall be covered with little ornamental flowerets, by colouring all alike, and letting each contain two parts of yellow and one part of blue and one of red, as separate and pure colours, the distant hue will be that of citrine: the same effect will result if the flowers are coloured variously, while the same proportions of the primaries are preserved throughout. I can conceive of no decorative effects more subtle, rich, and lovely than those of which I now speak.

Imagine three rooms, all connected by open archways, and all decorated with a thousand flower-like ornaments, and these so coloured, in this mingled manner, that in one room blue predominates, in another red, and in another yellow; we should then have a beautiful tertiary bloom in each—a subtle mingling of colour, an exquisite delicacy and refinement of treatment, a fulness such as always results from a rich mingling of hues, and an amount of detail which would interest when closely inspected; besides which, we should have the harmony of the general effect of the three rooms, the one appearing as olive, another as citrine, and the other as russet.

This mode of decoration has this advantage, that it not only gives richness and beauty, but it also gives purity. If pigments are mixed together they are thereby reduced in intensity, as we have already seen; but if placed side by side, when viewed from a distance the eye will mix them, but they will suffer no diminution of brilliancy.

With the view of cultivating the eye, Eastern works cannot be too carefully studied. The Indian Museum should be the home of all who can avail themselves of the opportunity of study which it affords; and the small Indian department of the South Kensington Museum should not be neglected, small though it is.[18] Chinese works must also be considered, for they likewise supply most valuable examples of colour harmony; and although they do not present such a perfect colour bloom as do the works of India, yet they are never inharmonious, and give clearness and sharpness, together with great brilliancy, in a manner not attempted by the Indians.

The best works of Chinese embroidery are rarely seen in this country; but these are unsurpassed by the productions of any other people. For richness, splendour, and purity of colour,

---

[18] It may not be generally known, but nearly all our large manufacturing towns have, in connection with the Chamber of Commerce, a collection of Indian fabrics, filling several large volumes, which were prepared, at the expense of Government, under the superintendence of Dr. Forbes Watson, and which were given to the various towns on the condition that they be accessible to all persons who are trustworthy. Although these collections do not embrace the costly decorated fabrics, yet much can be learned from them, and the combinations of colour are always harmonious. A much larger collection is now in course of formation.

together with a delicious coolness, I know of nothing to equal them.

The works of the Japanese are not to be overlooked, for in certain branches of art they are inimitable, and as colourists they are almost perfect. On the commonest of their lacquer trays we generally have a bit of good colouring, and their coloured pictures are sometimes marvels of harmony.

As to the styles of colouring adopted by the nations referred to, I should say that the Indians produce rich, mingled, bloomy, *warm* effects—that is, effects in which red and yellow prevail; that the Chinese achieve clearness, repose, and *coolness*—a form of colouring in which blue and white prevail; and that the Japanese effects are *warm*, simple, and quiet.

Besides studying the works of India, China, and Japan, study those also of Turkey and Morocco, and even those of Algeria, for here the colouring is much better than with us, although not so good as in the countries first named. No aid to progress must be neglected, and no help must be despised.[19]

---

[19] The South Kensington Museum has a very interesting collection of art-works from China and Japan; but the latter are chiefly lent. It is a strange thing that the perfect works of the East are so poorly illustrated in this national collection, while costly, yea, very costly works of inferior character, illustrative of Renaissance art, swarm as thickly as flies in August. This can only be accounted for by the fact that the heads of the institution have a feeling for pictorial rather than decorative art, and the Renaissance ornament is that which has most of the pictorial element. To me, the style appears to

With the view of refining the judgment further in respect to colour, get a good colour-top,[20] and study its beautiful effects. See also the "gas tubes" illuminated by electricity, as sold by opticians, and let the prism yield you daily instruction. Soap-bubbles may also be blown, and the beautiful colours seen in them carefully noted. These and any other available means of cultivating the eye should constantly be resorted to, as by such means only can we become great colourists.

As to works on colour, we have the writings of Field, to whom we are indebted for valuable discoveries; of Hay, the decorator, and friend of the late David Roberts, but some of his ideas are wild and Utopian; of Chevreul, whose work will be most useful to the student; and the small catechism of colour by Mr. Redgrave, of the South Kensington Museum, which is excellent. The student will also do well to carefully study the excellent manual of "Colour" by Professor Church, of Cirencester College.

---

owe its very weakness to this fact, for decorative art should be wholly ideal. Pictorial art is of necessity more or less imitative.
[20] Not the so-called colour or "chameleon" top sold in the toy-shops, but the more scientific toy procurable of opticians, together with the perforated discs of Mr. John Graham, M.R.C.S., of Tunbridge, Kent.

CHAPTER III.

FURNITURE.

Having considered those principles which are of primary importance to the ornamentist, we may commence our notice of the various manufactures, and try to discover what particular form of art should be applied to each, and the special manner in which decorative principles should be considered as applicable to various materials and modes of working.

We shall first consider furniture, or cabinet-work, because articles of furniture occupy a place of greater importance in a room than carpets, wall-papers, or, perhaps, any other decorative works; and, also, because we shall learn from a consideration of furniture those structural principles which will be of value to us in considering the manner in which all art-objects should be formed if they have solid, and not simply superficial, dimensions.

In the present chapter, I shall strive to impress the fact that design and ornamentation may be essentially different things, and that in considering the formation of works of furniture these should be regarded as separate and distinct. "Design," says Redgrave, "has reference to the construction of any work both for use and beauty, and therefore includes its ornamentation also. Ornament is merely the decoration of a thing constructed."

The construction of furniture will form the chief theme of this chapter, for unless such works are properly constructed they cannot possibly be useful, and if not useful they would fail to answer the end for which they were contrived.

But before commencing a consideration of the principles involved in the construction of works of furniture, let me summarise what is required in such works if they are to assume the character of art-objects.

1. The general form, or mass form, of all constructed works must be carefully considered. The aspect of the "sky-blotch" of an architectural edifice is very important, for as the day wanes the detail fades and parts become blended, till the members compose but one whole, which, when seen from the east, appears as a solid mass drawn in darkness on the glowing sky; this is the sky-blotch. If the edifice *en masse* is pleasing, a great point is gained. Indeed, the general contour should have primary consideration. In like manner, the general form of all works of furniture should first be cared for, and every effort should be made at securing to the general mass beauty of shape.

2. After having cared for the general form, the manner in which the work shall be divided into primary and secondary parts must be considered with reference to the laws of proportion, as stated in a former chapter.

3. Detail and enrichment may now be considered; but while these cannot be too excellent, they must still be subordinate in obtrusiveness to the general mass, or to the aspect of the work as a whole.

4. The material of which the object is formed must always be worked in the most natural and appropriate manner.

5. The most convenient or appropriate form for an object should always be chosen, for unless this has been done, no reasonable hope can be entertained that the work will be satisfactory; for the consideration of utility must in all cases precede the consideration of beauty, as we saw in our first chapter.

Having made these few general remarks, we must consider the structure of works of furniture. The material of which we form our furniture is wood. Wood has a "grain," and the strength of any particular piece largely depends upon the direction of its grain. It may be strong if its grain runs parallel with its length, or weak if the grain crosses diagonally, or very weak if the grain crosses transversely. However strong the wood, it becomes comparatively much weaker if the grain crosses the piece; and however weak the wood, it becomes yet weaker if the grain is transverse or diagonal. These considerations lead us to see that *the grain of the wood must always be parallel with its length whenever strength is required.*

For our guidance in the formation of works of furniture, I give the following short table of woods arranged as to their strength:—

Iron-wood, from Jamaica—very strong, bearing great lateral pressure.

Box of Illawarry, New South Wales—very strong, but not so strong as iron-wood.

Mountain ash, New South Wales—about two-thirds the strength of iron-wood.

Beech—nearly as strong as mountain ash.

Mahogany, from New South Wales—not quite so strong as last.

Black dog-wood of Jamaica—three-fourths as strong as the mahogany just named.

Box-wood, Jamaica—not half as strong as the box of New South Wales.

Cedar of Jamaica—half as strong as the mahogany of New South Wales.[21]

Wood can be got of sufficient length to meet all the requirements of furniture-making, yet we not unfrequently find the arch structurally introduced into furniture, while it is absurd to employ it in wooden construction of any kind. The arch is a most ingenious invention, as it affords a means of spanning a large space with small portions of material, as with small stones, and at the same time gives great strength. It is, therefore, of the utmost utility in constructing stone buildings; but in works of furniture, where we have no large spaces to span, and where wood is of the utmost length required, and is stronger than our requirements demand, the use of the arch becomes structurally foolish and absurd. The folly of this mode of structure becomes more apparent when we notice that a wooden arch is always formed of one or two

---

[21] For full particulars on this subject see "Catalogue of the Collection illustrating Construction and Building Material," in the South Kensington Museum, and the manual of "Technical Drawing for Cabinetmakers," by E. A. Davidson.

pieces, and not of very small portions, and when we further consider that, in order to the formation of an arch, the wood must be cut across its grain throughout the greater portion of its length, whereby its strength is materially decreased; while if the arch were formed of small pieces of stone great strength would be secured. Nothing can be more absurd than the practice of imitating in one material a mode of construction which is only legitimate in the case of another, and of failing to avail ourselves of the particular mode of utilising a material which secures a maximum of desirable results.

While I protest against the arch when structurally used in furniture, I see no objection to it if used only as a source of beauty, and when so situated as to be free from strain or pressure.

One of the objects which we are frequently called upon to construct is a chair. The chair is, throughout Europe and America, considered as a necessity of every house. So largely used are chairs, that one firm at High Wycombe employs 5,000 hands in making common cane-bottomed chairs alone; and yet we see but few chairs in the market which are well constructed. All chairs having curved frames—whether the curve is in the wood of the back, in the sides of the seat, or in the legs—are constructed on false principles. They are of necessity weak, and being weak are not useful. As they are formed by using wood in a manner which fails to utilise its qualities of strength, these chairs are offensive and absurd. It is true that, through being surrounded by such ill-formed objects from our earliest infancy, the eye often fails to be offended with such works as would offend it were they new to it; but this does not show that they are the less offensive, nor that they are not constructively wrong. Besides, whenever wood is cut across the grain, in order that we get anything approaching the requisite strength, it has to be much thicker and more bulky than would be required were the wood cut with the grain; hence such furniture is unnecessarily heavy and clumsy.

Fig. 26 represents a chair which I have taken the liberty of borrowing from Mr. Eastlake's work on household art.[22] This chair Mr. Eastlake gives as an illustration of good taste in the construction of furniture; but I give it as an illustration of that which is essentially bad and wrong. The legs are weak, being cross-grained throughout, and the mode of uniting the upper and lower portions of the legs (the two semicircles) by a circular boss is defective in the highest degree. Were I sitting in such a chair, I should be afraid to lean to the right or the left, for fear of the chair giving way. Give me a Yorkshire rocking-chair, in preference to one of these, where I know of my insecurity, much as I hate such.

A chair is a stool with a back-rest, and a stool is a board elevated from the ground or floor by supports, the degree of elevation being determined by the length of the legs of the person for whom the seat is made, or by the degree of obliquity which the body and legs are desired to take when the seat is in use. If the seat is to support the body when in an erect sitting posture, about seventeen to eighteen inches will

---

[22] The title of the work is "Hints on Household Taste." It is well worth reading, as much may be learned from it. I think Mr. Eastlake right in many views, yet wrong in others, but I cannot help regarding him somewhat as an apostle of ugliness, as he appears to me to despise finish and refinement.

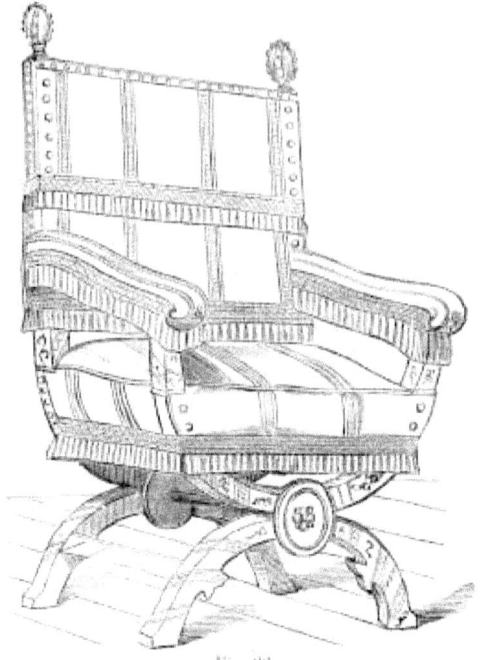

Fig. 26.

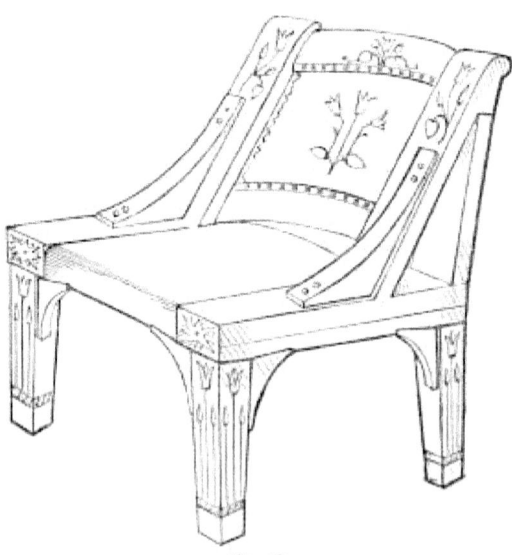

Fig. 27.

96

be found a convenient height for the average of persons; but if the legs of the sitter are to take an oblique forward direction, then the seat may be lower.

A stool may consist of a thick piece of wood and of three legs inserted into holes bored in this thick top. If these legs pass to the upper surface of the seat, and are properly wedged in, a useful yet clumsy seat results. In order that the top of the stool be thin and light, it will be necessary that the legs be connected by frames, and it will be well that they be connected twice, once at the top of each leg, so that the seat may rest upon this frame, and once at least two-thirds of the distance from the top. The frame would now stand alone, and although the seat is formed of thin wood it will not crack, as it is supported all round on the upper frame.

A chair, I have said, is a stool with a back. There is not one chair out of fifty that we find with the back so attached to the seat as to give a maximum of strength. It is usual to make a back leg and one side of the chair-back out of one piece of wood—that is, to continue the back legs up above the seat, and cause them to become the sides of the chair-back. When this is done the wood is almost invariably curved so that the back legs and the chair-back both incline outwards from the seat. There is no objection whatever to the sides of the back and the legs being formed of the one piece, but there is a great objection to either the supports of the back or the legs being formed of cross-grained wood, as much of their strength is thereby sacrificed. Our illustrations (Figs. 27 to 32) will give several modes of constructing chairs such as I think legitimate; but I will ask the reader to think for himself upon the construction of a chair, and especially upon the proper means of giving due support to the back.

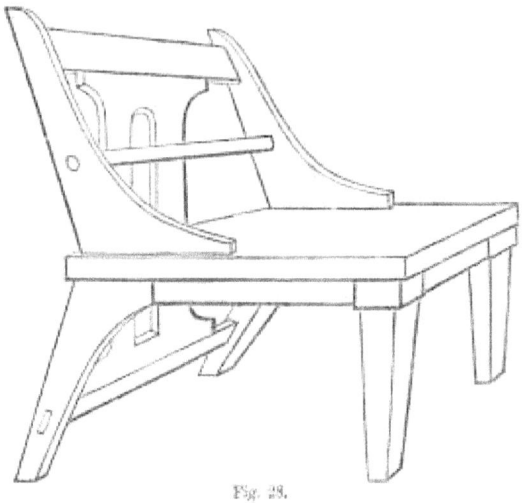

Fig. 48.

I have given, in an axiomatic form, those principles which should guide us in the construction of works of furniture, and endeavoured to impress the necessity of using wood in that manner which is most natural—that is, "working" it with the grain (the manner in which we can most easily work it), and in that way which shall secure the greatest amount of strength with the least expenditure of material. I wish to impress my readers with the importance of these considerations, for they lie at the very root of the successful construction of furniture. If the legs of chairs, or their seat-frames, or the ends or backs of couches, are formed of wood cut across the grain, they must either be thick and clumsy, or weak; but, besides this, the rightly constituted mind can only receive pleasure from the contemplation of works which are wisely formed. Daily contact, as we have before said, with ill-shaped objects may have more or less deadened our senses, so that we are not so readily offended by deformity and error as we might be; yet, happily for us, directly we seek to separate truth from error, the beautiful from the deformed, reason assists the judgment, and we learn to feel when we are in the presence of the beautiful or in contact with the degraded.

My illustrations will show how I think chairs should be constructed. Fig. 26 is essentially bad, although it has traditional sanction, hence I pass it over without further comment. Fig. 27 is in the manner of an Egyptian chair. It serves to show the careful way in which the Egyptians constructed their works. The curved rails against which the back would rest are the only parts which are not thoroughly correct and satisfactory in a wood structure. Were the curved back members metal, the curvature would be desirable and legitimate. The back of this chair, if the side members were connected by a straight rail, would have immense strength (the backs of some of *our* chairs are of the very weakest), and if well made it is a seat which would endure for centuries. Fig. 28 is a chair of my own designing, in which I have sought to give strength to the back by connecting its upper portion with a strong cross-rail of the frame.

Fig. 29 is a chair slightly altered from one in Mr. Eastlake's work on "Household Taste;" as shown in our illustration, it is a correctly formed work. Fig. 30 is an arm-chair in the Greek style, which I have designed. Fig. 31 is a Lady's chair in the Gothic style; Fig. 32, a lady's chair in early Greek. These I have prepared to show different modes of structure; if the legs are fitted to a frame (the seat-frame), as in the early Greek chair just alluded to, they should be very short, as in this instance, or they must be connected by a frame below the seat, as in Figs. 33 and 34. The best general structure is that in which the front legs pass to the level of the upper surface of the seat.

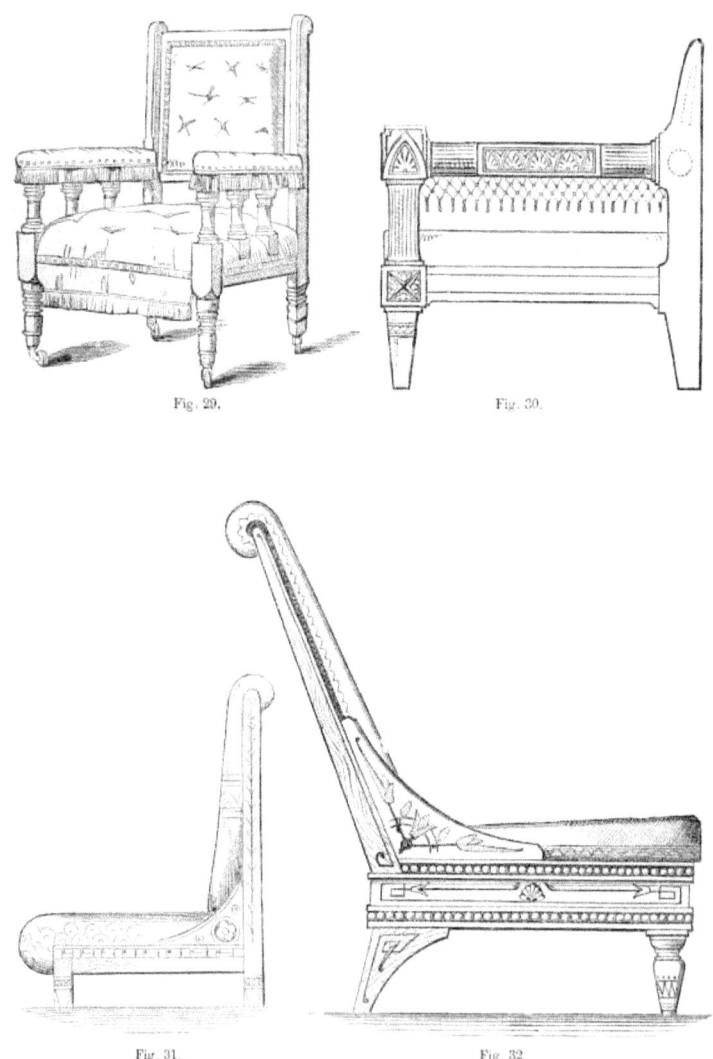

Fig. 29.

Fig. 30.

Fig. 31.

Fig. 32.

Fig. 33 is a copy of a chair shown by Messrs. Gillow and Co., of Oxford Street, in the last Paris International Exhibition. In many respects it is admirably constructed. The skeleton brackets holding the back to the seat are very desirable adjuncts to light chairs; so are the brackets connecting the legs with the seat-frame, as these strengthen the entire chair. The manner in which the upper rail of the back passes through the side uprights and is "pinned" is good. The chief, and only important, fault in this chair is the bending of the back legs, involving their being cut against the grain of the wood.

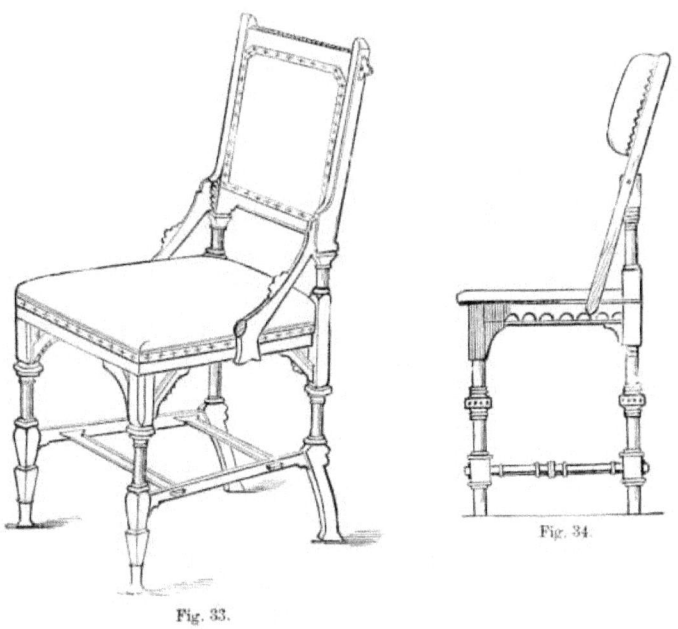

Fig. 34.

Fig. 33.

Fig. 31 is a chair from Mr. Talbert's very excellent work on "Gothic Furniture." It shows an admirable method of supporting the back. Fig. 35 I have designed as a high-backed lounging chair. With the view of giving strength to the back,

I have extended the seat, and arranged a support from this extension to the upper back-rail, and this extension of the seat I have supported by a fifth leg. There is no reason whatever why a chair should have four legs. If three would be better, or five, or any other number, let us use what would be best.[23]

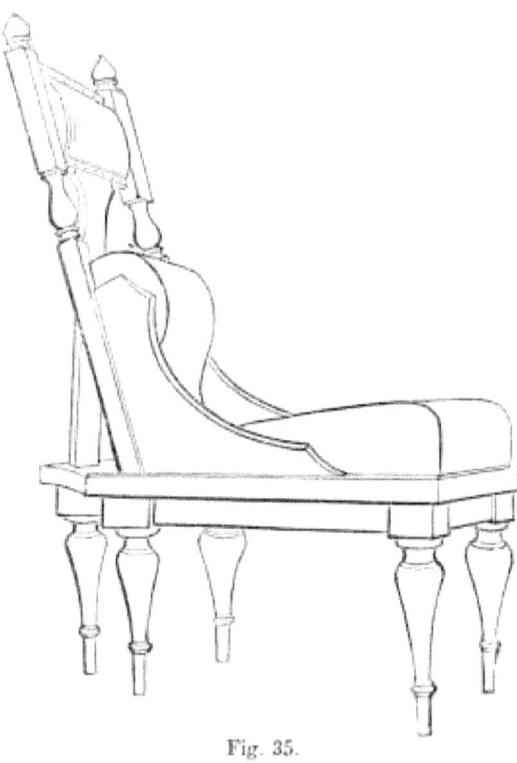

Fig. 35.

I have now given several illustrations of modes of forming chairs. I might have given many more, but it is not my duty

---

[23] In my drawing, the stuffing of the back has been accidentally shown too much rounded.

to try and exhaust a subject. What I have to do is simply point out principles, and call attention to facts. It is the reader who must think for himself—first, of the principles and facts which I adduce; secondly, of the illustrations which I give; thirdly, of other works which he may meet with; and fourthly, of further means of producing desirable and satisfactory results than those set forth in my illustrations.

As it cannot be doubted that a well-constructed work, however plain or simple it may be, gives satisfaction to those who behold it—while a work of the most elaborate character fails to satisfy if badly constructed—we shall give a few further illustrations of structure for other articles of furniture, besides chairs, which have become necessary to our mode of life.

Fig. 36 is one of my sketches for Greek furniture, designed for a wealthy client. It was formed of black wood. Here the frame of the seat is first formed, and the legs are inserted beneath it, and let into it, while the wood-work of the end of the couch stands upon it, being inserted into it. This appears to have been the general method with the Greeks of forming their furniture, yet it is not so correct structurally as Fig. 37, another of my sketches, where the end and the leg are formed of one piece of wood. The first formation (that of Fig. 36) would bear any amount of pressure from above, but it is not well calculated for resisting lateral pressure; while the latter would resist this lateral pressure, but would not bear quite the same amount of pressure from above. The latter, however, could bear more weight than would ever be required of it, and would be the more durable piece of furniture.

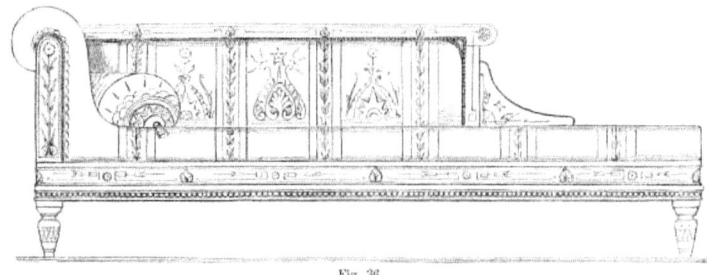

Fig. 36.

Fig. 38 gives a legitimate formation for a settee; the cutting-out, or hollowing, of the sides of the legs is not carried to an extreme, but leaves a sufficiency of strong wood with an upright grain to resist all the pressure that would be placed on the seat, and the lower and upper thickened portions of the legs act as the brackets beneath the seat in Fig. 33. The arch here introduced is not used structurally, but for the sake of a curved line, and acts simply as a pair of brackets. This illustration is also from Mr. Talbert's work. Fig. 39 is a table such as we occasionally meet with. I see no objection to the legs leaning inwards at the top; indeed, we have here a picturesque and useful table of legitimate formation. Fig. 40 is the end elevation of a sideboard from Mr. Talbert's work. Mark the simplicity of the structure. The leading or structural lines are straight and obvious. Although Mr. Talbert is not always right, yet his book is well worthy of the most careful consideration and study; and this I can truly say, that it compares favourably with all other works on furniture with which I am acquainted.

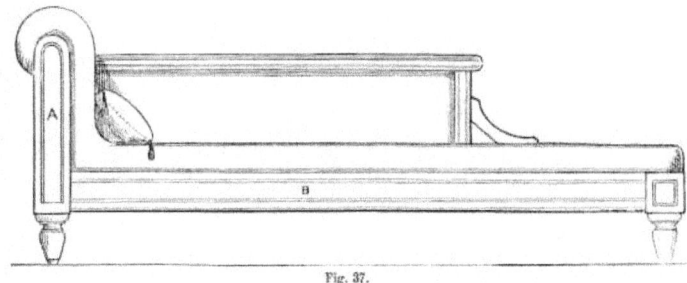

Fig. 37.

The general want which we perceive in modern furniture is simplicity of structure and truthfulness of construction. If persons would but think out the easiest mode of constructing a work before they commence to design it, and would be content with this simplicity of structure, we should have very different furniture from what we have. Think first of what is wanted, then of the material at command.

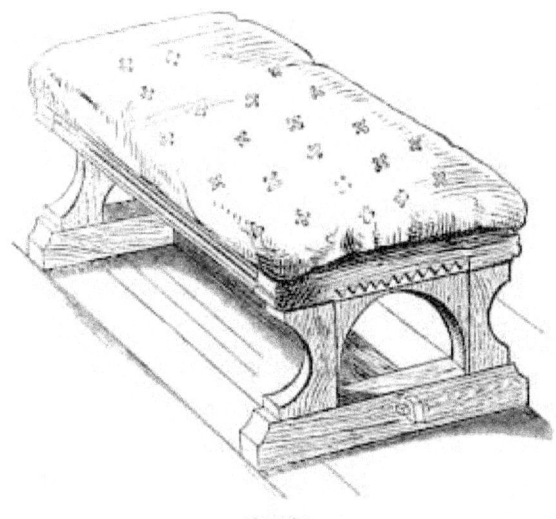

Fig. 38.

I fear that I have very feebly enforced and very inefficiently illustrated the true principles on which works of furniture should be constructed; and yet I feel that the structure of such works is of importance beyond all other considerations. Space is limited, however, and I must pass on; hence I only hope that I have induced the reader to think for himself, and if I have done so I shall have fulfilled my desire, for his progress will then be sure.

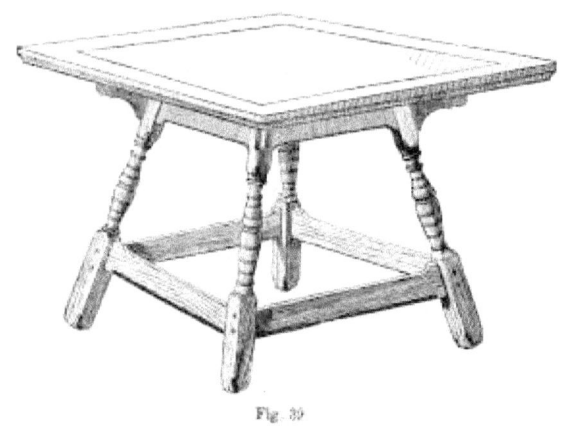

Fig. 39

Respecting structure I have but a few general remarks further to make, and all these are fairly embraced in the one expression, "Be truthful." An obvious and true structure is always pleasant. Let, then, the "tenon" and the "mortise" pass through the various members, and let the parts be "pinned" together by obvious wooden pins. Thus, if the frame of a chair-seat is tenoned into the legs, let the tenon pass through the leg and be visible on the outer side, and let it be held in its place by glue and wooden pins—the pins being visible. Yet they need not protrude beyond the surface; but why hide them? In this way that old furniture was made which has endured while piece after piece of modern furniture, made with invisible joints and concealed nails and screws, has perished. This is a true structural treatment, and is honest in expression also.

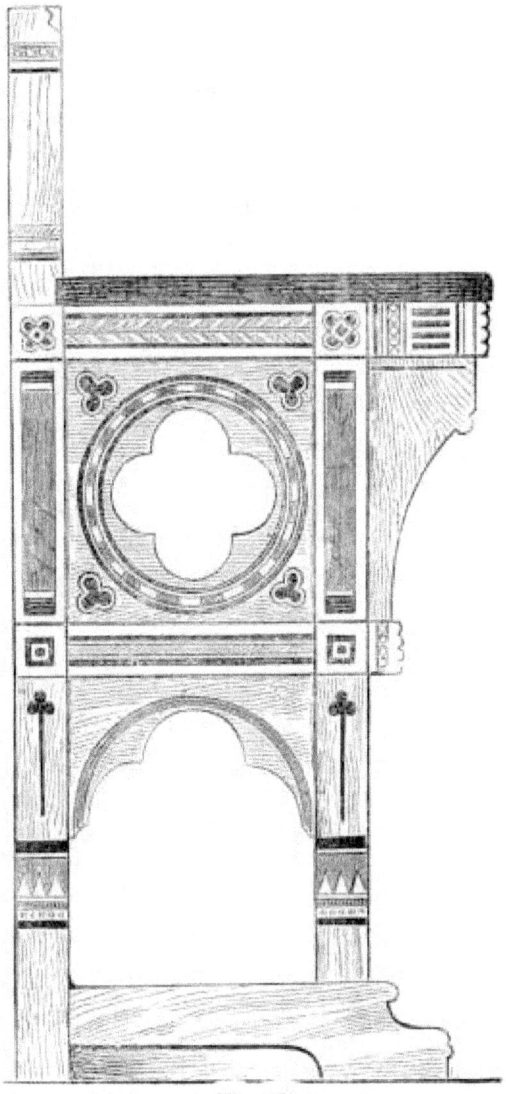

Fig. 40.

I do not give this as a principle applicable to one class of furniture only, but to all. When we have "pinned" furniture with an open structure (see the back of chair, Fig. 33), the mode of putting together must of necessity be manifest; but in all other cases the tenons should also go through, and the pins by which they are held in their place be driven from one surface to the other side right through the member.

In the commencement of this chapter on furniture, I said that after the most convenient form has been chosen for an object, and after it has been arranged that the material of which it is to be formed shall be worked in the most natural or befitting way, that then the block-form must be looked to, after which comes the division of the mass into primary parts, and lastly, the consideration of detail.

As to the block-form, let it be simple, and have the appearance of appropriateness and consistency. Its character must be regulated, to an extent, by the nature of the house for which the furniture is intended, and by the character of the room in which it is to be placed. All I can say to the student on this part of the subject is this: Carefully consider good works of furniture whenever opportunity occurs, and note their general conformation. A fine work will never have strong architectural qualities—that is, it will not look like part of a building formed of wood instead of stone. There is but small danger of committing any great error in the block-form, if it be kept simple, and to look like a work in wood, provided that the proportions of height to width and of width and height to thickness are duly cared for.

After the general form has been considered, the mass may be broken into primary and secondary parts. Thus, if we have to construct a cabinet, the upper part of which consists of a cupboard, and the lower portion of drawers, we should have to determine the proportion which the one part should bear to the other. This is an invariable rule—that the work must not consist of equal parts; thus, if the whole cabinet be six feet in height, the cupboards could not be three feet while the drawers occupied three feet also. The division would have to be of a subtle character—of a character which could not be readily detected. Thus the cupboard might be three feet five inches, and the drawers collectively two feet seven inches. If the drawers are not all to be of the same depth, then the relation of one drawer, as regards its size, to that of another must be considered, and of each to the cupboard above. In like manner the proportion of the panels of the doors to the styles must be thought out; and until all this has been done no work should ever be constructed.

Next comes the enrichment of parts. Carving should be sparingly used, and is best confined to mouldings, or projecting or terminal ends. If employed in mouldings, those members should be enriched which are more or less completely guarded from dust and injury by some overhanging member. If more carving is used, it should certainly be a mere enrichment of necessary structure—as we see on the legs and other uprights of Mr. Crace's sideboard, by Pugin (Fig. 41). I am not fond of carved panels, but should these be employed the carving should never project beyond the styles surrounding them, and in all cases of carving no pointed members must protrude so as to injure the person or destroy the dress of those who use the piece of furniture. If carving is used sparingly, it gives us the impression that it is valuable; if it is lavishly employed, it appears to be comparatively worthless. The aim of art is the production of repose. A large work of furniture which is carved all over cannot produce the necessary sense of repose, and is therefore objectionable.

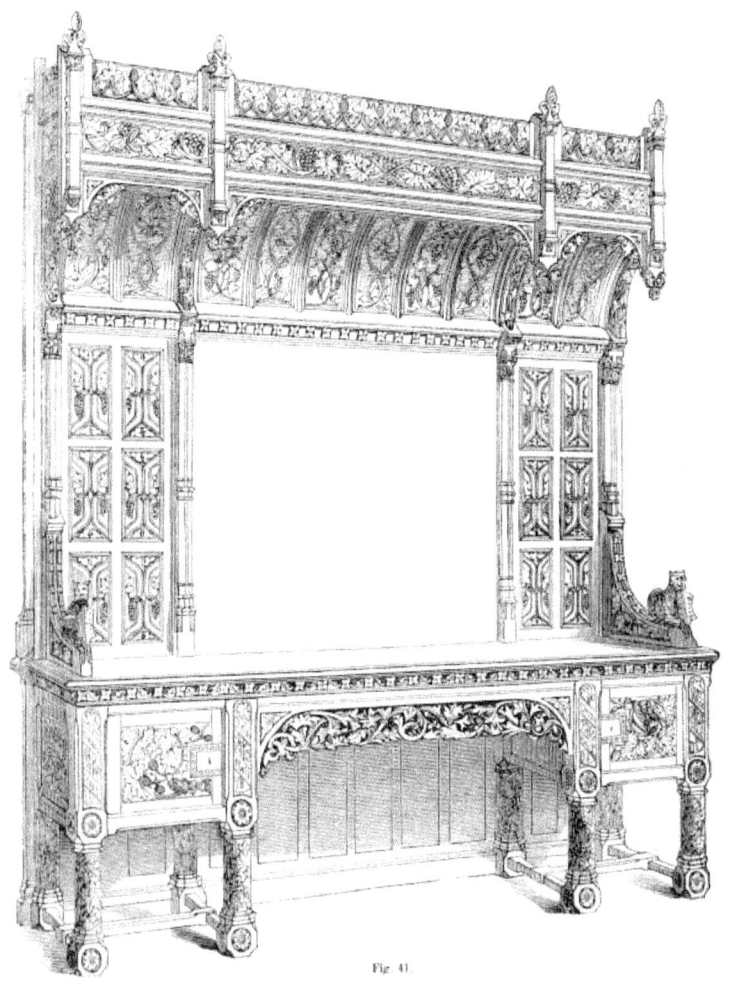

Fig. 41

There may be an excess of finish in works of carving connected with cabinet-work; for if the finish is too delicate there is a lack of effect in the result. A piece of furniture is not a miniature work, which is to be investigated in every detail. It is an object of utility, which is to appear beautiful in a room, and is not to command undivided attention; it is a work which is to combine with other works in rendering an apartment beautiful. The South Kensington Museum purchased in the last Paris International Exhibition, at great cost, a cabinet from Fourdonois; but it is a very unsatisfactory specimen, as it is too delicate, too tender, and too fine for a work of utility—it is an example of what should be avoided rather than of what should be followed. The delicately carved and beautiful panels of the doors, if cut in marble and used as mere pieces of sculpture, would have been worthy of the highest commendation; but works of this kind wrought in a material that has a "grain," however little the grain may show, are absurd. Besides, the subjects are of too pictorial a character for "applied work"—that is, they are treated in too pictorial or naturalistic a manner. A broad, simple, idealised treatment of the figure is that which is alone legitimate in cabinet work.

Supports or columns carved into the form of human figures are always objectionable.

Besides carving, as a means of enrichment, we have inlaying, painting, and the applying of plaques of stone or earthenware, and of brass or ormolu enrichments, and we have the inserting of brass into the material when buhl-work is formed.

Inlaying is a very natural and beautiful means of enriching works of furniture, for it leaves the flatness of the surface undisturbed. A great deal may be done in this way by the employment of simple means. A mere row of circular dots of black wood inlaid in oak will often give a remarkably good effect; and the dots can be "worked" with the utmost ease. Three dots form a trefoil, four dots a quatrefoil, six dots a hexafoil, and so on, and desirable effects can often be produced by such simple inlays.

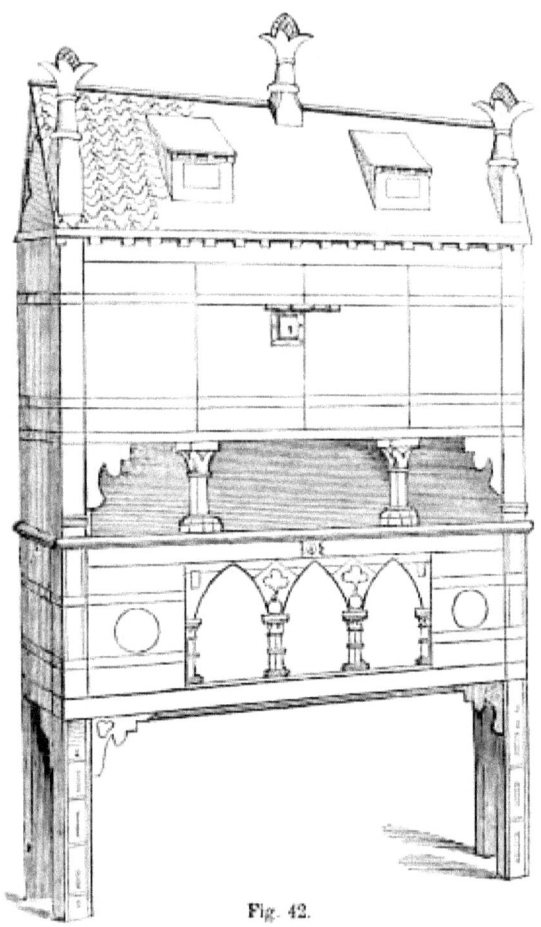

Fig. 42.

Panels of cabinets may be painted, and enriched with ornament or flatly-treated figure subjects. This is a beautiful mode of decoration very much neglected. The couch (Fig.

37) I intended for enrichment of this kind. If this form is employed, care should be exercised in order that the painted work be in all cases so situated that it cannot be rubbed. It should fill sunk panels and hollows and never appear on advancing members.

I am not fond of the application of plaques of stone or earthenware to works of furniture. Anything that is brittle is not suitable as an enrichment of wood-work, unless it can be so placed as to be out of danger.

Ormolu ornaments, when applied to cabinets and other works in wood, are also never satisfactory. They look too separate from the wood of which the work is formed—too obviously applied; and whatever is obviously *applied* to the work, and is not a portion of its general fabric, whether a mass of flowers even if carved in wood or an ormolu ornament, is not pleasant.

Buhl-work is often very clever in character and skilfully wrought, but I do not care for it. It is of too laborious a nature, and thus intrudes upon us the sense of labour as well as that of skill. As a means of enrichment, I approve of carving, sparingly used, of inlays, and of painted ornament in certain cases; and by the just employment of these means the utmost beauty in cabinet-work can be achieved. Ebony inlaid with ivory is very beautiful.

In order to illustrate my remarks respecting cabinets, sideboards, and similar pieces of furniture, I give an engraving of a sideboard executed by Mr. Crace, from the design of Mr. A. Welby Pugin (the father), to which I have before alluded (Fig. 41), and a painted cabinet by Mr. Burgess (Fig. 42), the well-known Gothic architect, whose architecture must be admired. Both of these works are worthy of study of a very careful kind.

In the sideboard, notice first the general structure or construction of the work, then the manner in which it is broken into parts, and lastly, that it is the structural members which are carved. If this work has faults, they are these: first, the carving is in excess—thus, the panels would have been better plain; and, second, in some parts there is a slight indication of a stone structure, as in the buttress character of the ends of the sideboard.

To the cabinet much more serious objections may be taken.

1st. A roof is a means whereby the weather is kept out of a dwelling, and tiles afford a means whereby small pieces of material enable us to form a perfect covering to our houses of a weather-proof character. It is very absurd, then, to treat the roof of a cabinet, which is to stand in a room, as if it were an entire house, or an object which were to stand in a garden.

2nd. The windows in the roof, which in the case of a house let light into those rooms which are placed in this part of the building, and are formed in a particular manner so as the more perfectly to exclude rain, become simply stupid when placed in the roof of a cabinet. These, together with the imitation tiled roof, degrade the work to a mere doll's house in appearance.

3rd. A panelled structure, which is the strongest and best structure, is ignored; hence strong metal bindings are necessary.

The painting of the work is highly interesting, and had it been more flatly treated, would then have been truthful, and would yet have lent the same interest to the cabinet that it now does, even if we consider the matter from a purely pictorial point of view.

Before we pass from a consideration of furniture and cabinet-work generally, we must notice a few points to which we have as yet merely referred, or which we have left altogether unnoticed. Thus we have to consider upholstery as applied to works of furniture, the materials employed as coverings for seats, and the nature of picture-frames and curtain-poles; we must also notice general errors in furniture, strictly so called.

When examining certain wardrobes and cabinets in the International Exhibition of 1862, I was forcibly impressed with the structural truth of one or two of these works. One especially commended itself to me as a fine structural work of classic character. Just as I was expressing my admiration, the exhibitor threw open the doors of this well-formed wardrobe to show me its internal fittings, when, fancy my feelings at beholding the first door bearing with it, as it opened, the two pilasters that I conceived to be the supports of the somewhat heavy cornice above, and the other door bearing away the third support, and thus leaving the superincumbent mass resting on the thin sides of the structure only, while they appeared altogether unable to perform the duty imposed upon them. "Horrible! horrible!" was all I could exclaim.

Some of the most costly works of furniture shown by the French in the last Paris International Exhibition were not free from this defect; and this is strange, for to the rightly constituted mind this one defect is of such a grave character as to neutralise whatever pleasure might otherwise be derived from contemplating the work. We see a man, a genius perhaps—a man having qualities that all must admire; but he has one great vice—one sin which easily besets him. While the man has excellent and estimable qualities, we yet avoid him, for we see not the excellences but the vice. It is so with such works of furniture as those of which we have been speaking, for their defects are such as impress us more powerfully than their excellences.

Respecting these works of furniture, this should be said: they are more or less imitative of works of a debased art-period—of a period in which structural truth was utterly disregarded—yet this is no reason why we should copy the defects of our ancestors.

Infinitely worse than the works just spoken of, is falsely constructed Gothic furniture, where the very truthfulness of structure is openly set before us. Not long since I was staying with a client whose house is of Gothic style. Being about to furnish drawings for the decorations of this mansion, I was carefully noting the character of the architecture and of the furniture, which latter had been designed and manufactured expressly for the house by a large Yorkshire firm of cabinet-makers. The structure of the furniture appeared just, the proportions tolerably good, the wood honest, and the inlays judicious; but, can it be imagined, the whole was a mere series of frauds and shams—the cross-grain ends of what should be supports were attached to the fronts of drawers, pillars came away, and such falsity became apparent as I never before saw. How any person could possibly produce such furniture, be he ever so degraded, I cannot think. I have seen works that are bad, I have seen falsities in art, but I never before saw such falsity of structure and such uncalled-for deception as these works presented. The untrue is always offensive; but when a special effort is made at causing a lie to appear as truth, a double sense of disappointment is experienced when the untruthfulness is discovered.

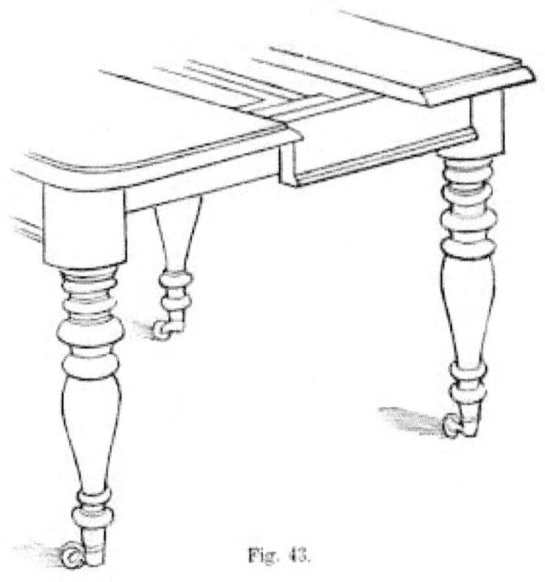

Fig. 43.

In his work on "Household Taste," to which I have before alluded, Mr. Eastlake objects, and I think very justly, to the character of an ordinary telescopic dining-table. He says: "Among the dining-room appointments, the table is an article of furniture which stands greatly in need of reform. It is generally made of planks of polished oak or mahogany laid upon an insecure framework of the same material, and supported by four gouty legs, ornamented by the turner with mouldings which look like inverted cups and saucers piled upon an attic baluster. I call the framework insecure, because

I am describing what is commonly called a 'telescope' table, or one which can be pulled out to twice its usual length, and, by the addition of extra leaves in its middle, accommodate twice the usual number of diners. Such a table cannot be soundly made in the same sense that ordinary furniture is sound; it must depend for its support on some contrivance which is not consistent with the material of which it is made. Few people would like to sit on a chair the legs of which slid in and out, and were fastened at the required height by a pin; there would be a sense of insecurity in the notion eminently unpleasant. You might put up with such an invention in camp, or on a sketching expedition, but to have it and use it under your own roof, instead of a strong and serviceable chair, would be absurd. Yet this is very much what we do in the case of the modern dining-room table. When it is extended it looks weak and untidy at the sides; when it is reduced to its shortest length the legs appear heavy and ill-proportioned. It is always liable to get out of order, and from the very nature of its construction must be an inartistic object. Why should such a table be made at all? A dining-room is a room to dine in. Whether there are few or many people seated for that purpose, the table might well be kept of a uniform length, and if space is an object it is always possible to use in its stead two small tables, each on four legs. These might be placed end to end when dinner parties are given, and one of them would suffice for family use. A table of this kind might be solidly and stoutly framed, so as to last for ages, and become, as all furniture ought to become, an heirloom in the family. When a man builds himself a house on freehold land, he does not intend that it shall only last his lifetime; he bequeaths it in sound condition to posterity. We ought to be ashamed of furniture which is continually being replaced; at all events, we cannot possibly take any interest in such furniture. In former days, when the principles of good joinery were really understood, the legs of such a large table as that of the dining-room would have been made of a very different form from the lumpy, pear-shaped things of modern use."

In nearly all these remarks I agree with Mr. Eastlake, and especially in his remark that, owing to the very nature of its construction, a modern dining-table must be an inartistic object. No work can be satisfactory in which any portions of the true supporting structure or frame are drawn apart; and this occurs to a marked degree in this table, as is shown in Mr. Eastlake's illustration, which we here copy (Fig. 43).

Falsities of structure, although not so glaring as that of the telescopic dining-table, are everywhere met with in our shops, and, curious as it may appear, the great majority of the works offered to the public are not only false in structure, but are utterly offensive to good taste in every way, and are formed almost exclusively of wood cut across the grain, which secures to the article the maximum amount of weakness. Figs. 44, 45, 46, and 47 are examples of utterly bad furniture.

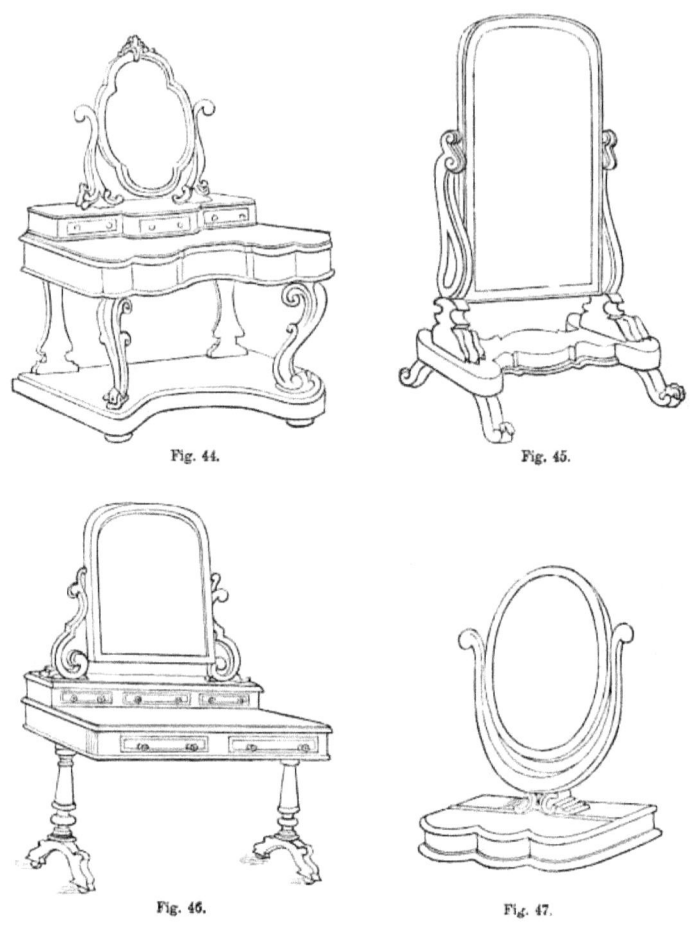

Fig. 44.

Fig. 45.

Fig. 46.

Fig. 47.

Another falsity in furniture is veneering—a practice which should be wholly abandoned. Simple honesty is preferable to false show in all cases; truthfulness in utterance is always to be desired. It was customary at one time to veneer almost every work of furniture, and even to place the grain of the veneer in a manner totally at variance with the true structure of the framework which it covered. This was a method of making works, which might in their unfinished state be satisfactory, appear when finished as most unsatisfactory objects. Since this time much progress has been made in a knowledge of truthful structure and of truthful expression, yet this method of giving a false surface by means of veneer is not wholly abandoned as despicable and false.

A few months back I had occasion to visit a cabinet warehouse in Lancashire, and the owner called my attention to the fine grain of some old English oak, and remarked that certain pieces of furniture were of solid wood. Upon investigation, however, I discovered that while the furniture in question was made throughout of oak, the bulk of the structure was of common wainscoting, and the surface was veneered with English oak. I confess that I would much rather have had the furniture without its false exterior, and daily my love for fine grain in wood gets less. I think that this arises from the fact that strong grain in wood takes from the "unity" of the work into which it is formed, and tends to break it up into parts, by rendering every member conspicuous. What is wanted in a work of furniture, before all other considerations, is a fine general form—a harmony of all parts—so that no one member usurps a primary place—and this it is almost impossible to achieve if a wood is employed having a strongly marked grain.

With us a room is considered as almost unfurnished if the windows are not hung with some kind of drapery. The original object of this drapery was that of keeping out a draught of air, which found its way through the imperfectly fitting windows; and the antitype of our window-hangings was a simple curtain, formed of a material suitable to achieve the purpose sought. Such a curtain was legitimate and desirable, and would contrast strangely with the elaborate festooning and quadrupled curtains of our present windows. We daily see yards of valuable material, arranged in massive and absurd folds, shutting out that light which is necessary to our health and well-being; a pair of heavy stuff curtains and a pair of lace curtains being hung at each window, each curtain consisting of a sufficient amount of material to more than cover the window of itself. An excess of drapery is always vulgar, while a little drapery usefully and judiciously employed is pleasant.

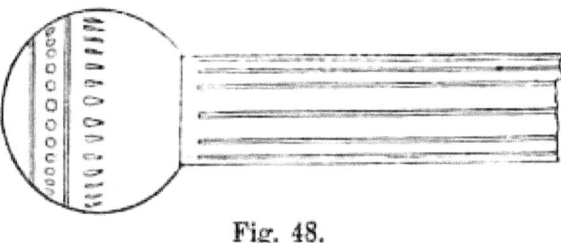

Fig. 48.

Many windows that are well made, and thus keep out all currents of air, need no curtains. If the window mouldings are of an architectural character, and are coloured much darker than the wall, so as to become an obvious frame to the window, and thus do for the window what a picture-frame does for a picture, no curtains will be required. I have recently had a wonderfully striking illustration of this. Two adjoining rooms are alike in their architecture; one is decorated, and has the window casement of such colours as strongly contrast, while they are yet harmonious, with the wall. Before the room was decorated, and the windows were thus treated, a general light colour prevailed, both on the wood-work and on the walls of the room, and curtains were hung at the windows in the usual way. With the altered decorations, the windows became so effective that I at once saw the undesirability of rehanging the curtains, and yet not one of all my friends has observed that there are no curtains to the windows; while if the curtains are removed from the adjoining room, where the window-frames are as light as the walls, the first question asked is, "Where are your curtains?"

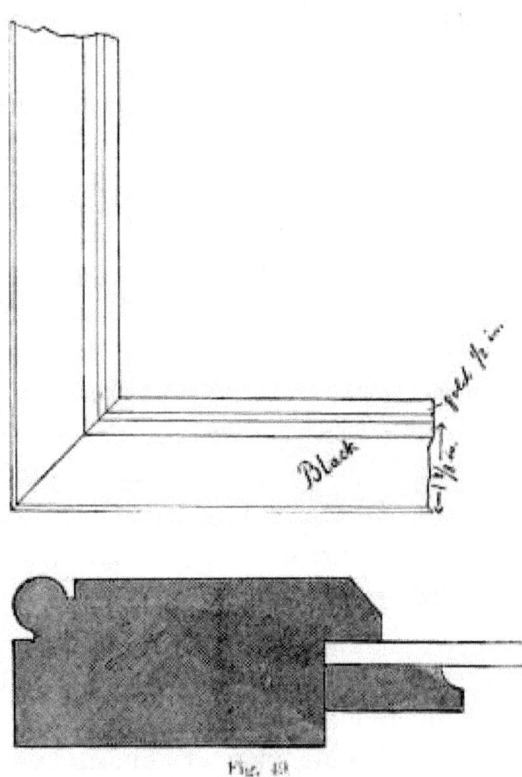

Fig. 48

Curtains should be hung on a simple and obvious pole (Fig. 48). All means of hiding this pole are foolish and useless. This pole need not be very thick, and is better formed of wood than of metal, for then the rings to which the curtains are attached pass along almost noiselessly. The ends of the pole may be of metal, but I prefer simple balls of wood. The pole may be grooved, and any little enrichments may be introduced into these grooves, providing the carving does not come to the surface, and thus touch the rings, which by their motion would injure it. Whatever is used in the way of enrichment should be of simple character, for the height at which the curtain pole is placed would render fine work altogether ineffective.

As to upholstery, I would say, never indulge in an excess. A wood frame should appear in every work of furniture, as in the examples we have given. Sofas are now made as though they were feather beds; they are so soft that you sink into them, and become uncomfortably warm by merely resting upon them, and their gouty forms are relieved only by a few inches of wood, which appear as legs. Stuffing should be employed only as a means of rendering a properly constructed seat comfortably soft. If it goes beyond this it is vulgar and objectionable. Spring stuffing is not to be altogether commended; a good old-fashioned hair-stuffed seat is more desirable, as it will endure when springs have perished. As to the materials with which seats may be covered I can say little, for they are many. Hair cloth, although very durable, is altogether inartistic in its effect. Nothing is better than leather for dining-room chairs; Utrecht velvet, either plain or embossed, looks well on library chairs; silk and satin damasks, rep, plain cloth, and many other fabrics are appropriate to drawing-room furniture. Chintz I am not fond of as a chair covering, and in a bed-room I would rather have chairs with plain wooden seats than with cushions covered with this glazed material.

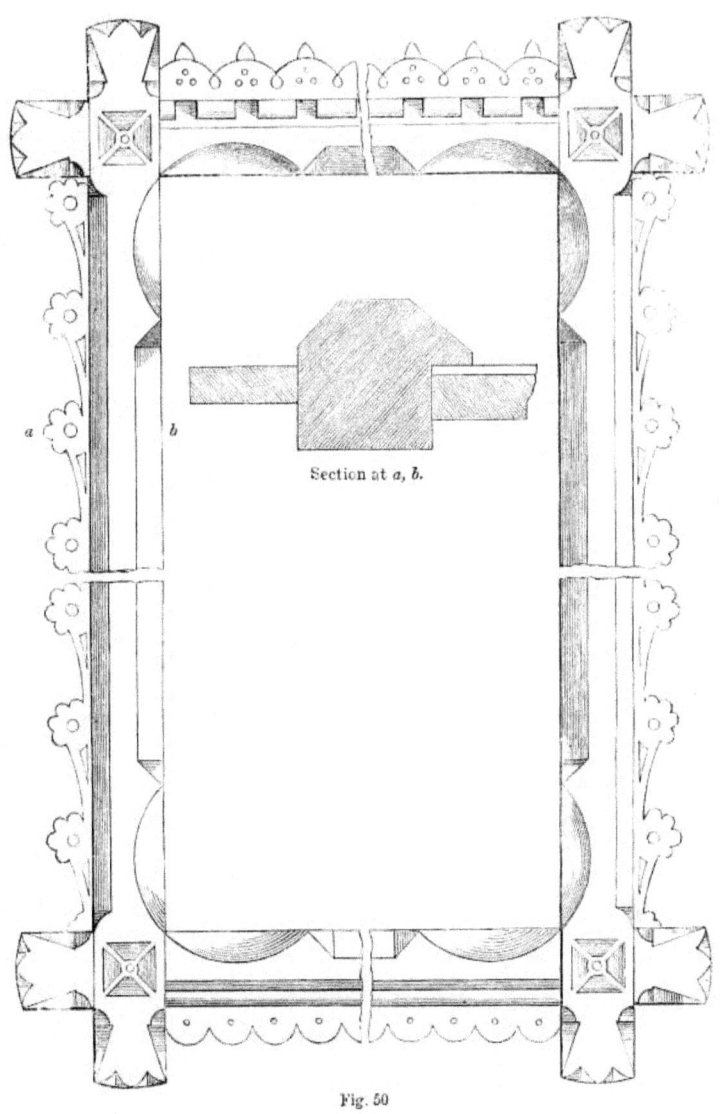

Section at *a, b.*

Fig. 50

With a mere remark upon picture-frames I will finish this chapter. Picture-frames are generally elaborately carved mouldings, or are simple mouldings covered with ornaments, which, whether carved or formed of putty, are overlaid with

125

gold leaf; they are, indeed, highly ornamented gilt mouldings. I much prefer a well-formed, yet somewhat simple, black polished moulding, on the interior of which runs a gold bead (Fig. 49). A fanciful yet good picture-frame was figured in the *Building News* of September 7th, 1866, which we now repeat (Fig. 50).

CHAPTER IV.

DECORATION OF BUILDINGS.

DIVISION I.—GENERAL CONSIDERATIONS—CEILINGS.

Having considered furniture, the formation of which requires a knowledge of construction, or of what we may term structural art, we pass on to notice principles involved in the decoration of surfaces, or in "surface decoration," as it is usually called. We commence by considering how rooms should be decorated; yet, in so doing, we are met at the very outset with a great difficulty, as the nature of the decoration of a room should be determined by the character of its architecture. My difficulty rests here. How am I to tell you what is the just decoration for a room, when the suitability of the decoration is often dependent upon even structural and ornamental details; and when, in all cases, the character of the decoration should be in harmony with the character of the architecture? Broadly, if a building is in the Gothic style, all that it contains in the way of decoration, and of furniture also, should be Gothic. If the building is Greek, the decorations and furniture should be Greek. If the building is Italian, all its decorations and furniture should be Italian, and so on.

But there are further requirements. Each term that I have now employed, as expressive of a style of architecture, is more or less generic in character, and is therefore too broad for general use. What is usually termed Gothic architecture, is a group of styles having common origin and resemblances, known to the architect as the Semi-Norman or Transition style, which occurred in the twelfth century under Henry II. (it was at this time that the pointed arch was first employed). The Early English, which was developed in the end of the twelfth and early part of the thirteenth century, under Richard I., John, and Henry III.; the Decorated, which occurred at the end of the thirteenth, and early portion of the fourteenth century, under Edward I., Edward II., and Edward III.; the Perpendicular, which occurred at the latter part of the fourteenth, and through the greater portion of the fifteenth century, under Richard II., Henry IV., V., and VI., Edward IV. and V., and Richard III.; and, lastly, the Tudor, which occurred at the end of the fifteenth, and the beginning of the sixteenth century, under Henry VII. and Henry VIII. All these styles are popularly spoken of as one, and are expressed by the one term—Gothic. It is so also, to an extent, with the Greek, Roman, and Italian styles, for each of these appears in various modifications of character, but into such details we will not enter: it must suffice to notice that the character of the decoration must be not only broadly in the style of the architecture of the building which it is intended to beautify, but it must be similar in nature to the ornament produced at precisely the same date as the architecture which has been employed for the building.

It must not be supposed that I am an advocate of reproducing works, or even styles of architecture, such as were created in times gone by, for I am not. The peoples of past ages carefully sought to ascertain their wants—the wants resulting from climate—the wants resulting from the nature of their religion—the wants resulting from social arrangements—the wants imposed by the building material at command. We, on the contrary, look at a hundred old buildings, and without considering our wants, as differing from those of our forefathers, take a bit from one and a bit from another, or we reproduce one almost as it stands, and thus we bungle on, instead of seeking to raise such buildings as are in all respects suited to our modern requirements.

Things are, however, much better in this respect than they were. Bold men are dealing with the Gothic style in its various forms. Scott, Burgess, Street, and many others are venturing to alter it; and thus, while it is losing old characteristics, and is acquiring new elements, it is already assuming a character which has nobility of expression, truthfulness of structure, and suitability to our special requirements. In time to come, further changes will doubtless be made; and thus the style which arose as an imitation of the past will have become new, through constantly departing from the original type, and as constantly adopting new elements.

I have said that the decoration of a building should be brought about by the employment of such ornament as was, in time past, associated with the particular form of architecture employed in the building to be decorated, if a precisely similar form of architecture previously existed. Let not the ornament, however, be a mere servile imitation of what has gone before, but let the designer study the ornament of bygone ages till he understands and *feels* its spirit, and then let him strive to produce new forms and new combinations in the spirit of the ornament of the past.

This must also be carefully noted—that the ornament of a particular period does not consist merely of the forms employed in the architecture, drawn in colour on the wall, or the ceiling, as the case may be. The particular form of ornament used in association with some forms of Gothic architecture was very different in character from what we might expect from the nature of the architecture itself, and did not to any extent consist of flatly-treated crockets, gable ends, trefoils, cinque-foils, etc. The ornament of the past must be studied in its purity, and not from those wretched attempts at the production of Gothic decoration which we often see.

In what we may call the typical English house of the present day there is really no architecture, and if such a building is to be decorated it is almost legitimate to employ any style of ornamentation. In such a case I should choose a style which has no very marked features—which is not strongly Greek, or strongly Gothic, or strongly Italian; and if there is the necessary ability, I should say try and produce ornaments having novelty of character, and yet showing your knowledge of the good qualities of all styles that are past. If this is attempted, care must be exercised in order to avoid getting a mere combination of elements from various styles as one ornament. Nothing can be worse than to see a bit of Greek, a fragment of Egyptian, an Alhambraic scroll, a Gothic flower, and an Italian husk associated together as one ornament; unless this were done advisedly and in order to meet a very special want, such an ornamental composition would be detestable. What I recommend is the production of new forms; but the new composition may have the vigour of the best Gothic ornament, the severity of Egyptian, the intricacy of the Persian, the gorgeousness of the Alhambra, and so on, only it must not imitate in detail the various styles of the past.

Now as to the decoration of a room. If one part only can be decorated, let that one part be the ceiling. Nothing appears to me more strange than that our ceilings, which can be properly seen, are usually white in middle-class houses, while the walls, which are always in part hidden, and even the floor, on which we tread, should have colour and pattern applied to them; and of this I am certain, that, considered from a decorative point of view, our ordinary treatment is wrong.

We glory in a clear blue sky overhead, and we speak of the sky as increasing in beauty as it becomes deeper and deeper in tint. Thus the depth of the tint of the Italian sky is familiar to us all. Why, then, make our ceilings white? I often ask this question, and am told that the whiteness renders the ceiling almost invisible; hence it is preferred. This idea is very absurd; first, because blue is the most ethereal and most distant of all colours (see Chap. II.); and, second, do we not build a house with the view of procuring shelter? hence why do we seek to realise the feeling that we are without a covering over our heads? We only like a white ceiling because we have been accustomed to such from infancy, and because we have been taught to regard a clean white ceiling as all that is to be desired. I knew a Yorkshire lady who, upon being asked by her husband whether she would like the drawing-room ceiling decorated, replied that she thought not, as she could not then have it re-whitewashed every year. The idea was clean certainly. Blue, I have said, is ethereal in character; it is so, and may become exceedingly so if of medium depth and of a grey hue; hence, if a mere atmospheric effect was sought, it would be desirable that this colour be used on the ceiling rather than white. But, as we have just said, invisibility of the ceiling is absurd, as it is our protection from the weather. Further, the ceiling may become an object of great beauty, and it can be seen as a whole. Why then neglect the opportunity of arranging a beautiful object when there is no reason to the contrary? We like a beautiful coloured vase, or, if we do not, we can have it whitewashed, or even dispense with it altogether. We like beautiful walls, or we would have them whitewashed also; indeed, we like our surroundings generally beautiful. Why not, then, have beautiful ceilings, especially as they can be seen complete, while the wall is in part hidden by furniture and pictures?

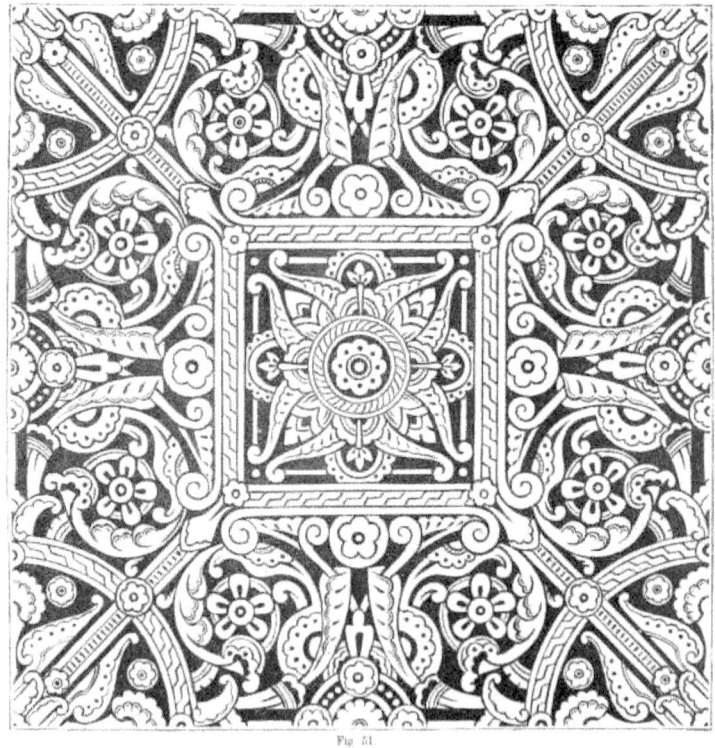

Fig. 51

I will suppose that we have an ordinary room to deal with. First, take away the wretched plaster ornament in the centre of the ceiling, for it is sure to be bad. There is not one such ornament out of a thousand that can be so treated as to make the ceiling look as well as it would do without it. Now place all over the ceiling a flat painted or stencilled pattern, a pattern which repeats equally in all directions (as Fig. 51), and let this pattern be in blue (of any depth) and white, or in blue (of any depth) and cream-colour, and it is sure to look well (the blue being the ground, and the cream-colour or white the ornament).

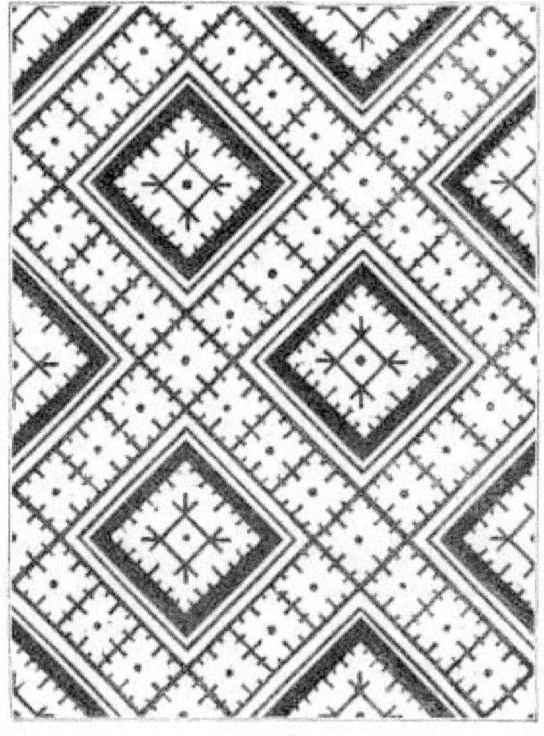

Fig. 52.

Simple patterns in cream-colour on blue ground, but having a black outline, also look well (Fig. 52); and these might be prepared in paper, and hung on the ceiling as common paper-hangings, if cheapness is essential. Gold ornaments on a deep blue ground, with black outline, also look rich and effective. These are all, however, simple treatments, for any amount of colour may be used on a ceiling, provided the colours are employed in very small masses, and perfectly mingled, so that the effect produced is that of a rich coloured bloom (see Chap. II.). A ceiling should be beautiful, and should also be manifest; but if it must be somewhat indistinct, in order that the caprices of the ignorant be humoured, let the pattern be in middle-tint or pale blue and white only.

I like to see the ceiling of a room covered all over with a suitable pattern, but I do not at all object to a large central ornament only, or to a centre ornament and corners; especially if the cornice is heavy, so as to give compensating weight to the margin. I have recently designed and seen carried out one or two centre ornaments for drawing-rooms, which ornaments were twenty-one feet in diameter. A centre ornament, if properly treated, may be very large without looking heavy; it may, indeed, extend at least two-thirds of the way from the centre to the margin of the ceiling. I do not speak of plaster ornaments, but of flat decorations.

If the ceiling is flat all ornament placed upon it must not only be flat also, but must not fictitiously represent relief, for no shaded ornament can be pleasant when placed as the decoration of a flat architectural surface.

I have already noticed that the decoration of a room should be in character with its architecture, but that while this should be so, the ornament applied by way of enrichment should not be a servile copy of the decorative forms employed in ages gone by, but should be such as is new in character, while yet of the spirit of the past.

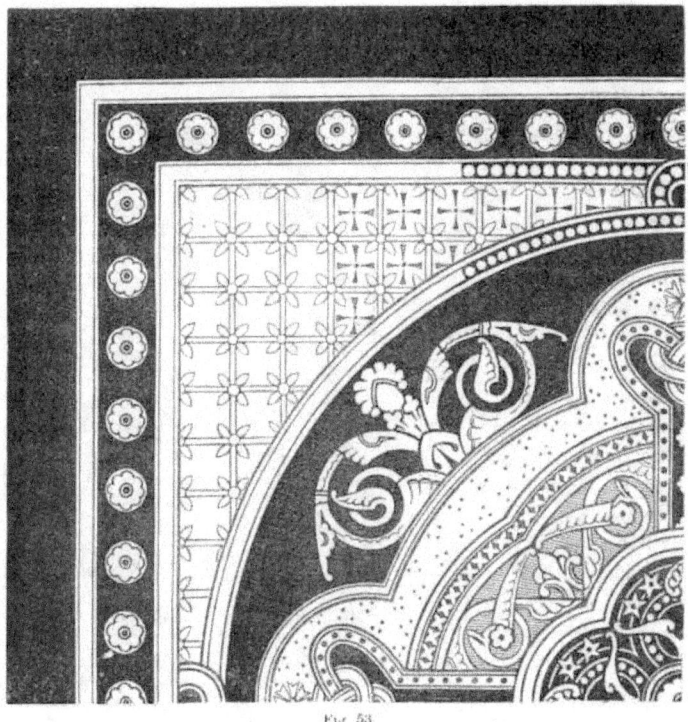

Fig 53.

Many circumstances tend to determine the nature of the decoration which should be applied to a ceiling: thus, if a ceiling is structurally divided into square panels, the character of the ornament is thereby restricted, and should these panels be large it will probably be desirable that each be fitted with the same ornament; while if they are small three or four different patterns may be employed, if arranged in some orderly or methodical manner.

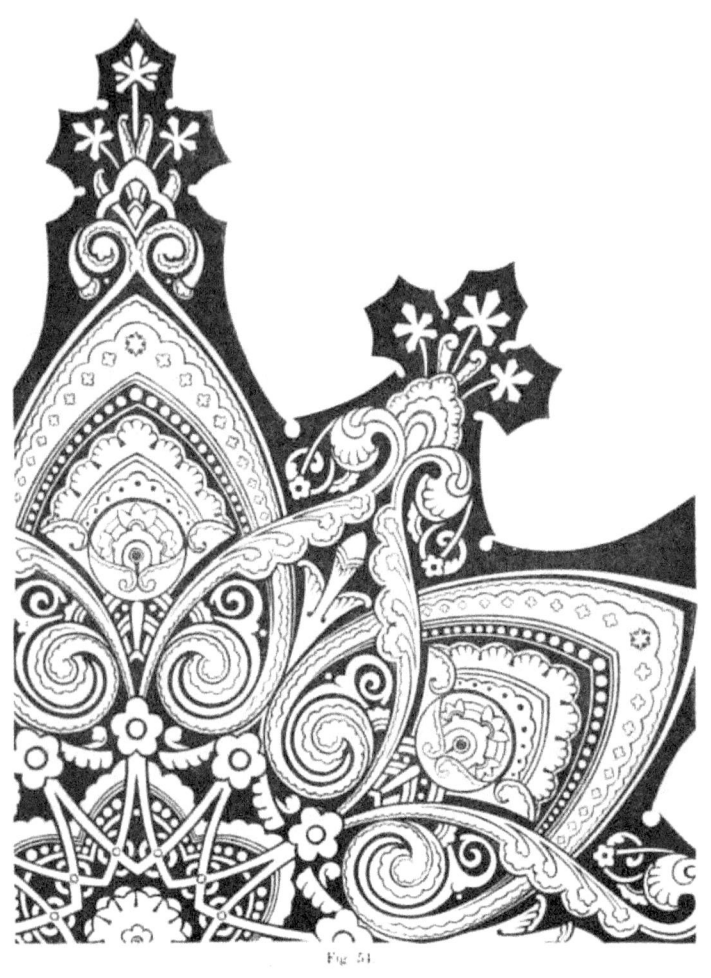

Fig 54

A ceiling may also have the joists or beams visible upon it: in this case the decoration would have to be of a very special character. The bottoms of the joists might have a string pattern upon them (a running pattern), as the "Greek key," or guilloche; whilst the sides might have either a running pattern, or a pattern with an upward tendency, as the "Greek honeysuckle;" and the ceiling intervening between the joists might have a running pattern, or better, a star, or diaper pattern, or it might have bands running in the opposite direction to the joists, so as, with them, to form squares, which squares might be filled with ornament.

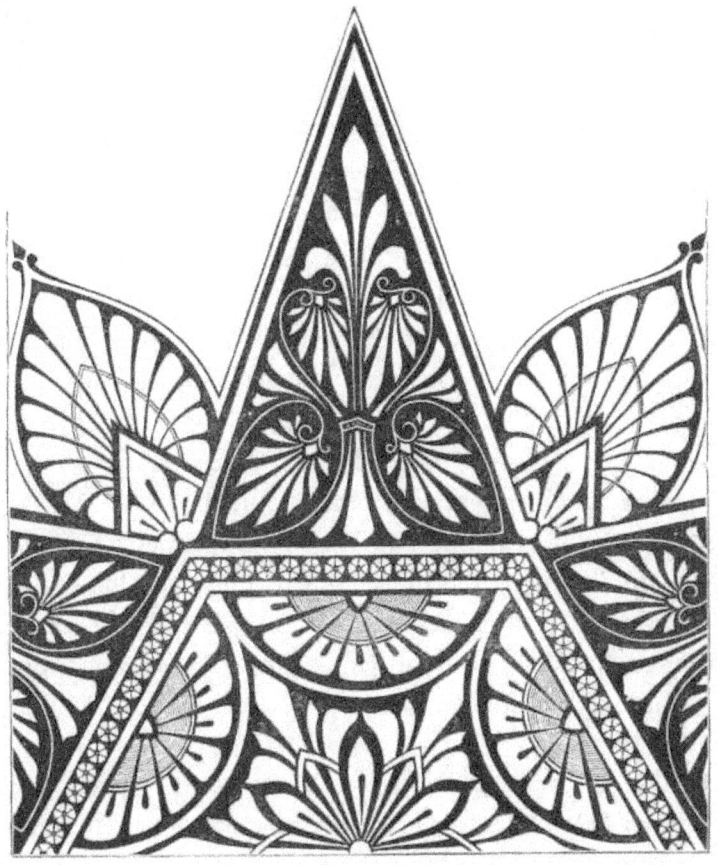

Fig. 55.

If, however, the ceiling is flat, and is not divided into sections structurally, almost any "setting out" of the surface may be employed, as Fig. 53; or a large centre ornament, as Figs. 54 and 55; or a rosette distributed over the entire surface, as Fig. 56. In any case it is not necessary or even desirable that the ornament be in relief upon the ceiling. Flatly treated ornaments may be employed with advantage, and all fictitious appearance of relief, as we have already said, must be avoided.

There are so many different ways of setting out ceilings, that I cannot attempt even to make any suggestions. I would simply say, however, Avoid an architectural setting out, if there are no structural members; for ornament which is flat may spread in any manner over a surface without even appearing to need structural supports. As to the colour of a ceiling if there is to be no ornament upon it, let it be a cream-colour (formed of white with a little middle-chrome) rather than white. Cream-colour always looks well upon a ceiling, and gives the idea of purity. A grey-blue is also a very desirable colour for a ceiling, such as is formed of pale ultramarine, white, and a little raw umber, just sufficient to make the blue slightly grey (or atmospheric). In depth this blue should be about half-way between the ultramarine and white. Another effect which I like is produced by the full colour of pure (or almost pure) ultramarine. In this case the cornice should be carefully coloured, and pale blue and white should prevail in it, but a little pure red must be present.

A further and very desirable effect is produced by placing pale cream-coloured stars irregularly over the pale blue, or even the deep blue ceiling, or by placing pale blue stars upon the cream-coloured ceiling. The stars should vary for an ordinary room ceiling (say a room sixteen feet square by ten feet high) from about three inches from point to point down to one inch; the larger stars having six points; others being smaller and with five points; and the small ones having, some four points, and some three. If such stars are irregularly (without order) intermixed over the ceiling, and yet are somewhat equally dispersed, a very pleasing and interesting effect will thereby be produced. This effect is in much favour with the Japanese. The stars, however, should be smaller if placed on a deep, than on a pale, blue ground.

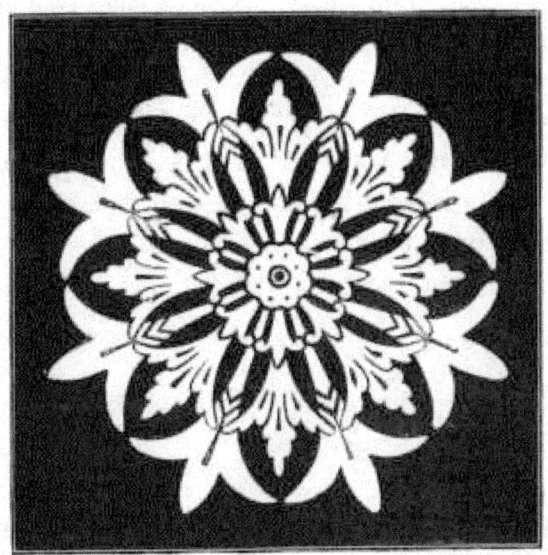

Fig. 56.

Another good effect is produced by giving the ceiling the colour of Bath, or Portland, stone, and starring it with a deeper tint of the same colour. This effect is improved by each star having a very fine outline of a yet darker tint of the same colour.

I should recommend those interested in the decoration of ceilings to study carefully the Egyptian, Alhambra, and Greek Courts at the Crystal Palace, Sydenham, especially the two last named; also to notice the ceiling in St. James's Great Hall, Piccadilly, London, and the ceiling of Ushaw College chapel near Durham. The ceilings in the Oriental Courts, by

Mr. Owen Jones, at the South Kensington Museum are worthy of careful notice; but the Renaissance ceilings in other parts of the Museum are both wrong in principle and are bad examples of their style. The structurally formed glass ceiling of the Crystal Palace Bazaar in Oxford Street, London, and still better, the ceiling of Mr. Osler's glass warehouse in Oxford Street, are well worthy of note.

On the Continent we very frequently meet with ceilings on which large pictures have been painted, as in the Louvre and the Luxembourg in Paris; and the authorities of the South Kensington Museum are making efforts to introduce this style into England, but such pictorial ceilings are in every way wrong.

1st. A ceiling is a flat surface, hence all decoration placed upon it should be flat also.

2nd. A picture can only be correctly seen from one point, whereas the decoration of a ceiling should be of such a character that it can be properly seen from any part of the room.

3rd. Pictures have almost invariably a right and wrong way upwards. A picture placed on a ceiling is thus wrong way upwards to almost all the guests in the room.

4th. In order to the proper understanding of a picture, you must see the whole of its surface at one time; this is very difficult to do without almost breaking your neck, or being on your back on the floor, if the picture is on the ceiling; whereas an ornament which consists of repeated parts may render a ceiling beautiful without requiring that the whole ceiling be seen at the one glance.

Most of the French pictorial ceilings are so painted that they are properly seen when the spectator stands with his back close to the fire. This is very awkward, as the rules of society do not allow us to stand in this position before company. Pictorial works are altogether out of place on a ceiling; they ought to be framed and hung right way upwards upon walls where they can be seen. We have a well-known painted ceiling at the Greenwich Hospital.

Arabesque ceilings, such as that of the Roman Court at the Crystal Palace, are also very objectionable.

What can be worse than festoons of leafage, like so many sausages, painted upon a ceiling, with griffins, small framed pictures, impossible flowers, and feeble ornament, all with fictitious light and shade? But not content with such absurdities and incongruities, the festoons often hang upwards on vaulted or domed ceilings, rather than downwards. Such ornaments arose when Rome, intoxicated with its conquests, yielded itself up to luxury and vice rather than to a consideration of beauty and truth.

Decorations like these were to an extent again revived by the great painter Raphael; but it must ever be remembered that Raphael, while one of the greatest of painters, was no ornamentist. It requires all the energy of a life to become a great painter; and it requires all the energy of a life to become a great ornamentist; hence it is not expected that the one man should be great at the two arts.

In all ages when decorative art has flourished, ceilings have been decorated. The Egyptians decorated their ceilings, so did the Greeks, the Byzantines, the Moors, and the people of our Middle Ages, and a light ceiling appears not to have been esteemed as essential, or as in many cases desirable. It is strange that so few of our houses and public buildings contain rooms with decorated ceilings; but the want is already felt, the fashion has set in, and many are at this present moment being prepared. We must get simple modes of enrichment for general rooms—modes of treatment which shall be effective, and yet not expensive—and then we may hope that they will become general.

DIVISION II.—DECORATIONS OF WALLS.

We must now devote ourselves to the consideration of wall decoration, or to the manner in which ornament should be applied to walls with the view of rendering them decorative.

It will appear absurd to say that all ornament that is applied to a wall should be such as will render the wall more beautiful than it would be without it; but this statement is needed, for I have seen many walls ornamented in such a manner, that they would have looked much better if they had been perfectly plain, and simply washed over with a tint of colour.

To ornament is to beautify. To decorate is to ornament. But a surface cannot be beautified unless the forms which are drawn upon it are graceful, or bold, or vigorous, or true, and unless the colours applied to it are harmonious. Yet how many walls do we meet with even in good houses—walls of corridors, walls of staircases, walls of dining-rooms, walls of libraries, and, indeed, walls of every kind of room—which are rendered offensive, rather than pleasing, by the decorations they bear.

A wall may look well without decoration strictly so called, and this statement leads me to notice the various ways in which walls may be treated with the view of rendering them beautiful.

A wall may be simply tinted either with "distemper" colour, or oil colour "flatted." Distemper colour gives the best effect, and is much the cheapest, but it is not durable, and cannot be washed. Oil colour when flatted makes a nice wall, whether "stippled" or plain, and is both durable and washable. An entire wall should never be varnished.

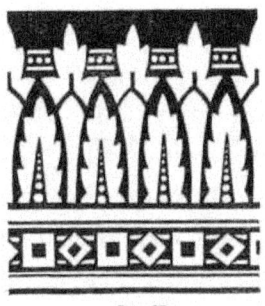

Fig. 57.

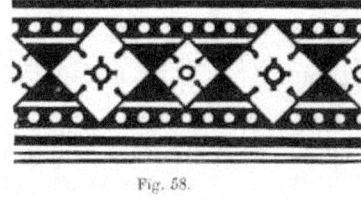

Fig. 58.

I say that a wall can look well even if not decorated. Let me give one or two instances; but, perhaps, I had better give treatments for the entire room, including the ceiling, and not for the wall simply.

Fig. 59.

A good effect of a very plain and inexpensive character would be produced by having a black skirting, a cream-colour wall (this colour to be made of the colour called middle-chrome and white, and to resemble in depth the best pure cream), a cornice coloured with pale blue of greyish tint, with deep blue, white, and a slight line of red, and a ceiling of blue of almost any depth. The ceiling colour to be pure French ultramarine, or this ultramarine mixed with white and a touch of raw umber (the cornice blues to be made in the same way). The red in the cornice to be deep vermilion if very narrow (one-sixteenth of an inch), or carmine if broad.[24]

---

[24] In some parts of the country it is customary to wash the cornice over with quick-lime. If this has been done the lime must be carefully removed, for lime will turn carmine black.

144

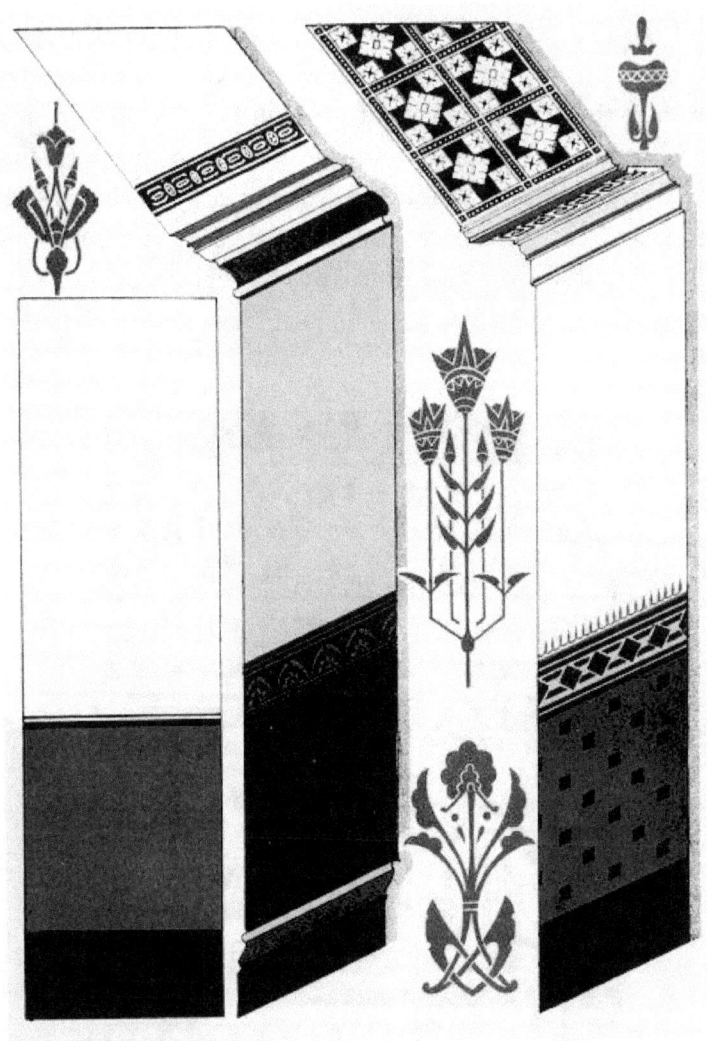

DECORATIVE DESIGN.
Illustrating Cornice, Ceiling & Wall Colouring.

A room of a slightly more decorative character would be produced by making the lower three feet of the wall of a different colour (by forming a dado) from the upper part of the wall: thus, if the other parts of the room were coloured as in the example just given, the lower three feet might be red (vermilion toned to a rich Indian red with ultramarine blue) or chocolate (purple-brown and white, with a little orange-chrome); this lower portion of the wall being separated from the upper cream-coloured portion by a line of black an inch broad, or better by a double line, the upper line being an inch broad, and the lower line three-eighths of an inch, the lines being separated from each other by five-eighths of the red or chocolate.

Fig. 60.

I like the formation of a dado, for it affords an opportunity of giving apparent stability to the wall by making its lower portion dark; and furniture is invariably much improved by being seen against a dark background. The occupants of a

146

room always look better when viewed in conjunction with a dark background, and ladies' dresses certainly do. The dark dado gives the desired background without rendering it necessary that the entire wall be dark. If the furniture be mahogany, it will be wonderfully improved by being placed against a chocolate wall.

The dado of a room need not be plain; indeed, it may be enriched to any extent. It may be plain with a bordering separating it from the wall, such as Figs. 57, 58, and 59, or the coloured border on Plate I. (frontispiece); or it may have a simple flower regularly dispersed over it; or it may be covered with a geometrical repeating pattern, in either of which cases it would have a border; or it may be enriched with a specially designed piece of ornament, as Fig. 60. This particular pattern should not, however, be enlarged to a height of more than twenty to twenty-four inches; but if of this width, and above a skirting of twelve or fifteen inches, it would look well.

I have designed two or three narrow dado papers for Messrs. Wylie and Lockhead, of Glasgow, which are about eighteen inches broad, and are printed in the direction of the length of the paper, so as to save unnecessary joins; and Messrs. Jeffrey and Co., of Essex Road, Islington, are issuing a complete series of my decorations for walls, dados, and ceilings.

If the dado is enriched with ornament, and the cornice is coloured, and a pattern spreads all over the ceiling, the walls can well be plain, but they may be covered with a simple "powdering" as the patterns in Fig. 61, if these are in soft colours, or with patterns such as those set forth in colours on Plate I.; but these, especially that on the blue ground, would only be used where a very rich effect is desired.

147

Fig. 61.

A good room would be produced by pattern Fig. 52 being on the ceiling in dark blue and cream-colour, by the cornice being coloured with a prevalence of dark blue, the walls being cream-colour down to the dado; the border separating the dado from the wall being black ornament on a dull orange-colour; and by the dado being chocolate with a black rosette upon it; the skirting boards being bright black. The dado may or may not be varnished; the upper part of the wall can only be "dead" (not varnished—dull). If the room is high a bordering may run round the upper portion of the wall, about three to four inches below the cornice; such a border as Fig. 62 may he employed in dull orange and chocolate.

A citrine wall comes well with a deep blue, or blue and white ceiling, if blue prevails in the cornice, and this wall may have a dark blue (ultramarine and black with a little white) dado, or a rich maroon dado (brown-lake). If the blue dado is employed the skirting should be indigo, which, when varnished and seen in conjunction with the blue, will appear as black as jet. (See the coloured examples on Plate II., and remarks on colour)

Walls are usually papered in middle-class houses. I must not object to this universal custom; but I do say, try to avoid showing the joinings of the various strips. In all cases where possible cut the paper to the pattern, and not in straight lines, for straight joinings are very objectionable. If you use paper for walls, use it artistically, and not as so much paper. Let a dado be formed of one paper, the dado bordering (dado rail) of a suitable paper bordering; the upper part of the wall being covered by another paper of simple and just design, and of such colour as shall harmonise with the dado. Proceed as an artist, and not as a mere workman. Think out an ornamental scheme, and then try to realise the desired effect. Avoid all papers in which huge bunches of flowers and animals or the human figure are depicted. The best for all purposes are those of a simple geometrical character, or in which designs similar to those in Fig. 61 are "powdered" or placed at regular intervals over a plain ground.

Fig. 62.

Just as the ceiling ornament must accord in character with the architecture of the room in which it is placed, so must the wall decoration be of the same style as the architecture of the room. Indeed, whatever we have said respecting the harmony of the ceiling decoration with the architecture of the building, applies equally to the ornamentation of the wall.

It has been customary to arrange walls into panels when decorating them, and of this mode of treatment we give one illustration (Fig. 63); yet nothing can be more absurd than such a treatment, unless the wall is architecturally (structurally) arched. A wall may be so formed that some parts are thick, so as to give the required strength, while other portions are thin. In such a case the wall would be formed of arched recesses and thickened piers alternately. This being the case, the decoration should be so applied as to emphasise, or render apparent, this arched structure; but if the wall is of one thickness throughout, its division into arches is absurd and foolish.

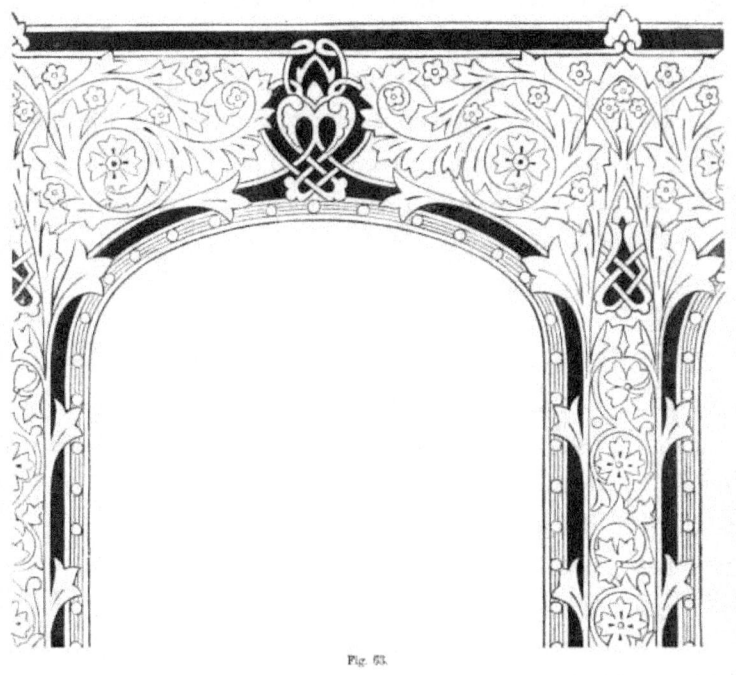

Fig. 63.

We sometimes see great follies, and even gross untruths, perpetrated with the view of bringing about the so-called decoration of a room. Thus it is not unfrequently that we meet with imitation pillars, recesses, and arches as the so-called ornamentation of a room.

In low music halls we are not surprised by such decorations, for we do not look for truth or any manifestation of delicacy of feeling in such places. Falsity and the untrue appear in natural juxtaposition with the debased and the vulgar. Sham marble pillars, a fictitious and merely imitative architecture, an assumed and unreal, yet coarse and vulgar, gorgeousness, are the natural adjuncts of immorality and vice; but such falsities cannot be tolerated in the abodes of those who pretend to purity and truth, nor in the buildings which they frequent; yet even the new Albert Hall has sham marble pillars (I say this to our shame), and but recently I visited a church near Edgware, in which there is a display of false decoration such as I never before saw. Here we find sham pillars, giving a false architecture; sham niches, containing sham statues; sham clouds, forming an absurd ceiling; and almost every falsity which a falsely constituted mind could perpetrate.

How strange it is that in a church, where purity and truth are taught, the whole of the decorations should be a sham! It is said that if you want to hear a fierce quarrel, and to see true hatred, you must seek it in religious sects and among theological discussionists. On the same principle, I suppose, we must prepare ourselves for a display of the worst art-falsity in the sacred edifice. Perhaps the idea is that of contrast. As the teetotal lecturer had a drunken man by him as a frightful example of what was to be avoided, so the decorations of this church may be intended as a warning, rather than as an example of what should be followed. Happily such churches as this are rare, and it can be truly said that ecclesiastical architecture and decoration has made great strides with us in recent years, and that in very many instances it is rigidly truthful as well as beautiful.

Before leaving the consideration of wall decorations, I must object to all imitations, as sham marbles, granites, etc., for no wall can be satisfactory which is to any extent a display of false grandeur; and this is curious, that in many cases it costs more to produce an imitation marble staircase than it would to line the same walls with the marbles imitated. I have known a case in which the imitation has cost double what the genuine stone would have cost, and such a case is not exceptional, for hand-polished work is always expensive. To imitations of marbles and granites, as I have already said, I strongly object, and of the genuine stone I am not fond, unless sparingly and judiciously used. My objections to its free use are these:—1st. Harmony of colour depends upon great exactness of tint. This exactness is rarely attainable in the case of two marbles. One stone may, however, be brought into direct and perfect harmony with a coloured wall, by the tint of the wall being carefully suited to the marble. 2nd. The true artist thinks less of the costliness of the material of which he forms his works than of the art-effect produced. Thus the old Greeks, who were full of art-feeling and refinement, coloured the buildings which they constructed of white marble, and they certainly thereby improved them; for colour, if harmoniously employed, lends to objects a new charm—a charm which they would not without it possess. I must further say, before leaving our present subject, that all walls, however decorated, should serve as a background to whatever stands in front of them. Thus they must retire even behind the furniture by their unobtrusiveness.

The order of arrangement in furnishing must be this. The living beings in a room should be most attractive and conspicuous, and the dress of man should be of such a character as to secure this. Ladies can now employ any amount of colour in their attire; but poor man, however noble, cannot by his dress be distinguished from his butler; and, worst of all, both are dressed in an unbecoming and inartistic manner. Next come the furniture and draperies— the one or the other having prominence according to circumstances; then come the wall and floor, both of which are to serve as backgrounds to all that stands in front of them. In decorating walls, or in judging of the merit or suitability of wall decorations, this must always be taken into consideration, that they are but enriched backgrounds; and it should also be remembered that the nature of the enrichment applied is determined, to a great extent, by the character of the architecture of the building of which the wall forms a part.

We come now to consider wall-papers, which are hangings prepared with the view of enabling us to decorate our walls at comparatively small cost. I may confess that I am not very fond of wall-papers under any circumstances. I prefer a tinted or painted wall. Yet they are largely used, and will be for a long time to come. I have already said that if wall-papers are used they should not be joined together with straight lines, and that we ought to consider them as so much art-material which should be used artistically.

As to the nature of the pattern which a wall-paper should have, it is almost impossible to speak, as there are endless varieties; but as a rule it may be said that those consisting of small, simple, repeated parts, which are low-toned or neutral in colour, are the best. Most wall-paper patterns are larger than is desirable. The pattern can scarcely be too simple, and it should in all cases consist of flat ornament.

If the ornament is very good, and the pattern is the work of a true artist, it may be larger, for then the parts will be balanced and harmonised in a manner that could not be expected from a less skilful hand; but even if by the most talented designer, it must ever be remembered that he has designed it at random, and not as a suitable decoration for any particular room. The man who selects the pattern for a particular wall must choose that which is suitable to the special case.

The effect of a wall-paper is materially affected by many circumstances. Thus, by the quantity of light admitted to the room—whether the room is dark or light; by the aspect, whether it receives the sun's rays direct or does not; by the character of the light, as whether direct from the sky, or reflected from a green lawn, or red-brick wall. All these things must be considered, and what looks well in the pattern-book may look bad on a wall.

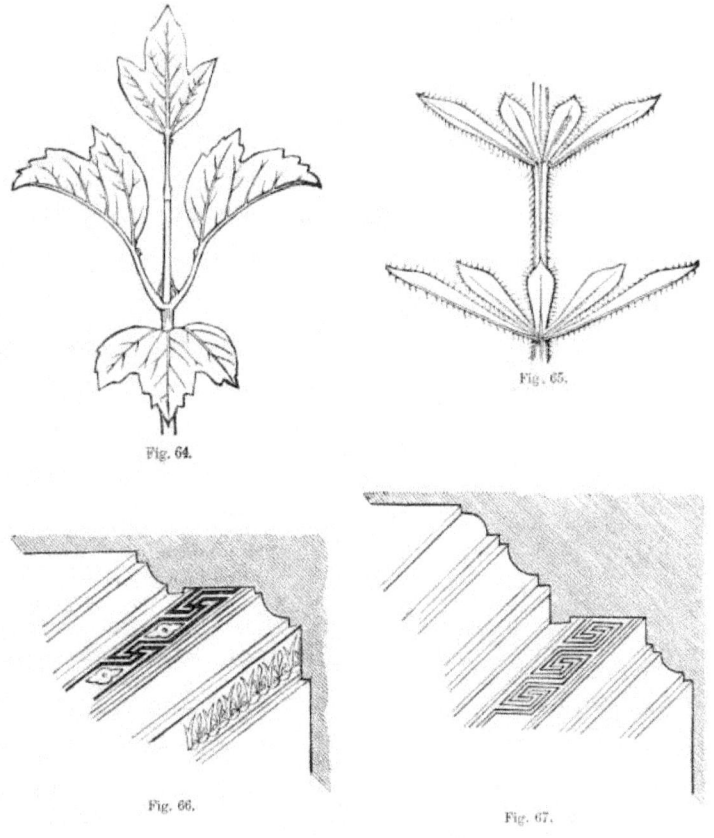

Fig. 64.

Fig. 65.

Fig. 66.

Fig. 67.

As to colour, the best wall-paper patterns are those which consist of somewhat strong colours in very small masses—

masses so small that the general effect of the paper is rich, low-toned, and neutral, and yet has a glowing colour-bloom; but these are rarely to be met with.

It was a fashion some time since to make wall-papers in imitation of woven fabrics, and this fashion has not wholly disappeared yet, absurd though it be. It arose through the accident of a designer of wall-paper patterns having been a shawl pattern designer, and having a number of small shawl patterns on hand, which he disposed of as wall-paper patterns. A pattern which is suitable for a woven fabric is rarely suitable to a printed fabric, and especially when the one pattern is to be seen in folds on a moving object, and the other flat on a fixed surface. And at all times imitation by one material of another is untruthful, and it becomes specially absurd when we think that almost every material is capable of producing some good art-effect which no other material can. We should always seek to make each material as distinctive in its art-character as we can, and to cause each to appear as beautiful as possible in that particular manner in which it can most naturally be worked.

A word should be said about the particular character which a wall-paper pattern should have, but the remarks which I am now about to make will apply equally to all patterns employed as wall decorations. If we view trees or plants, as we see them against the sky as a background, they are objects which point upwards and have a bilateral symmetry—their halves are alike (Figs. 64 and 65)—or are more or less irregular in form, and when seen in this view we may regard them as natural wall decorations. Our wall patterns, then, may point upwards, as in Fig. 61, and be bilateral or otherwise; but it must be remembered that when the flowers of a primrose protrude from a bank they are regular radiating, or star, ornaments. I think that it is legitimate for us to use on a wall star, or regular radiating ornaments, as well as those having an upward tendency.

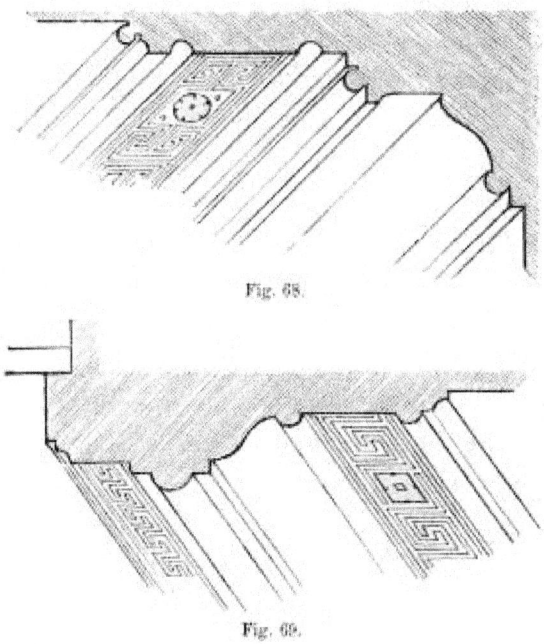

Fig. 68.

Fig. 69.

I have said that when seen from the side plants are bilateral, or are more or less irregular. As I have referred to plants as furnishing us with types of ornament, I should not be doing rightly were I to leave this statement in its present form; for the tendency of the vital force of all plants is to produce structures of rigidly symmetrical character; but insects, which eat buds and leaves, and blights, winds, and frosts, so act upon plants as to destroy their normal symmetry, hence we find an apparent want of symmetry in the arrangement of the parts of plants.

Respecting the colouring of cornices, a few words should be said. 1st. Bright colours may here be employed. 2nd. As a rule, get red in shadow or in shade, blue on flat or hollow surfaces, especially those that recede from the eye, and yellow on rounded advancing members. 3rd. Use for red either vermilion or carmine; for blue, ultramarine either pure or with white; for yellow, middle chrome much diluted with white. 4th. Use red very sparingly, blue abundantly, the pale yellow in medium quantity.

Besides primary colours, none others need be used on the cornice. It is a mistake to use many, or dull, colours, here, but gold may be used instead of yellow. With the view of explaining the principles which we have just enunciated by diagrams, we give four illustrations (Figs. 66, 67, 68, 69), which I advise the student to try and colour in accordance with the principles just set forth.

CHAPTER V.

CARPETS.

It is not my intention in this chapter to consider in detail the various kinds of carpet which are common in our market, nor even to review the history of their manufacture, interesting as it would be to do so; for we must confine ourselves more particularly to an examination of the art-qualities which they present, and to the particular form of pattern which may be applied to them with advantage.

Although we cannot here enter into a consideration of the manufacture of carpets, I cannot too strongly recommend all who intend preparing designs for them to consider minutely the powers of the carpet loom; for the nature of the effect produced will depend to a large extent upon the knowledge which the designer possesses of the capabilities of the manufacture for which he designs patterns. In the case of any manufacture it is highly desirable, if not absolutely essential, that the designer of the patterns to be wrought should be acquainted with the process by which his design is to be converted into the particular material for which the pattern has been prepared; for this knowledge, even when not absolutely essential, gives an amount of freedom and power which nothing else can supply.

The carpets most extensively in use are "Brussels;" but there are many other kinds both of better and inferior qualities. "Kidderminster carpet" (a carpet not now made by even one Kidderminster manufacturer) is a common fabric suited to the bedrooms of middle-class houses; but the art-capabilities of this material are very small, as it can only have two colours in any line running throughout its length. This carpet consists of two thicknesses, which are imperfectly united, and is not durable. "Brussels carpeting," now made chiefly in Great Britain, is a good carpet for general purposes. Its surface consists of loops, and it may have five, or, if made of extra quality, six colours in any line running throughout its length. If with five colours in the same line the carpet will, in a sense, consist of five thicknesses of worsted; yet these are united into one fabric. In some cases a "Brussels carpet" is woven of very close texture, with the loops cut through; thus we have a "velvet pile" or "Wilton carpet"—a fabric which is very rich-looking, and durable.

Those called real "Axminster" carpets are, perhaps, the best made. They are formed by the knotting together of threads by hand, consequently any number of colours may be used in their formation; but such are necessarily most costly. "patent Axminster" carpet is made by a double process of hand-weaving, by which fine results are achieved, and any number of colours used. In the first weaving a rough "cloth" is formed, which is cut into strips called "chenille threads," and these are again woven into the carpet. This process is most ingenious, and the carpets produced by it are very good; but they are costly.

Some few years since a most ingenious process of manufacturing what are known as "tapestry" carpets was patented—a process resembling in its nature that of the patent Axminster manufacture, but differing in this particular, that the "warp" threads are coloured by printing, and thus the first process of weaving is dispensed with. These carpets are, like Brussels, made with a looped surface, and also with a pile. They cannot be said to compare in any way with the patent Axminster carpets, which are of a pretentious and costly character, nor even with a good "Brussels;" but they are low in price, and meet a want, as is proved by their enormous sale.

Besides these varieties of carpet there are a number of kinds of foreign production, most of which are hand-made, and are very beautiful. By far the greater number of these have a "pile," although this is sometimes rough and uneven, yet rarely, if ever, inartistic; but a few are without pile; still these are not without that indescribable something which renders them estimable in the eye of an artist.

Having hastily noticed the chief kinds of carpet in use in this country, and we might say in almost all countries, we come to the question—what form of pattern, or what character of ornament, should form the "enrichment" of such a fabric?

When speaking in a previous chapter of wall decorations, we noticed that a wall-paper pattern, or, indeed, a wall pattern of any kind, might desirably have an upward direction and a bilateral symmetry. This can never be the case, however, with a carpet pattern, which must be equally extended all over the surface, or have a simple radiating symmetry, as Fig. 56; and this rule will apply whether the pattern be simple or complicated. It is not wrong, as we have said before, to have a radiating pattern on a wall, but it is wrong to have a bilateral pattern on a floor.

The reason of this is obvious. If such an object as we have indicated is placed on a wall, from whatever point the occupants of the room may view it, it is yet right way upwards to them; but if such an object were placed on a floor it would be wrong way upwards, or sideways, or oblique to most of those who viewed it; and to employ a pattern of this character in such a position is highly absurd, when a pattern can as readily be formed which will avoid this unpleasantness. What would we think were we asked to view a picture, or even to visit an apartment containing such, were this work of art presented to our view in an inverted manner? We should feel astonished at the absurdity; yet this would be no worse than expecting us to view a carpet while the pattern is to us in an inverted position.

And the principle which we have just set forth is one taught by a consideration of plants. If we wander over the moor, where we tread on Nature's carpet, we find that all the little plants which nestle in the short mossy grass are "radiating ornaments"—that is, they are pretty objects which consist of parts spreading regularly from a centre.

I cannot too strongly advise the young ornamentist to study the principles on which Nature works. Knowledge of the laws which govern the development of plant-growth is very desirable; but it is not our place to *imitate* even the most beautiful of plant-forms—this being the work of the pictorial artists. Yet it is ours to study Nature's laws, and to observe all her beauty, even to her most subtle effects, and then we may safely pillage from her all that we can *consistently* adapt to our own purposes. But in order that we produce ornament, we must infuse mind or soul into whatever we borrow from her.

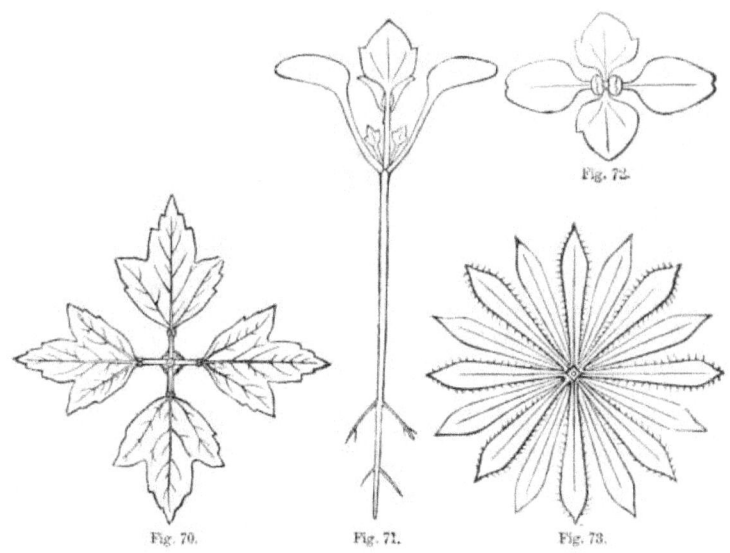

Fig. 72.

Fig. 70.   Fig. 71.   Fig. 73.

With the view of more fully impressing the manner in which Nature teaches us principles which we may apply in art, and of aiding the student in his inquiries, we will give one or two illustrations. Thus Fig. 64 is a drawing of a spray of the guelder rose (*Viburnum opulus*) when seen from the side, or, as I might express it, when viewed as a wall decoration; and Fig. 70 is the same spray as seen from above, or, to use the same manner of expression, when seen as a floor pattern. Further, Fig. 71 represents a young plant of a species of speedwell (*Veronica*) as a wall ornament, and Fig. 72, the same plant when seen as a floor ornament; and Figs. 65 and 73 represent a portion of the goosegrass (*Galium Aparine*) as seen in the same two views.

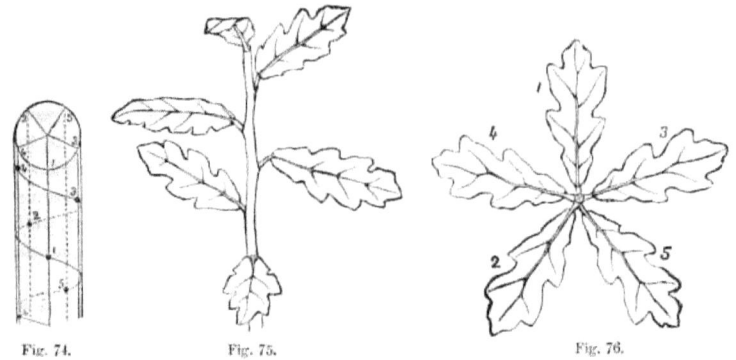

Fig. 74.   Fig. 75.   Fig. 76.

From these illustrations we see that plants furnish us with types of two essentially different ornaments, which are adapted to the decoration of the two positions of wall and floor, and may be introduced with truthful expression and effect into wall-paper or carpet.

Fig. 77.   Fig. 78.   Fig. 79.

Even when the leaves appear somewhat dispersed upon the stem, a principle of order can yet be distinctly traced in the manner of their arrangement, as is diagrammatically expressed in Figs. 74, 75, 76; and here, also, the top view gives us a regular radiating ornament.[25]

The same law prevails in the flower that we have traced as existing in the arrangement of leaves upon the stem: thus Fig.

---

[25] The spray here represented is that of the oak, and the diagram (Fig. 74) shows the orderly spiral manner in which the leaves spring from the stem.

77, which represents the London pride (*Saxifraga umbrosa*), affords an example of a regular radiating flower, which we find so placed, in different examples, as to appear as a floor or wall ornament; and Figs. 78 and 79, the former being the flower of the speedwell (Veronica), and the latter that of the common pansy (*Viola tricolor*), furnish us with illustrations of bilateral flowers intended only as wall ornaments. In order to secure our seeing the pansy only laterally, it is furnished with a bent stalk; hence it never rests horizontally upon the summit of its stem, but always hangs so that it is perfectly seen only from the side.

There are cases, however, in which bilateral flowers are placed horizontally; but it is very interesting to notice that when this occurs the disposition or arrangement of the flowers is such as to restore the radiating symmetry. Thus, if we take the candytuft (*Iberis*) or the common hemlock (*Conium*), we find that while each flower is bilateral in character, the flowers are yet arranged around a centre in such a manner that the smaller portion of each flower points to the centre of the flower-head, while the larger parts point outwards from the centre of the group. These, then, are the teachings of plants, to which we are called upon to hearken.

The above illustrations are not only useful examples of the suggestions of plant-forms to the ornamentist, but form excellent material to the art-student for the conventional treatment of leaves and sprays, buds and blossoms. They will also serve to indicate the kind of plant-forms that should be chosen for decorative purposes. Students of this branch of art would find it a useful practice to make a collection of flowers and plants or parts of plants that appear to offer features similar to those of which we have been writing, and test their capabilities for decorative purposes, by endeavouring to arrange them for the ornamentation of wall and floor, as we have treated the plant-forms indicated in this chapter.

We have now seen the principle on which all carpet patterns should be constructed as distinctive from wall patterns, and in order to impress the necessity of giving a radiating basis to the ornaments placed upon carpets, and not a bilateral structure, we have referred to the principle of plant growth, where we noticed that all plants, when viewed as floor ornaments (when viewed from above), are of a radiating character; whereas if they are seen as wall or vertical ornaments, they are either radiating or bilateral. This is a necessity of a carpet pattern, that it have a radiating structure, or, in other words, that it point in more than two directions.

Man naturally accustomed to tread on grass, when brought into a state of civilisation, seeks some covering for his floor which shall be softer to the tread and richer in colour than stone or brick. And in our northern climate he seeks also warmth; hence he chooses not a mere matting, or lattice of reeds, but a covering such as shall satisfy his requirements.

In early times our floors appear to have been strewn with sand—a custom still lingering in some country districts; then came the habit of strewing reeds over the floor, and on the part of the opulent, sweet-scented reeds (*Acorus calamus*). And it is curious to notice, in connection with this subject, that one of the charges brought by Henry VIII. against Cardinal Wolsey was that of extravagance in the use of sweet reeds. This use of reeds was succeeded by the employment of mats of simple appearance, formed of a kind of grass, and these by the introduction of wool mats, which, at first, were chiefly imported, but afterwards manufactured in our own country. The wool mats were in their turn replaced by carpets, which gradually increased in size till their proportions became such as to cover the entire floor on which they were placed.

This brief history brings us to notice what is required of a carpet:—it should be soft in texture, rich in appearance, and of "bloomy" effect.

We may add to these requirements by saying that a carpet should also be a suitable background to all works of furniture or other objects placed upon it, and that in character it should accord with the objects with which it is associated in any particular apartment.

Considering more fully these requirements, we notice that a carpet should be soft. This is very desirable, for softness gives a sense of comfort, and with softness is generally combined durability of the fabric; but softness can scarcely be regarded as an art-quality. Yet as the art which an object bears is more leniently viewed when the fitness of the object to the purpose for which it is intended is apparent, we may safely regard softness as a very desirable quality of a carpet.

The Eastern carpets are pre-eminent in this quality of softness, and of English-made carpets "Brussels" and tapestry are the least satisfactory in this way; as usually made, they have a hard "backing." A kind of Brussels carpeting with a soft back has recently been brought out, but at present it is not general in the trade. If the carpet employed in any apartment as a floor covering is harsh in character, it is desirable to place soft felt under it (felt for this purpose can be got at carpet warehouses), or evenly spread soft hay, for by so doing the wear of the fabric will be greatly increased, and the pleasure of walking on it will also be correspondingly greater.

The next quality of a carpet is richness. No carpet is satisfactory which is "washy" or faded in appearance. There must be "depth" of effect, a "fulness" of art-quality. Hangings may be delicate, wall-decorations soft in tint, but a carpet must be rich and "full" in effect, yet a general softness of tone is desirable.

But this richness must be of singular character, for the most desirable effect which a carpet can present is that of a glowing neutral bloom.

I hope that my language does not appear mystical to the general reader or young student. To the ornamentist I think it will be intelligible. What I wish to say is that the effect should be glowing, or radiant, or bright, as opposed to dull, quiet, or heavy; that it should be such as results from the use of a predominance of bright and warm colours, rather than of cold and neutral hues; that it should be neutral, inasmuch as it should not present large masses of positive colour, hut should have an equality of rich harmonious colours throughout; that it should be "bloomy," or have the effect of a garden full of flowers, or better, of the slope of a Swiss alp, where the flowers combine to form one vast harmonious "glow" of colour. This is the effect which a carpet should present, yet it should never present flowers, imitatively rendered, as its ornamentation. Such imitative renderings are not to be produced by the ornamentist; they must come from the pictorial artist, for they are pictures. They cannot form suitable backgrounds to furniture and living objects, for they are positive, and not neutral, in their general effect. A picture, also, will not bear repetition: whoever heard of one person having two copies of the same picture in one room? Yet a pictorial group of flowers may be seen repeated many times over a floor, which is very objectionable. The effect to be produced is that of a rich "colour-bloom;" but the skilled ornamentist will achieve this without violating any laws of fitness, and will gently and delicately hint at the beauty of a profusion of blossom through his tenderly formed pattern.

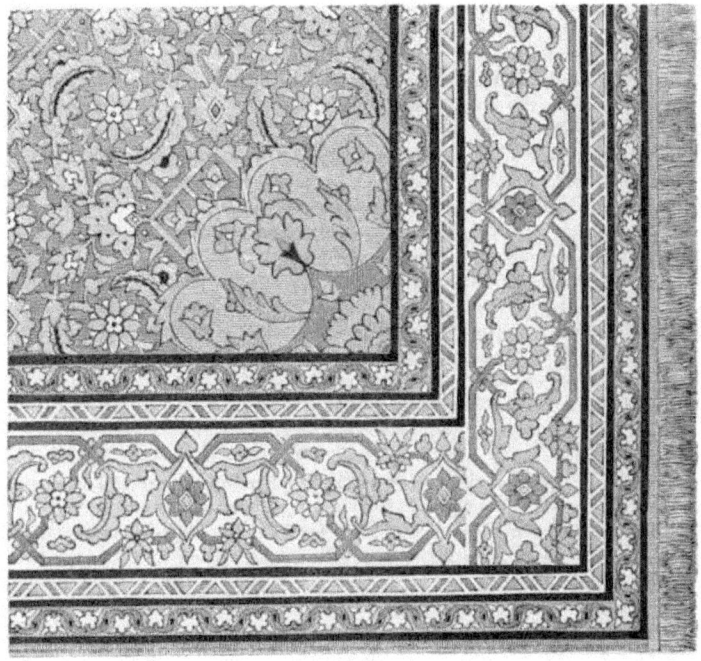

Fig. 80.

Yet a carpet must be neutral in its general effect, as it is the background on which objects rest. Neutrality of effect is of two kinds. Large masses of tertiary or neutral colours will achieve its production, so also will the juxtaposition of the primary colours in small quantities, either alone or with the secondary colours, and black or white; but there will be this difference between the two effects—that produced by low-toned colours will be simply neutral, while that produced by the primary colours will be "bloomy" as well as neutral, and if yellows and reds slightly predominate in the intermingling of colours, the effect will be glowing or radiant.

The radiant, or glowing, bloomy neutrality of effect is that which it is most desirable that a carpet should present.

This effect is rarely produced in English carpets, owing either to the want of skill on the part of the ornamentist, who is unable to produce such works; the want of judgment on the part of the manufacturer, whereby he fails to produce such patterns; or the want of taste on the part of the consumer, owing to which he buys works of a more vulgar character. I have designed carpets in which I have sought to realise as much of this effect as I could with six colours—the number to which I have been limited by the conditions of manufacture, and fortunately these appear to be commanding a large sale, and to be setting a fashion in carpets; but those who wish to study these bloomy effects in their more perfect forms, must do so in the carpets of India, Persia, Smyrna, and Morocco, but especially in the Indian rugs.

Some of the carpets from India are perfect marvels of colour-harmony, and of radiant bloom. They appear to glow as a bed of flowers in the sunshine, and yet they are neutral in their general effect, and when placed in an apartment do not usurp a primary place, as does any pictorially treated pattern.

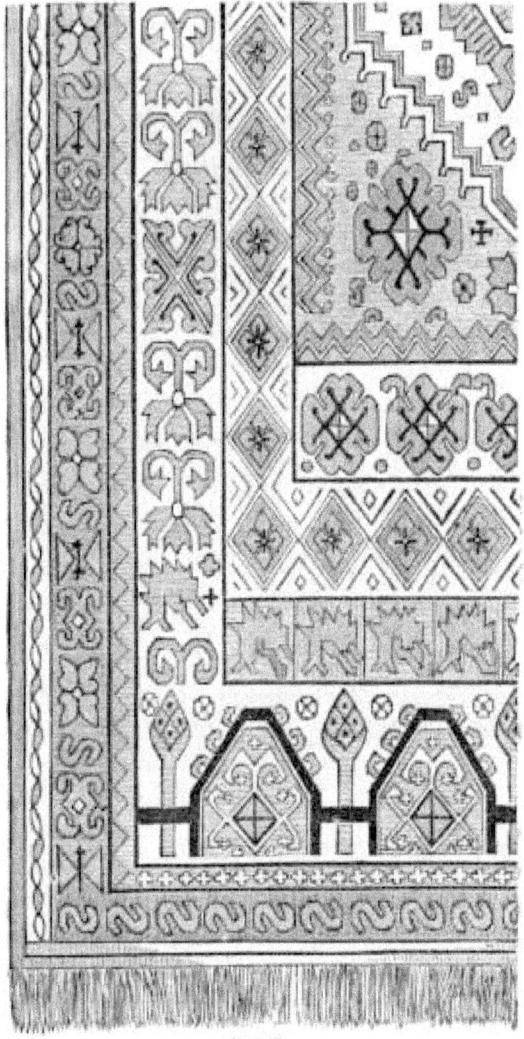

Fig. 81.

This "bloom" was seen to perfection in one or two silk rugs which were shown at the International Exhibition of 1862 in London, and it was not much less apparent in some of the carpets from India shown in the Paris Exhibition of 1867.

Most Indian carpets have this colour-bloom to some extent, and few are unworthy of careful study.

Persian carpets (Fig. 80) are also models of what carpets should be; they are less radiant than many of the Indian works, but are almost more mingled in colour-effect. In pattern many of the Indian and Persian carpets are identical, being traditional, yet in colour they differ, and both are worthy of much consideration.

The Morocco carpets (Fig. 81) differ again from both those of India and Persia, and even to a greater degree than the Persian carpet differs from the Indian. In these there is often a prevalence of soft yellows and juicy yellow-greens, intermingled with reds, blues, and grey-whites, in such a manner as to produce a most harmonious and artistic effect. To the young student, and to any who may desire to cultivate his taste in respect to such matters, I say, Study the carpets of the East most carefully, especially those of India, Persia, and Morocco.

Indian carpets, such as we have just referred to, may be seen at the museum in the building of the new India Office at Whitehall, which museum is open free to the public.

As to the nature of the pattern which may be applied to a carpet, we have "all-over" patterns, or patterns spreading regularly all over the surface; "geometrical" patterns, or those which have an apparent regularity of structure; and panel patterns, or those in which particular parts are, as it were, framed off from other parts.

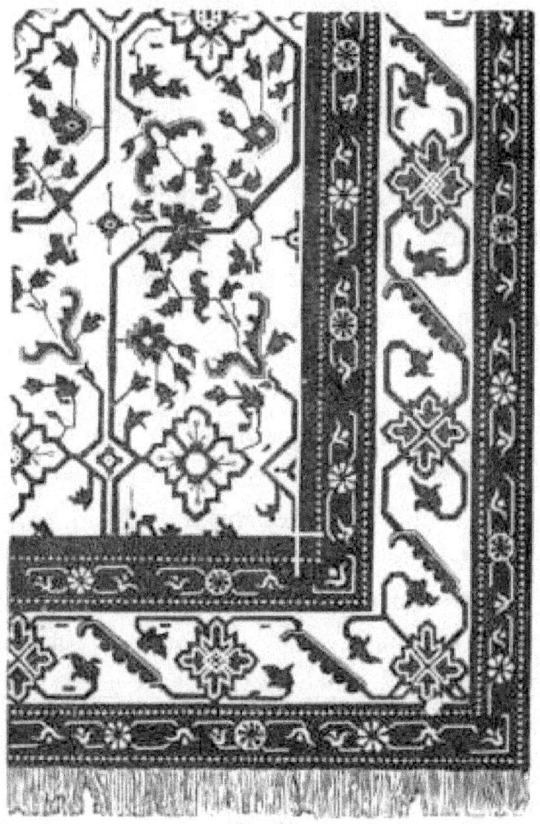

Fig. 82.

First, as to "all-over" patterns. These are what we almost always find in both Indian and Persian carpets, and are, undoubtedly, the true form of decoration for a woven floor covering. What is desirable is an evenly spread pattern, such as will give richness without destroying the unity of the entire effect. The pattern may have parts slightly accentuated or emphasised beyond other parts, but not strongly so, and this emphasising of parts must be arranged with the view of securing to the pattern special interest. Thus, if a carpet is

173

viewed at a distance it should not appear as devoid of all pattern, but through the slight predominance of certain leading features (in Indian carpets, generally of ornamental flowers) the plan of the design should be indicated. More detail should be apparent when the work is seen from a nearer point of view, and still more upon close inspection; but in no case should any parts appear strongly pronounced, or otherwise than refined and beautiful, and in no case should there be a want of interest manifested by the pattern.

Carpet patterns are generally better if founded on a geometrical plan. In this way most of the Indian and Persian patterns are constructed. A geometrical plan secures to the design a manifestation of order and thought in its formation. Panel patterns, unless very carefully managed, become coarse. In some Indian carpets we find a sort of panel in which the colour of the ground is changed from that of the general ground of the carpet, but here the panel has usually a truly ornamental form, and is, indeed, rather a large ornament than a sort of frame enclosing a distinct space. Whenever a panel occurs in an Indian, Persian, or Moorish carpet, it is so managed, and its surroundings are such, as to cause it to appear as a part natural to the general design; but it is far otherwise with the panel patterns which we occasionally see in our shop-windows as the produce of native industry, and it is far otherwise with those which are used in vast quantities by the Americans. Judging from the carpets which they order, I imagine that nowhere on earth is taste in matters of decorative art so depraved as it is in America. It is true that the great floral patterns have ceased to be demanded by them, but they are only replaced by coarse, raw-looking panel patterns, coloured in the most vulgar manner, and without even a hint at refinement or harmony of colour. Let the pattern be "loud" and inharmoniously coloured, and the chances of its sale in the American market are great.

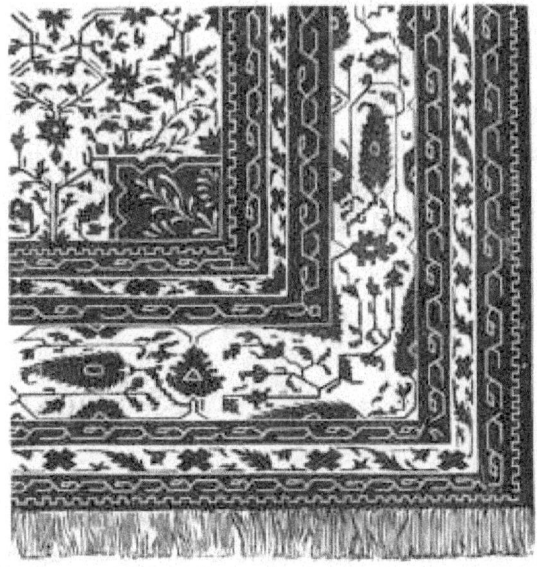

Fig. 83.

But we must not forget that even in our own country bad patterns sell equally as well as good, inartistic patterns as well as those which are of a more refined character, and that even here in Great Britain more of the indifferent, if not of the very bad, sells than of the good. Let us cast the beam, then, from our own eye, before we try to extract it from that of another.

The ground colour of a carpet may vary much, as we all know; it may be black, blue, red, green, or white, or any other colour. If the ground of a carpet is pure white, it is almost impossible that it look well. When I make this assertion I am often told that some of the Indian carpets which I so much admire have white grounds. This is a mistake. Some of them have light grounds, but not pure white. They have light cream-grey, or green-white grounds, but not pure white, and this variety of tone altogether alters the case. Yet even with a light-toned ground it is not an easy matter to make a carpet which shall appear as a suitable background to the furniture of a room; it can be done, but it is a thing difficult to achieve. The safest and best ground for a carpet is black or indigo blue. If on this a closely fitting, well-studied pattern be arranged, drawn in small masses of bright colour, a beautiful bloomy effect may be achieved, and a glance at our best shop-windows will show that the most satisfactory carpets are coloured in this way.

As to the size of the pattern we can say but little, as this will be determined by the coarseness or fineness of the fabric. In a Brussels carpet each stitch is about the one-tenth of an inch square. In some Turkey carpets each stitch is a quarter of an inch square. It is obvious that a much smaller and finer pattern can be produced in Brussels than in Turkey carpet.

A carpet pattern is best small, or at least small in detail if not in the extent of the design. A pattern may repeat three or four times in the width of the fabric (twenty-seven inches if Brussels), or but one figure may be shown, yet in this latter case the detail of the pattern may be as great as in the former. That degree of smallness which is compatible with tolerable distinctness of detail is desirable. For this reason Turkey carpets are not altogether satisfactory; no fine pattern can be worked in them, and besides this they have no colour-bloom and little colour-harmony. In some respects they are good, but altogether they are not satisfying.

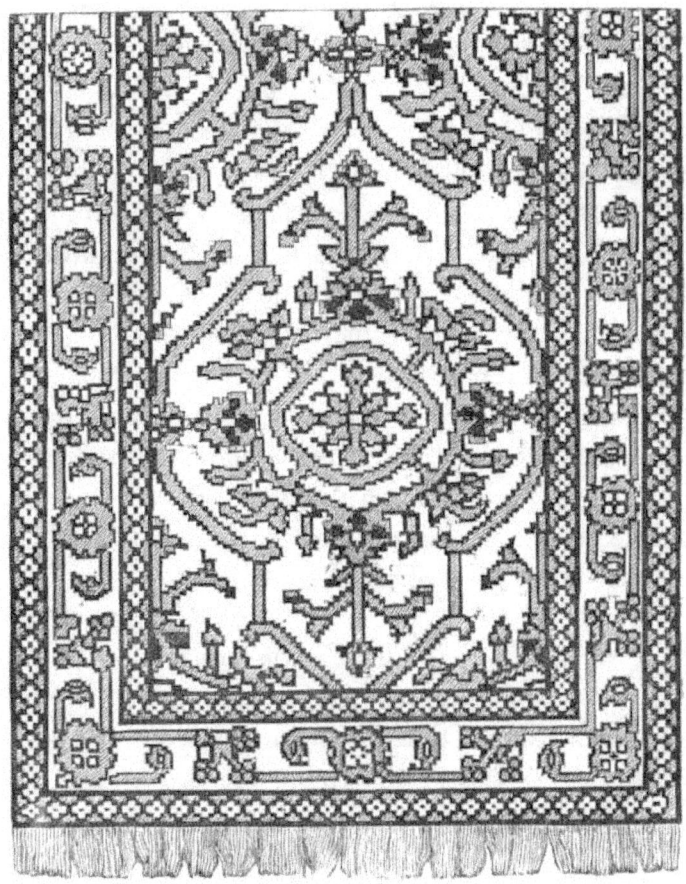

Fig. 84.

Before I close these remarks upon carpets, let me say that, as designers, manufacturers, and consumers, we are one and all timid of new things. We want daring—the energy to produce new things, to manufacture them, to use them. What if the pattern is "extreme," if it is better than others? what if Mrs. Grundy should think us eccentric?—better be eccentric than ever harping on one monotony. If we could but bear calmly the derisive smiles of the ignorant, art-progress would be easy.

With us carpets cover the entire floor. In London these carpets are nailed to the boards, and but seldom taken up. In some parts of England we find rings sewn around the under edge of the carpet, which rings are looped to the heads of nails. Carpets so furnished can be more readily removed for cleaning than those which are nailed to the floor. Square carpets, such as the Turkey, Indian, and Persian, are spread loosely on the boards, and can be taken up and shaken without difficulty. This is unquestionably the most healthy plan of using a carpet, and it is also an artistic plan. If the outer portion of the room floor is formed of inlaid wood of simple and suitable pattern, and a loose square carpet is spread in the centre, we have an artistic effect, and the desirable knowledge that cleanliness is also attainable with a reasonable expenditure of labour.

Before we leave the consideration of carpets we will state in axiomatic form the conditions which govern the application of ornament to them, as reference can more easily be made to short concise sentences than to more extended remarks.

1st. Carpet patterns may with advantage have a geometrical formation, for this gives to the mind an idea of order or arrangement.

2nd. When the pattern has not a geometrical basis, a general evenness of surface should be preserved.

3rd. Carpets are better not formed into "panels," as though they were works of wood or stone; on the contrary, they should have a general "all-over" effect without any great accentuation of particular parts. The Indian and Persian carpets meet this requirement.

4th. While a carpet should present a general appearance of evenness, parts may yet be slightly "pronounced" or emphasised, so as to give to the mind the idea of centres from which the pattern radiates.

5th. A carpet should, in some respects, resemble a bank richly covered with flowers; thus, when seen from a distance the effect should be that of a general "bloom" of colour; when viewed from a nearer point it should present certain features of somewhat special interest; and when looked at closely new beauties should make their appearance.

6th. As a floor is a flat surface, no ornamental covering placed on it should make it appear otherwise.

7th. A carpet, having to serve as a background to furniture, should be of a somewhat neutral character.

8th. Every carpet, however small, should have a border, which is as necessary to it as a frame is to a picture.

Having thus summarised the principles that govern the application of ornament to carpets, we may proceed to notice the conditions governing the decoration of other woven fabrics.

CHAPTER VI.

CURTAIN MATERIALS, HANGINGS, AND WOVEN FABRICS GENERALLY.

In the consideration of hangings of various kinds, we have first to notice the nature of the cloth on which the pattern is to be worked—whether it is of open or close texture. Fabrics of an open character should bear upon them a larger pattern than those which are thicker or closer. The openness or closeness of the fabric will thus determine, to an extent, the nature of the ornament which is to be placed upon it. Muslins, being open in character, should have larger patterns than calicoes, which are closer in texture, or the pattern will be indistinct in the one case or coarse in the other.

But not only does texture influence the pattern when considered as to coarseness or fineness, but also the nature of the cloth as regards material. Thus silk will bear greater fulness of colour than muslins or calico-prints, owing to the fact that the lustre of the material, by reflecting light to the eye of the observer, destroys a certain portion of the intensity of the effect of colour which a less reflective material would exhibit. Silk, as a material, also conveys to the mind an idea of costliness or worth, and wherever the material does so the pattern may be richer in colour than it should be in cheaper and commoner fabrics. If a pattern is in two tints of the same colour only, as in the case of those woven silks where the pattern is formed by the contrast of "tabby" and satin, it may be considerably larger than in those cases where it is rendered conspicuous by colours.

This latter remark will apply also to damask table-linen, and to all similar materials, as well as to dress fabrics, and draperies such as window hangings; but of these we shall say a word shortly.

The closeness or openness of a fabric should, then, be considered when we design patterns for its enrichment, and so should the nature of the material, as this will influence its deadness or lustre. But there are also other considerations which must not be lost sight of. If the pattern is to be wrought by printing, then one class of conditions must be complied with; if by weaving, then another class of requirements call for consideration.

The requirements of manufacture are much more numerous than might be supposed, and are in some cases very restrictive. The size of the repeat, the manner in which colour can be applied, the character of surface attainable, and many other considerations have to be carefully complied with before a pattern can appear as a manufactured article.

The chief fault of patterns, as applied to fabrics generally, is their want of simplicity—want of simple structure, want of simple treatment, want of simplicity of effect; and together with this we generally find largeness and coarseness of parts.

These errors arise chiefly out of a want of consideration of the capabilities of the material. What can be done with this or that particular fabric, is a question that we should carefully ask ourselves before we think of preparing a design. Have we colour at our disposal, or texture merely? and if colour, can it be employed freely or only sparingly? and can any desired colours be placed in juxtaposition or only certain tints? These are questions of great importance, and they should be asked and carefully considered before the first step is taken towards the formation of a pattern. Having ascertained what can be done with the material at command, let us ever remember that we should always endeavour to so employ the capabilities of a material as to conceal its weakness and emphasise its more desirable effects. If this consideration were always given by designers to the power which the material has of yielding effects, we should see, in very many instances, effects strangely different from those which we often encounter; and this remark applies to no class of fabrics more fully than to damask table-linen and coloured damask window hangings.

No satisfactory effect can be got in light and shade upon any woven or printed fabric; besides, to attempt such a mode of treatment is absurd. Light and shade belong only to pictorial art. The ornamentist when enriching a fabric deals only with a surface, and has no thought of placing pictures thereon; he has simply to enrich or beautify that which without his art would be plain and unornamental. A picture will never bear repetition. Who ever heard of a man having two copies of one picture in a room? Yet how much more absurd is it to repeat a little picture—perhaps a pictorially rendered flower—a hundred times over one surface! Besides this, a surface must always be treated, for decorative purposes, as a surface, and not in a manner calculated to deceive by giving apparent relief, or thickness, to that which is essentially without thickness. Take a common damask table-cover. This is by custom almost always white, although it would be better if of a deep cream-colour, or soft buff; and the pattern which it bears results from a change of surface only (why a margin of "ingrain" colour is not added, I could never see); yet in nine cases out of ten the pattern which is presented by such a fabric is a miserable shaded attempt at a pictorial treatment, and is also a thorough failure.

Simplicity of pattern naturally accords with a simple mode of production, and the means of producing pattern in damasks is certainly most simple. That there is a natural harmony between simplicity of pattern and simple means of producing an art-effect is obvious, for of all patterns that I have ever seen upon damask table-linen the simple spot, or dot, is the most satisfactory. If, combined with this spot, we have a border formed of a simple Greek "key-pattern," or of mere lines (a very usual border to good cloths), the effect is perfectly satisfying, and, as far as it goes, is highly to be commended.

It is curious that this spot is only sold in the better quality of table-linen (at least so they tell me in the City), and this shows that the wealthy, or, in other words, the educated, buy such patterns, as they prefer the true to the meretricious, while the false and showy devices which we see on the common cloths please only the common people of vulgar taste. I am not sure, however, that many persons, whose means are limited, would not buy spots and other simple, but correctly treated, patterns, if such were to be got in common qualities of damask; but when the pocket must govern the purchase, it is hard to say that the false is preferred to the true, if the true is not procurable with the means at command.

While I cannot withhold praise from this little spot, it must not be thought that I thereby give to it a high place as an art-work. Little is here attempted, and that little is done well. But let us analyse this pattern. First, the spots are of one tint throughout, if I may thus express myself—a tint, shall we say, which is the reverse of that of the ground. It is not shaded so that it may appear as a ball or globe, and is not graduated in "colour" in any way (were it graduated or shaded, feebleness of effect must inevitably accrue), but is a simple, honest spot, treated as a surface ornament. Secondly, this spot is geometrically arranged, or, in other words, has an orderly arrangement.

If an attempt is made at rendering a pictorial, or light-and-shade effect, in damask, an absurd failure can alone result, for depth of shade is not obtainable in the material; and, besides this, what appears as shade, when the cloth is seen from one point of view, appears as light if seen from another point of view. Nothing could be more absurd, then, than seeking to produce shaded effects with such means as are here at our disposal. But were the fabric capable of rendering such effects, it would still be wrong to employ them, as we deal only with the surface, and are seeking to enhance the value of, or beautify, a fabric, and not to cover it with pictures. In our simple spot we have those elements which may be extended into the richest and most artistic damask patterns. We have order—as indicated by the geometrical plan of the pattern—and an honest and simple expression, or application, of the capabilities of the material.

All table-covers should certainly have a border. Any object which is to be used as a whole looks unsatisfactory if it appears as though it were part of a whole. If a cloth is without border it is impossible to avoid the impression that it is a part of a larger cloth, and in every respect the general effect is decidedly unsatisfactory.

It is perhaps well that we notice one peculiarity of a table-cover before we dismiss the consideration of such fabrics, which is this, that while the central portion is seen flat, the border portion is viewed in folds; and here we come to one of the great peculiarities of most draperies, that of their being viewed not as flat surfaces, but in waves or folds. One portion of a table-cloth is, however, seen flat, but this is almost an exception in the case of draperies. Another exception to this rule of hangings appearing in folds, and that of a very complete character, occurs in silk damasks which are used as a rich lining to the walls of palaces and some mansions; but of table-cloths we will speak for the present.

The central part of a table-cloth, that portion which is always to be viewed as a flat surface, may be enriched with any diaper pattern that is simply treated, and this diaper pattern may be full of design, provided the parts are not too large or too small. It may also be formed of gracefully curved parts, or of straight lines or circles, or of any combination of these elements; but, preferably, not wholly of straight lines.

Were it not for the fact that much of this central portion of the cloth is to be covered by articles of the dinner-table, it might well be furnished with a central ornament, repeating only in quarters; but as such an ornament, in order that it be satisfying, requires to be seen as a whole, it is not desirable that such be here employed. A diaper pattern that repeats many times in the centre is preferable, as the pattern can then be seen in a satisfactory manner.

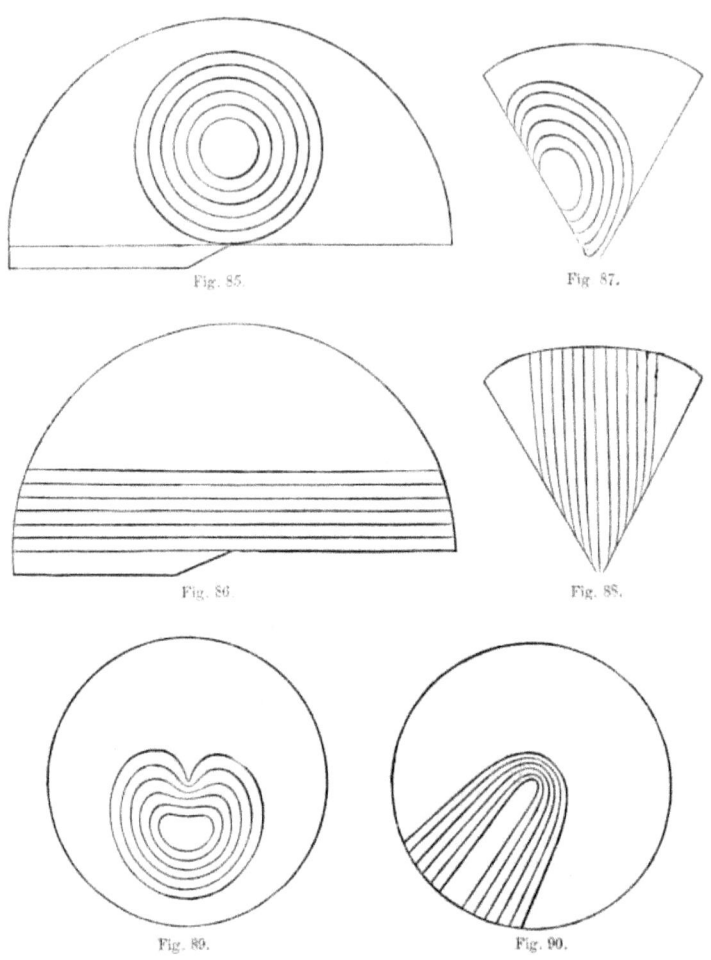

Fig. 85.

Fig. 87.

Fig. 86.

Fig. 88.

Fig. 89.

Fig. 90.

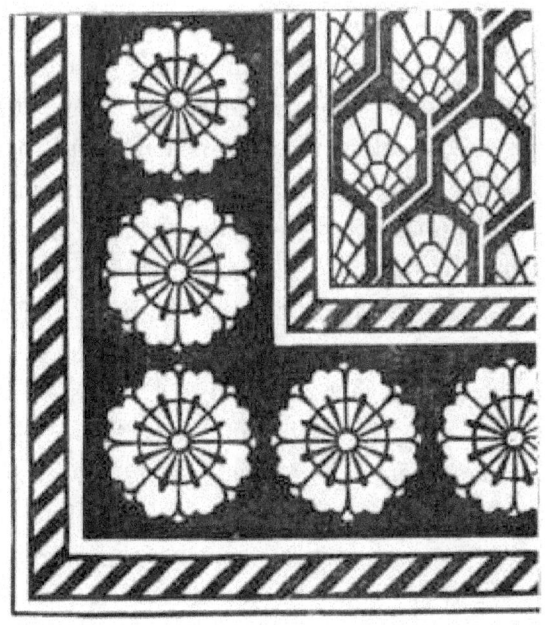

Fig. 91.

The border of a table-cloth, like all fabrics that are to be seen in folds, requires special treatment, for what looks well when seen as a flat surface may not look well when seen on a waved surface. Tender and graceful curves are lost when viewed upon folds, for they here appear as mere wormy lines. On the contrary, right lines, whether horizontal or diagonal, and circles, all look well when seen upon waved grounds. These lines become, owing to the folds of the fabric, curves of a subtle character. The manner in which lines become influenced by falling on a curved surface can be readily illustrated by forming semicircles of paper, and folding them into cones, after having drawn upon them a series of circles (Fig. 85) or straight lines (Fig. 86). If these cones (Figs. 87 and 88) are now viewed from above, or in such a manner that the eye rests over the apices, it will be seen that the circles have now become richly varied curves, each having somewhat the form of a blunt heart or cardioid (Fig. 89), and that the straight lines become horse-shoe-shaped (Fig. 90). These illustrations will be sufficient to show that what is plain when seen upon a flat surface may be delicate and satisfying if seen upon a curved surface; and will also lead us to understand that what may be delicate and refined when seen upon a flat surface may become feeble and unsatisfactory if falling upon a waved ground. I have said that stripes or straight lines, if *crossing* a folded fabric, are satisfactory. This is so in almost all cases, the only exception being in ladies' dresses. Here lines crossing the fabric are not satisfactory, as they become rings around the body, which appear to divide it into hoop-like strata. The patterns of dresses *may* consist of narrow, vertical stripes, as these are collected together at the waist of the figure, and fall into graceful curves with any motion of the body, but the very opposite is the case with window-hangings. All vertical stripes are here highly offensive, while horizontal stripes are thoroughly satisfactory.

A consideration of the window-hanging materials made in Spain, Algeria, and on the Morocco coast, will show us the beauty of horizontal stripes; and in some of the little Algerian warehouses, such as we have in Regent Street, London, and in the Rue de Rivoli in Paris, we see some of these fabrics of a most interesting character.

To state in a concise form the laws which should govern the application of ornament to certain fabrics which are to be seen in folds, I should say—

1st. Great simplicity of pattern is necessary.

2nd. Circles, straight lines crossing the fabric, and diagonal lines are all correct in such a case, and are improved by the folds, which form them into subtle and beautiful curves (Fig. 91).

3rd. If curves are tender and graceful, they become commonplace on a waved or folded ground.

4th. The size of the pattern should be considered in relation to the size of the folds of the material.

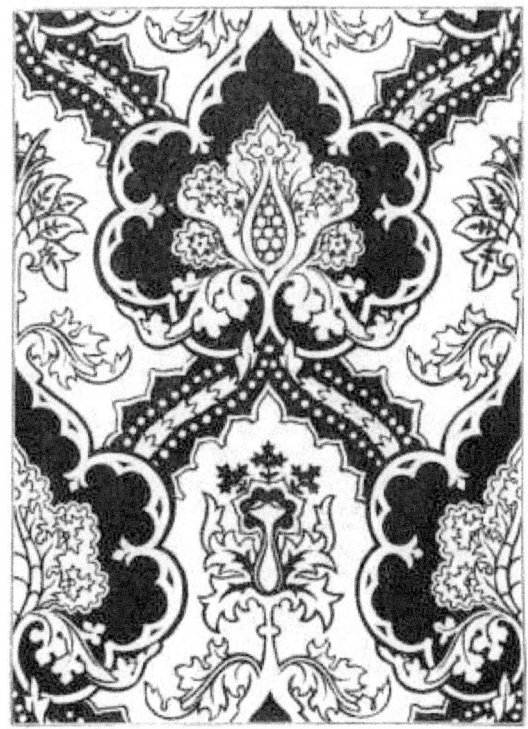

Fig. 92.

189

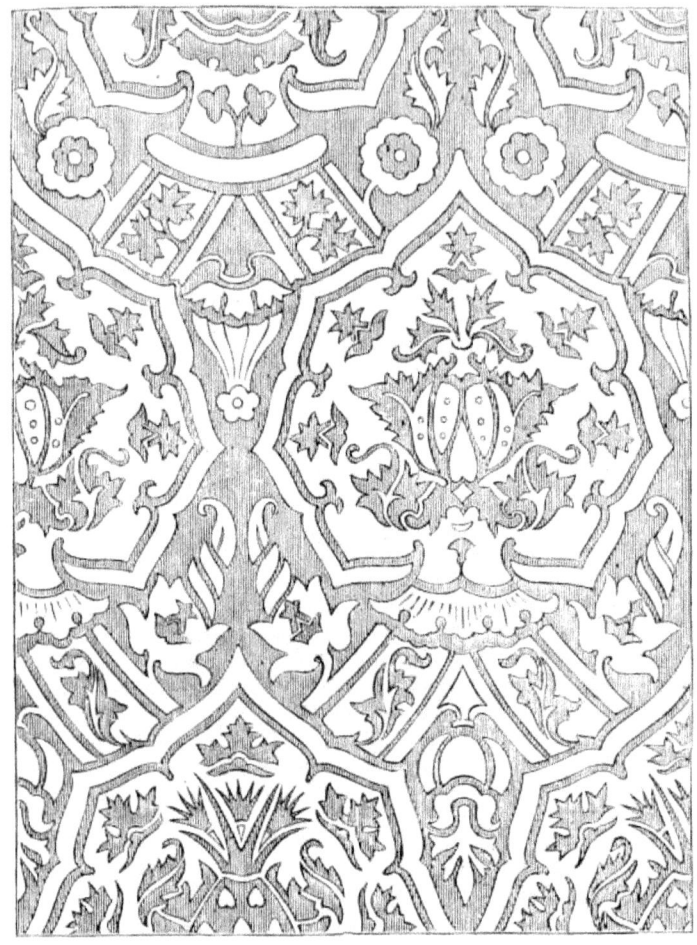

Fig. 93.

In Germany a kind of ornament is applied to rich stiff fabrics which is almost peculiar to the country. This ornament is rich, bold, hard or stiff in its lines, and in every way adapted for the decoration of a costly fabric which falls in large folds, the folds changing the hard and stiff lines into graceful curves. This should also be noted respecting these curious yet beautiful patterns, that they are always simple in plan,

190

however rich in detail, and are invariably founded on a geometrical basis. "German Gothic" is a name by which such ornament may be distinguished (flat Gothic ornament has always been quite distinct from the stone and metal ornaments of Gothic buildings, which have solid and not merely superficial form), see Figs. 92 and 93. This particular class of ornament forms the background to many old pictures, a most interesting collection of which exists in the museum of Cologne, and is certainly worthy of the most careful study.

As to flat silk wall-damasks, which are used in some of the upper-class houses as wall-papers are used in the middle-class houses, all that need be said is that they should be treated as wall decorations, and not as fabrics which are to be seen folded. Were I asked whether I approve of these damasks as wall coverings, I should say, "Certainly not." A wall is better treated as a wall, and not so covered with drapery as to leave space for vermin between the wall and its enrichment. There is also the further objection that the lines where the fabric is joined are visible, and these are most certainly objectionable.

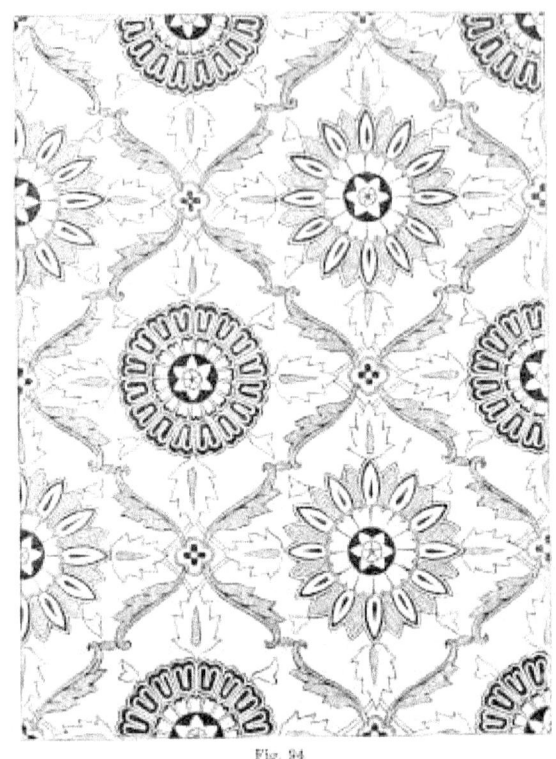

Fig. 94

Besides the illustrations of German ornament just given, we figure also a specimen of Indian embroidery on cotton (Fig. 94). I cannot too strongly recommend the designer of patterns for woven goods to study the native fabrics of India, exhibited at the Indian Museum, Whitehall.

Besides the collection here brought together, there is also in most of our manufacturing towns a large series of specimens of these cloths deposited with the Chamber of Commerce, and these can be consulted by all respectable members of the community. Speaking of these Indian fabrics, Mr. Redgrave says, in his Report on Design prepared for the Commissioners of the International Exhibition of 1851:—"These are almost wholly designed on the principles here presumed to be just ones—the ornament is always flat, and without shadow; natural flowers are never used imitatively or perspectively, but are conventionalised by being displayed flat and according to a symmetrical arrangement; and all other objects, even animals and birds, when used as ornament, are reduced to their simplest flat form. When colour is added, it is usually rendered by the simplest local hue, often bordered with a darker shade of the colour, to give it a clearer expression; but the shades of the flowers are rarely introduced. The cloth of gold figured in the loom (Fig. 95), and part of an Indian scarf (Fig. 96), illustrate fully these remarks. The ornament is geometrically and symmetrically arranged, flat, in simple tints, and bordered, as above described, with darker shades of the local colour. The principle of colour adopted is a balance of the complementaries red and green, in both cases with white introduced to give points of expression, and to lead the eye to the symmetrical arrangement of the ornament. In Fig. 95 purple is introduced to harmonise with the gold ground, a harmony very frequently used in the rich tissues of India. In Fig. 96 variety has been obtained by introducing two reds, giving an interchange of a lighter tint in every other flower in the border. The borders of these scarves are beautifully illustrative of the simple and graceful flowing lines which characterise Indian ornament; and in Fig. 96 we can observe the difference between the Eastern and the mediæval patterns—while the same principles are acknowledged in both, the latter are often stiffer and more angular than the graceful sprigs of this border. Both these works show how much beauty may be obtained by simple means, when regulated by just principles, and how perfectly unnecessary are the multiplied tints by which modern designers think to give value to their works, but which increase the difficulties of production out of all proportion to any effect resulting from them—nay, often even to the absolute disadvantage of the fabric. If we look at the details of the Indian patterns, we shall be surprised at their extreme simplicity, and be led to wonder at their rich and satisfactory effect; it will soon be evident, however, that their beauty results entirely from adherence to the principles above described. The parts themselves are often poor, ill-drawn, and common-place; yet, from the knowledge of the designer, due attention to the just ornamentation of the fabric, and the refined delicacy evident in the selection of *quantity* and the choice of tints, both for the ground, where gold is not used as a ground, and for the ornamental forms, the fabrics, individually and as a whole, are a lesson to our designers and manufacturers, given by those from whom we least expected it."

Much that Mr. Redgrave here says is worthy of careful consideration, and I can do no more than recommend the student to study these beautiful Indian fabrics, and consider them in conjunction with the remarks which we have made respecting them and fabrics in general.

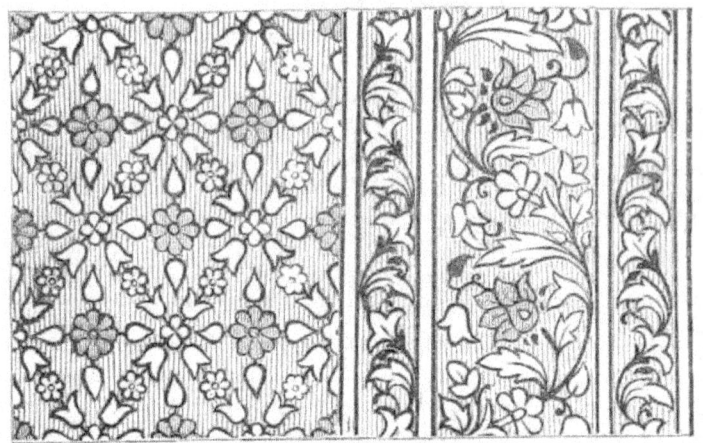

Fig. 95.

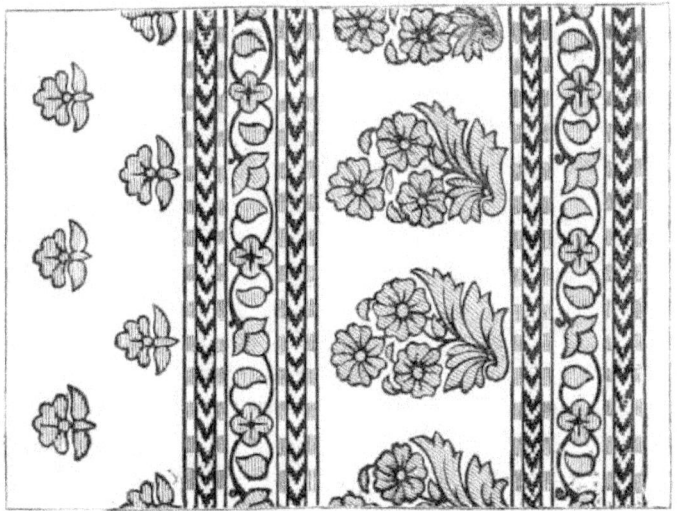

Fig. 96.

CHAPTER VII.

DIVISION I.

In this chapter I have to commence our consideration of pottery, and of hollow vessels especially; and this I do with considerable pleasure, as works in pottery enjoy a longer existence, though through the character of the material of which they are made they are more fragile, than those formed of almost any other substance. Many works of Greek pottery are known to us, and not a few such works by the ancient Egyptians, and these are preserved not as fragments merely, but as works in their entirety, and with the same beauty that they possessed when first they left the hands of the workman.

Clay is a most desirable material with which to form works of utility and of beauty, and this for many reasons. First, it is so inexpensive as to be almost valueless; secondly, it is easily formed into vessels of almost any required shape; thirdly, it is capable of being "worked" into shapes of great beauty by a momentary exercise of skill; fourthly, clay is naturally of many beautiful colours; fifthly, it is capable of receiving by application to its surface any amount of colour, and of preserving such colours as are applied to it in an unimpaired state for ages; and sixthly, it is susceptible of the highest art-finish, or the bold sketchy touch of the modeller's hand. I say that clay is a very desirable material for formation into vessels of various kinds, because of its inexpensive character. This quality of cheapness gives to the material an advantage over many other substances of a much more costly character, such as should not be overlooked, for the long existence which so many works of earthenware have had is mainly due to the worthlessness of the material of which they are composed. In my first chapter I gave an extract from the writings of Professor George Wilson, showing that gold and silver, while beautiful in themselves, and worthy to be fashioned into exquisite devices, are yet too tempting to the thief, and to all who are pressed for means, to remain long in the form of art-works. Families who have been reduced in circumstances, and have thereby been constrained to part with their old plate, have melted it, so as to hide their shame. To illustrate this, let me quote from the "Handbook of the Arts of the Middle Ages and Renaissance, as applied to the Decoration of Furniture, Arms, Jewels, etc., translated from the French of M. Jules Labarte, 1856." After giving the names of many workers in the precious metals, the author says:—"We may form some idea of what artists these Italian goldsmiths were of the fourteenth, fifteenth, and sixteenth centuries, and what admirable works they must have produced. But, alas! these noble works have almost all perished; their artistic worth proving no safeguard against cupidity or necessity, the fear of pillage, or the love of change. But a very few names even of those skilled artists have descended to us, and in making known those preserved to us in the writings of Vasari, Benvenuto, Cellini, and others, we can rarely point out any of their works as being still in existence.

"Cellini tells us that while Pope Clement VII. was besieged in the castle of St. Angelo, he received orders to unset all the precious stones that were upon the tiaras, the sacred vessels, and the jewels of the sovereign pontiff; and to melt down the gold, of which he obtained 200 pounds. How many artistic treasures must have perished in the crucible of Cellini." We now see clearly that while clay is a much more fragile material than either silver or gold, its very worthlessness, despite its fragility, gives to it length of years.

We have said that clay is easily formed into vessels of almost any required shape. This is so within certain limits. Throughout these chapters I have lost no opportunity of insisting upon the importance of working every material in a befitting manner, and in the most simple and easy way in which the material can be wrought. Almost every material can be simply "worked" in some way, or while in some particular condition.

Glass has a molten state in which it can be "blown" into the most beautiful of shapes, and this process of blowing is the work of but a few seconds. Glass has also a solid condition, yet as it can be formed into works of great beauty by the exercise of momentary skill, it would be extremely foolish to take a mass of the solid glass, and by laborious grinding form it into a bottle or a bowl. It fortunately happens that if a material is worked in its most simple and befitting manner, the results obtained are more beautiful and satisfying than those which are arrived at by any roundabout method of production. Glass should be formed into hollow vessels only when in its plastic condition, for it cannot be shaped into the form of such vessels as we require when in its solid state without the expenditure of much unnecessary, therefore wasteful, labour. But if a mass of crystal or marble is required to assume the form of a bowl or font, then the laborious process of grinding must be resorted to, for these substances have no plastic state.

The potter's wheel has been known from the earliest historic time, and this has at all times been the instrument with which the best earthen vessels have been formed. A mass of clay of suitable size is placed on a horizontal disc of wood, to which a rotary motion is imparted. The operator presses his thumbs into the centre of the clay, and then, by causing his fingers to approach his thumbs, manipulates the clay into a cup, a bowl, a vase, an earthen bottle, or whatever form he may please; and if skilful, the operator can form objects of marvellous beauty with a rapidity that astonishes all who see for the first time his mode of working.

If potters would but content themselves, in order to the production of such articles as we require in common life, with the "potter's wheel," we should be almost sure of a certain amount of beauty in domestic earthenware, but such is not the case. They make fancy moulds of plaster of Paris and of wire gauze, and roll out clay as the pastrycook does dough, and manipulate it as so much pie-crust, instead of applying to it simple skill. Neither a bowl nor a plate need have a scalloped edge, indeed they are much better without it; and if unnecessary, and even undesirable, absurdities were avoided, and a simple and natural method of working each material alone employed, a great improvement in art would speedily take place.

It is strange but true, that the worker in one material seems rarely to be satisfied with making his works look as well and as consistent as possible; he desires rather to form poor imitations of something else. We have all seen earthen jugs made in imitation of wicker-work, although to do so is obviously foolish, as no wicker vessel could hold water, and the thing imitated is much less beautiful than a thousand forms which clay is capable of assuming. Men's heads without brains are, or were at least, favourite jugs. Well, that there are many models for this idea in Nature, I doubt not; yet why we should copy them by making a jug in the form of a hollow head, I know not. I have in my possession a milk-jug, such as is common in the district of Swansea in South Wales, in the likeness of a cow. The tail is twisted into a handle; by a hole in the back the milk is admitted, and through the mouth it is ejected. A more wretched and coarse idea it is scarcely possible to conceive of, yet the vulgar admire this jug. Let us work the material in a simple and befitting manner, and satisfactory results are almost sure to accrue.

I have said that clay, as such, has many beautiful colours. Naturally clay is black, grey-white, red, brown, and yellow, and it is capable of assuming many desirable tints by the agency of chemical means. We do not use coloured clays as we should do. We want so much white—everything to look so clean. All ornamental ware, at least, should be artistic, and the art-effect should supersede that cold whiteness which the Dutch and the English mistake for cleanliness. A clay of good natural colour is not a thing to be hidden, or ashamed of.

Clay is capable, when glazed, of receiving any amount of colour, and of preserving these colours in their beauty for almost any length of time. These qualities are invaluable to the ornamentist. Colour is not always at his disposal. The goldsmith has difficulty in getting it, but to the potter it is very accessible. Colour is capable of giving to objects a charm which they could not possibly have without it. Let us use the power thus placed at our disposal rightly and well, and then the enduring character of the colour-harmonies which we produce may gladden posterity in ages yet to come.

Clay is susceptible of the highest art-finish, or of a bold sketchy treatment. Finish is very desirable in some cases. The cup which my lady uses in her boudoir should be delicate and fine, for what is worthy to approach the sacred lips of the occupant of a fair apartment but such a work as is tender and refined?

As a rule, however, we over-estimate the value of finish, and under-value bold art-effects. Excessive finish often (but by no means always) destroys art-effect. I have before me some specimens of Japanese earthenware, which are formed of a coarse dark brown clay, and are to a great extent without that finish which most Europeans appear so much to value, yet these are artistic and beautiful. In the case of cheap goods we spend time in getting smoothness of surface, while the Japanese devote it to the production of an art-effect. We get finish without art, they prefer art without finish.

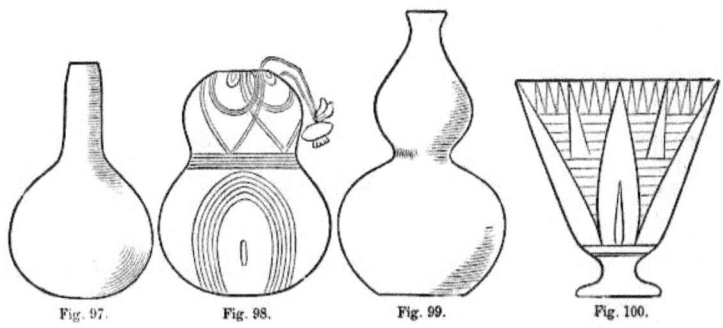

Fig. 97. Fig. 98. Fig. 99. Fig. 100.

We must now devote ourselves to a special consideration of the shapes of earthen vessels, and to the manner in which ornament should be applied to them.

In his primitive condition man appears to have used the shells of certain fruits as drinking vessels and bottles; and to this day we find many tribes of uncivilised or half-civilised men using the same class of vessels. "Monkey-pots" (the hard shells of the *Lecythis allaria*), the coverings of the Brazil nut (*Bertholetia excelsa*), and especially the rinds of the calabash and many species of gourd (Figs. 97 and 98), have been used in this way.[26] The first efforts made at the production of earthen vessels were mere attempts at copying in clay the forms of the fruit-shells which were in use as drinking vessels. After a power of forming earthen vessels, having a certain amount of perfection of manufacture, was gained, we still find the origin of the potter's art manifested by certain works. Thus in China, where the potter's art has so long been understood, we still find vessels made in the form of the bottle-gourd, just as was their custom in the days of their first manufacturing efforts (Fig. 99). Before considering the shapes of vessels from a utilitarian point of view, I should tell the student that certain shapes are characteristic of different nations and of different periods of time.

The Greek shapes, as we may call them—that is, the forms of those vessels which the Greeks produced—are of a particular class, and the vessels produced by the Egyptians are of a different type; while those of the Chinese, Indians, Japanese, and Mexicans again differ from each other, and from those of both the Greeks and the Egyptians. For grace of form the vessels of the old Greeks stand pre-eminent (Figs. 101 and

---

[26] All who are interested in this subject are referred to a paper published in the "Transactions of the Edinburgh Botanical Society," for 1859, by Professor George Wilson, on the "Fruits of the Cucurbitaceæ."

102); for simple dignified severity, those of the Egyptians (Fig. 100); for quaintness, those of the Mexicans (Fig. 103); for a combination of grace with dignity, those of the Chinese (Figs. 104 and 105); and for a combination of beauty with quaintness, those of the Japanese (Fig. 106); while in many respects the Indian shapes (Figs. 107 and 108) resemble those of the Japanese. Fig. 109 is a water vessel from Ha, and Figs. 110 and 111 are jugs from Morocco.

I cannot enter into any details respecting the characteristic forms of vessels produced by these various nations, but must content myself by giving a few illustrations of the various shapes, and leaving the matter with the learner for study. The British Museum, the South Kensington Museum, and the Indian Museum will aid him in his researches.

It has been said that the character of a people can be told by their water-vessels. As the consideration of this statement will lead us to see how perfectly a domestic utensil may answer the end which it should serve, I will extract from my "Art of Decorative Design" a few remarks on this subject.

This statement can well "be illustrated by the Egyptian and Greek water-vessels, the former of which has sides tapering to the top and slanting inwards, a small orifice, and a rounded base, and the mouth of the vessel bridged by an arched handle, the whole being constructed of bronze (Fig. 112); the latter consists of an egg-shaped body (the broad end being above) resting upon a secure foot, which is surmounted by a large, divergent, funnel-shaped member (Fig. 113). It has no handle over the orifice, but has one at either side.

"Not only do these vessels differ in form, but associated circumstances differ also; and it is this variation in circumstances which brought about the difference in form of the two water-vessels.

"The peculiarities of the Egyptian water-vessel are its formation of bronze, the roundness of its base, which renders it unfitted for standing, the narrowness of its mouth, and the handle arching the orifice; and of the Greek, its being wrought in clay, the secure base, the wide mouth, the contraction in the centre, and the handle at either side. We should judge from these vessels that the Egyptians drew water from a river, or some position which required that the vessel be attached to a cord and cast into the source of supply, for the roundness of the base at once points to this, it being a provision for enabling the vessel to fill by turning upon its side (were its base flat it would float on the water); it is also formed out of metal so as to facilitate this end. The arched handle not only points to the attachment of the vessel to a string in order that it be cast into the water, but also to the carrying the vessel pendent from the hand in the manner that pails are at present carried, and the contracted mouth restrains the splashing over of the water: and what this simple water-vessel points to we find to have been the case, for the Egyptians derived water from the Nile in the very manner that the vessel would indicate; but with the Greeks circumstances were different, and the shape of the vessel varies accordingly. The base is here flat, in order that the vessel may stand; the mouth is large, in order to collect the water which fell from above,—from the dripping-rocks and water-spouts. This being the manner in which water was gathered, a vessel formed of heavy metal was unnecessary; the contraction prevented the water from splashing over when carried, and up to this point the vessel was filled, and no higher; and the handles at the side show that it was carried on the head. But, in conjunction with this mode of carrying, there is another consideration of interest, which is, the centre of gravity is high. If we attempt to balance a stick, having one enlarged end, on the finger, it will be found necessary that the weight be at the top; and in balancing anything, it will be found that the object, in order that it ride steadily, have its point of greatest weight considerably elevated above its base. In the Greek water-vessel, which was carried balanced on the head, we find this condition fully complied with, the centre of gravity occupying a high position, while in the Egyptian vessel the centre of gravity was low; but where the vessel is to be carried underhand, it is as great an advantage to have the centre of gravity low as it is in the case of a coach, where security is thus gained just as the centre of gravity is lowered. The Greek water-vessel, then, consists of a cavity for holding water, a funnel to collect and guide the water, a base for the vessel to rest upon, and handles to enable it to be raised to the head, and the centre of gravity is high in order that it be readily balanced; and we should judge from this vessel that the Greeks procured water from dripping-rocks and water-spouts, and this is exactly what did occur. These are the direct teachings of the Egyptian and Greek water-vessels; yet how many circumstances and incidents of common life can be conceived as associated with these different forms of vessel. There is the gossip round the well, and the lingering by the river-side where the image of the date-palm is mirrored by the glassy surface of the waters. The effect of the noise of the splashing water upon the mind in the one case, combined with the comparatively loud and energetic speaking which would be necessary in order that the voice be not drowned by the noise, and of the calm tranquillity of the river-bank in the other, where the limpid water is ever flowing on in silent majesty, must be considerable. Then we have the potter's art essential to the production of the vessel in the one case, and the metal-worker's in the other—the digging of clay, the mining of metal, the kilns and smelting furnaces. We will not continue this portion of the subject further, and have brought forward this illustration in order to show how well-considered objects reveal to us the habits and customs of the peoples and nations in which they originated."

It will now be apparent that even a common object may result from such careful consideration that its form will at once suggest its use; but the object will only reveal the purpose for which it was created with definiteness of expression when it perfectly answers the end proposed by its formation. The advice which I must give to every designer is to study carefully exactly what is required, before he proceeds to form his ideas of what the object proposed to be created should be like, and then to diligently strive to arrange such a form for it as shall cause it to be perfectly suited to the want which it is intended to meet.

More will be said upon the subject of form when speaking of glass vessels and of silversmiths' work; and when considering these subjects we shall also give the law which governs the application of handles and spouts to vessels; and it is of the utmost importance that they be correctly placed in order that the vessel may be used with convenience. A word must now be said respecting the decoration of earthen vessels, but on this subject our remarks must be brief.

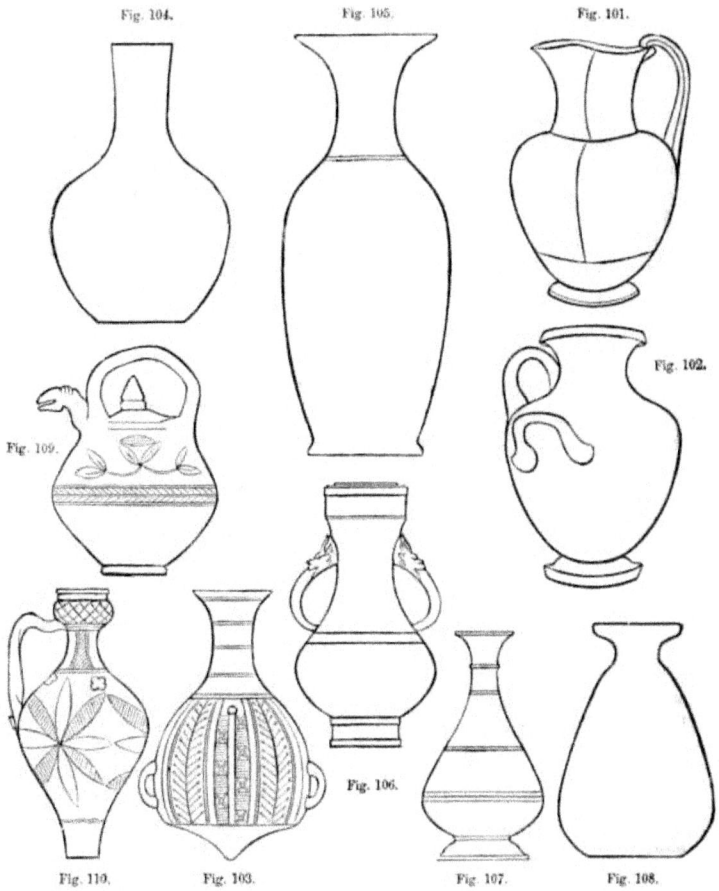

Fig. 104.   Fig. 105.   Fig. 101.

Fig. 109.

Fig. 102.

Fig. 110.   Fig. 103.   Fig. 106.   Fig. 107.   Fig. 108.

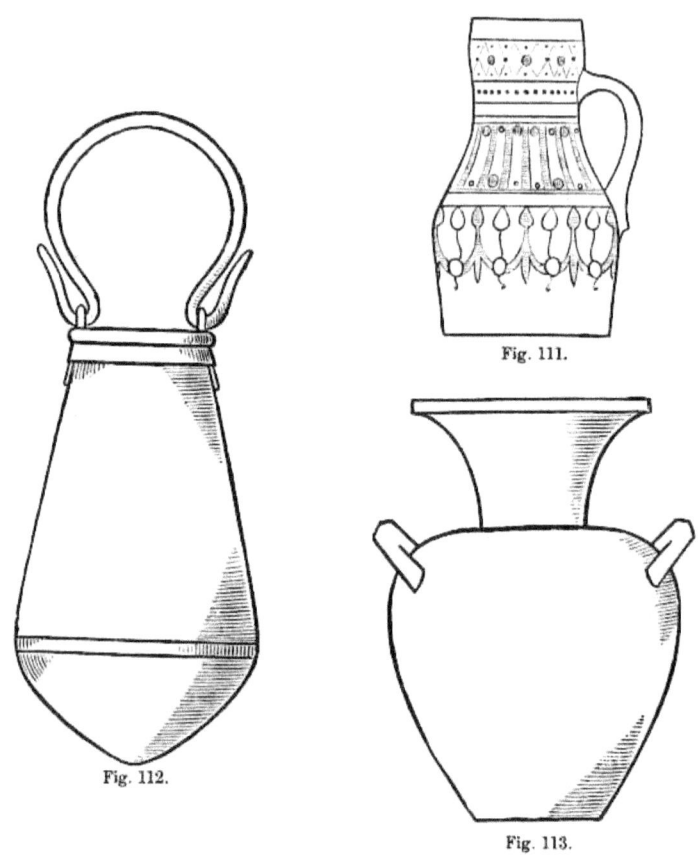

Fig. 111.

Fig. 112.

Fig. 113.

The object to which the decoration is applied must determine the nature of the ornament to be employed. In the case of a vessel which is to be in part hidden when in use, great simplicity of treatment should be adopted, and the ornament may with advantage consist of repeated parts. In the case of a plate, little or no ornament should be placed in the centre; but if there is a central ornament it should be a small, regular, radiating figure, consisting of like parts (Figs. 114 and 115). The border should also consist of simple members repeated, for it will then look well if portions are covered; and these remarks will apply equally to all kinds of plates, whether intended for use at dinner or dessert.

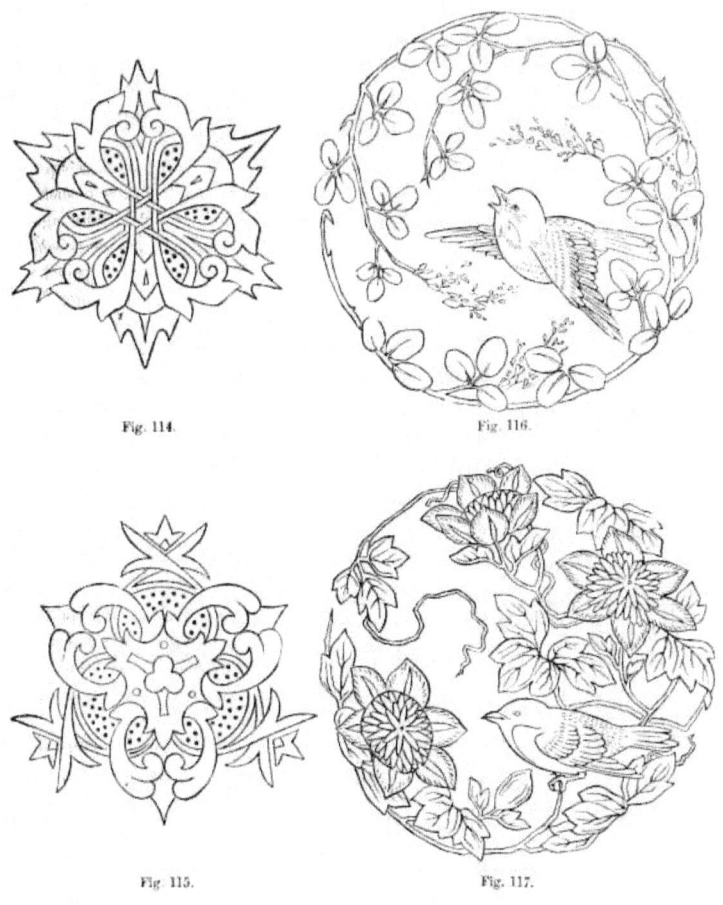

Fig. 114.

Fig. 116.

Fig. 115.

Fig. 117.

No plate should have a landscape painted upon it, nor a figure, nor a group of flowers. Whatever has a right and wrong way upwards is inappropriate in such a position, as whatever ornament a plate bears should be in all positions as fully right way upwards to the beholder as it can be. Besides, landscapes, groups of flowers, and figures are spoiled if in part hidden, provided they are satisfactory when the whole is seen.

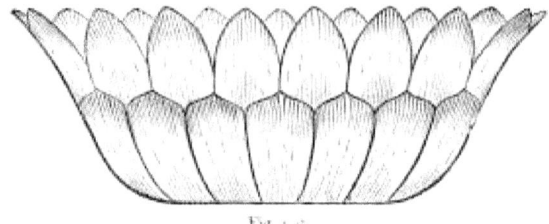

Fig. 105.

Plates may have a white ground, for it is desirable that those articles on which food is presented should manifest the utmost cleanliness, yet to a cream tint there can be no objection. I should, however, prefer white plates, with a rather deep blue, Indian red, maroon, or brown pattern upon them, and a pale buff table-cloth for them to rest upon.

In the case of cups and saucers the treatment should be similar to that of the plate. The saucer may have a simple border ornament, consisting of parts repeated, and little or no ornament in the central portion on which the cup rests. The cup may have an external border ornament, and a double narrow line of colour around the upper portion of the interior, but no other ornament is here required.

Whatever ornament is placed around a cup, or vase, or any tall object must be such as will not suffer by perspective, for there is scarcely any portion of the ornament that can be seen otherwise than foreshortened (Figs. 103 and 111). Let simplicity be the ruling principle in the decoration of all rounded objects, and ever remember that a line which is straight on a flat surface becomes a curve on a round surface.

I have given what is a correct decoration for a plate and cup and saucer, but there are other methods of treatment than those just named. The Japanese are very fond of placing little circular groups of flowers on plates, saucers, and bowls (Figs. 116 and 117). The Greeks had various methods of enriching their tazzas and vases with ornament, and the Egyptians were partial to the plan of rendering a cup as a lotus-flower (Fig. 100). But when they formed a cup thus, they were careful to draw the flower conventionally and ornamentally, and never produced an imitative work. The Chinese treat the flower of the sacred bean in the same way (Fig. 118).

What I have said has been addressed to the student. The remarks, however, made respecting the form chosen being that which is most suitable to the end proposed, and the conditions to which I shall make reference as governing the application of handle and spout to any object, are binding upon all who would produce satisfactory works; but to the genius who has power to produce beautiful and vigorous ornament, and whose taste has, by years of study and cultivation, become refined and judicious, I can give no rules, his own taste being his best guide.

DIVISION II.

When speaking of earthenware, I insisted upon the desirability of using every material in the easiest and most natural manner, and I illustrated my meaning by saying that glass has a molten condition as well as a solid state, and that while in the molten condition it can be "blown" into forms of exquisite beauty. Glass-blowing is an operation of skill, and an operation in which natural laws come to our aid, and I cannot too strongly repeat my statement that every material should be "worked" in the most simple and befitting manner; and I think that our consideration of the formation of glass vessels will render the reasonableness of my demand apparent.

Let a portion of molten glass be gathered upon the end of a metal pipe, and blown into a bubble while the pipe drops vertically from the mouth of the operator, and a flask is formed such as is used for the conveyance of olive oil (Fig. 119); and what vessel could be more beautiful than such a flask? Its grace of form is obvious; the delicate curvature of its sides, the gentle swelling of the bulb, and the exquisitely rounded base, all manifest beauty.

Here we get a vessel formed for us almost wholly by Nature. It is the attraction of gravitation which converts what would be a mere bubble, or hollow sphere of glass, into a gracefully elongated and delicately-shaped flask. This may be taken as a principle, that whenever a material is capable of being "worked" in a manner which will so secure the operation of natural laws as to modify the shapes of the objects into which it is formed, it is very desirable that we avail ourselves of such a means of formation, for the operation of gravitation and similar forces upon plastic matter is calculated to give beauty of form.

When clay is worked upon the potter's wheel, it is shaped by the operator's skill, and is sufficiently stiff to retain the shape given to it to a very considerable extent; yet the operation of gravitation upon it, so long as it has any plasticity whatever, is calculated to secure delicacy of form. This rule should ever be remembered by the art-student—that a curve is beautiful just as its origin is difficult to detect. In the formation of vases, bottles, etc., knowledge of this law is very important, and the operation of gravity upon hollow plastic vessels is calculated to give to their curves subtlety (intricate beauty) of character. Having arranged that the material shall be worked in the manner most befitting its nature, we must next consider what purpose the object to be formed is intended to serve.

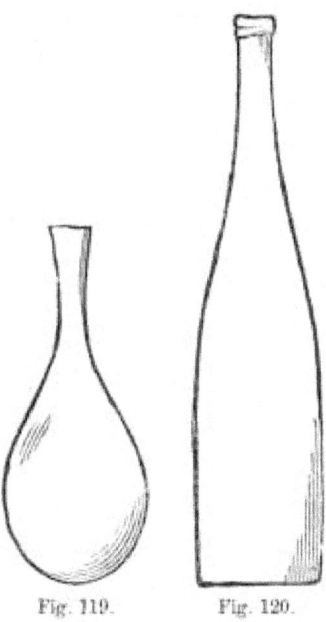

Fig. 119.   Fig. 120.

Take a common hock-bottle (Fig. 120) and consider it. What is wanted is a vessel such as will stand, in which wine can be stored. It must have a strong neck, so that a cork may be driven in without splitting it, and must be formed of a material that is not absorbent. Glass, as a material, admirably answers the want, and this bottle is capable of storing wine; it will stand, and has a rim around the neck such as gives to it strength. But, besides serving the requirements named, it is both easily formed and is beautiful. The designer must be a utilitarian, but he must be an artist also. We must have useful vessels, but the objects with which we are to surround ourselves must likewise be beautiful; and unless they are beautiful, our delicacy of feeling and power to appreciate Nature, which is full of beauties, will be impaired. A hock-bottle is a mere elongated bubble, with the bottom portion pressed in so that it may stand, and the neck thickened by a rim of glass being placed around it.

Here we have a bottle shaped by natural agency; it is formed of heavy glass, and the bubble was thick at its lower part, hence its elongated form; but if length is required in any bubble, and the glass is even light, it can always be given by swinging the bubble round from the centre, so that centrifugal force may be brought into play in the direction of its length; or if it has to be widened, this can as easily be done by giving to it a rotatory motion, whereby the centrifugal force is caused to act from the axis of the vessel outwards, and not from the apex to the base, as in the former instance. In either case a certain amount of beauty would appear in the shape produced, for Nature here works for us. (Compare the short, dumpy, yet beautiful bottle, in which we receive curaçao, with the hock-bottle, when the two natural modes of forming bottles will be illustrated.) Our wine-bottles are moulded, hence their ugliness. We work without Nature's assistance, and we reap ugliness as the reward.

Let us now consider what a decanter should be. In many respects, the wants which a decanter is intended to meet are similar to those which are met by the bottle, as just enumerated, but here is a great difference—a bottle is only *intended* to be filled once, whereas a decanter will have to be filled many times; and a bottle is made so that it can travel, while a decanter is not meant to be the subject of long journeys. It is true that a bottle may be refilled many times, but it is not intended that it should, as the fact that we use a funnel when we wish to fill it clearly shows, and without a funnel the vessel is not complete. All objects which are meant to be refilled many times should have a funnel-shaped mouth (see my remarks on the Greek water-vessel), but if a bottle had a distended orifice it would not be well adapted for transport. A decanter should have capacity for containing liquid; it should stand securely, and have a double funnel—a funnel to collect the fluid and conduct it into the bottle, and a funnel to collect it and conduct it out of the bottle. It must also be convenient to use and hold, and the upper funnel should be of such a character that it will guide the liquid in a proper direction when poured from the decanter.

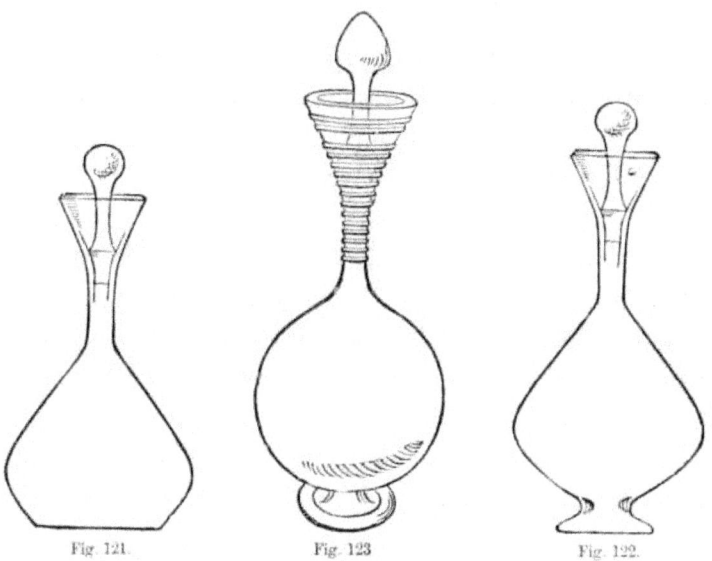

Fig. 121.   Fig. 123.   Fig. 122.

If we take a flask and flatten its base, and extend the upper portion of the neck slightly into the form of a funnel, we have all that is required of a decanter, with the exception of a permanent cork, which is a stopper (Fig. 121).

But as most decanters are intended to hold wine, the brilliancy of which is not readily apparent when that portion of the vessel which contains the liquid rests immediately upon the table, it is desirable to give to the vessel a foot, or, in other words, raise the body of the decanter so that light may surround it as fully as possible (Figs. 122 and 123).

In Figs. 124 to 135 I give a number of shapes of decanters and jugs, such as may be seen in our best shop-windows, and such as I consider desirable forms for such vessels; and in considering-the shape of such vessels, the character of the upper portion of the neck (the lip) must be regarded, as well as that of the body and base. Notice also whether the centre of gravity is high or low, and the position and character of the handle; but respecting the application of handles to vessels I will speak when considering silversmiths' work.

Besides decanters and bottles, glass is formed into tumblers, wine-glasses, flower-holders, and many other things; but the principles which we have already laid down will apply equally to all, for if the objects formed result from the easiest mode of working the material, and are such as perfectly answer the end proposed by their formation, and are beautiful, nothing more can be expected of them.

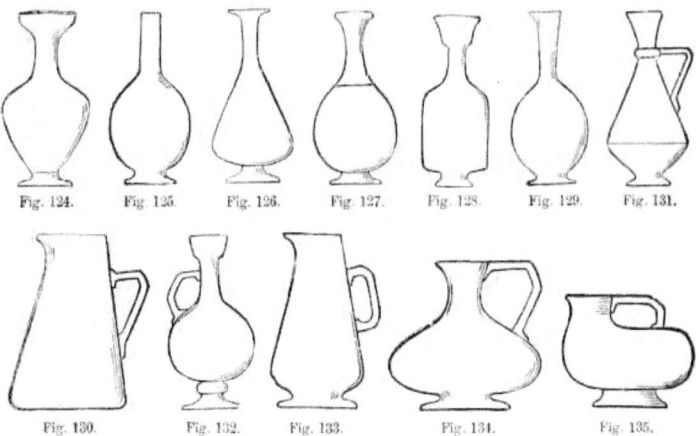

Fig. 124. Fig. 125. Fig. 126. Fig. 127. Fig. 128. Fig. 129. Fig. 131.

Fig. 130. Fig. 132. Fig. 133. Fig. 134. Fig. 135.

Many objects of fancy shape have been produced as mere feats of glass-blowing, and with some of these efforts I sympathise. Wherever the work produced is truly adapted to use, or where an artistic effect is achieved, the glass-blower has my warm sympathy; but if the effort is made at the production of novelty merely, the result gained is sure to be unsatisfactory. Much of the Venetian glass will illustrate these last remarks.

Fig. 136 is a very excellent and picturesque spirit-bottle; it is easy to hold, and quaint in appearance.[27] Figs. 137, 138, and 139 are Venetian glass vessels, wrought entirely at the furnace-mouth, and neither cut nor engraved—they are artistic, and of interesting appearance; while Fig. 140 is a work of Roman glass, in which the upper distension is useful if the liquid contains a sediment which it is not desirable to pour out with the liquid.

---

[27] In order that the nature of this bottle be better understood, I give a section of it at A as seen when cut through the central part.

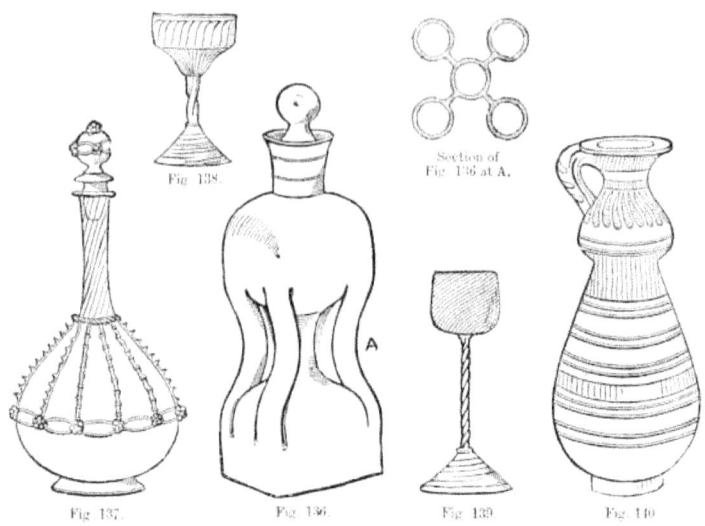

Fig. 138.

Section of
Fig. 136 at A.

Fig. 137.

Fig. 136.

Fig. 139.

Fig. 140.

There is one thing pertaining to table-glass that we do not now sufficiently consider, which is its capacity for colour. Our one idea in the formation of glass vessels is the imitation of crystal, unless we happen to produce a vessel of the strongest tint. With the exception of hock-glasses, which are generally either ruby-colour, dark green, or intense yellow-green, we rarely employ tinted glass on our tables. These three colours, which we usually employ in hock-glasses, are all too strong in tint for ordinary purposes, and they are coarse and vulgar. It is curious that we should confine ourselves to these colours when glass is capable of assuming the most delicate of shades, of appearing as a soft, subtle, golden hue of the most beautiful light tertiary green, lilac, and blue, and, indeed, of almost any colour.

Why, then, should we employ only two or three colours, and those of the most crude character? If the Roman and Greek glass of the British Museum be inspected, it will be seen that the Romans employed various soft and delicate tints, and why we should not do so I cannot see. For many reasons the colours of our hock-glasses are highly objectionable, but especially for two. First, as already stated, the colour is so strong that they appear as mere dark spots on the cloth, and altogether fail in imparting to the table a pleasant colour-effect; and, secondly, they utterly destroy the beauty of appearance which the wine would otherwise present.

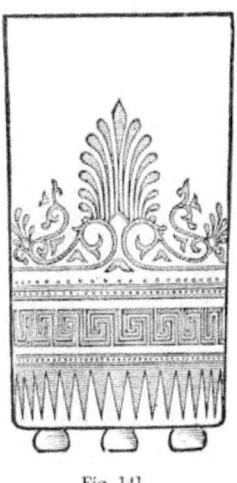 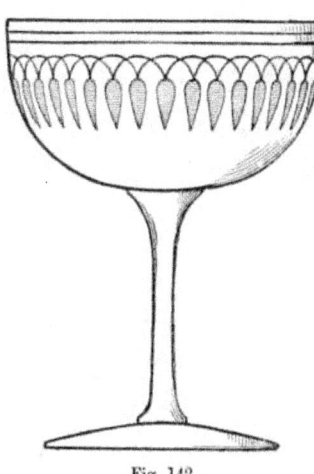

Fig. 141.   Fig. 142.

No glass which is to contain a liquid of pleasant colour should be so strong in tint as to mar the beauty of the contained fluid, and especially is this true when the colour of the glass is of an opposite character to that of the liquid: thus a red liquid placed in a strongly-coloured green glass becomes highly offensive in appearance, and yet we often see claret served in green hock-glasses. A dinner-table requires colour. Let the cloth be pale buff, or cream-colour, instead of white; and the glass water-vessels of very pale, but refined and various, tints; and the salt-cellars, if of glass, also coloured, in a tender and befitting manner, and a most harmonious effect will be produced. The flowers with which the table is adorned would then harmonise with the other things, and much beauty might be produced.

Respecting the ornamentation of glass, two methods of treatment are resorted to, which are "cutting" and "engraving." Both modes deal with glass as a hard, crystal-like substance; and consist in grinding the surface, and either leaving it "dead" or repolishing it. In the case of "cutting" a considerable portion of the substance of the glass is generally removed, and the surface is repolished; but in the case of "engraving" little more than the surface is generally acted upon, and the engraved portion remains dead.

Cutting may be employed in bringing about ornamental effects in glass, but it is rarely to be commended when so lavishly used as to be the chief means of giving form to the vessel; indeed, cutting should be sparingly and judiciously used. A vessel formed of glass should never be wholly shaped by cutting, as though it were a work of stone. If the neck of a decanter can be made more convenient by being slightly cut—if it can be so treated that it can be held more securely—then let it be cut; but in all cases avoid falling into the error of too much cutting which causes the work to appear laboured, for any work which presents the appearance of having been the result of much labour is as unpleasant to look upon as that work is pleasing which results from the exercise of momentary skill. There is a great art-principle manifested in the expression "Let there be light, and there was light."

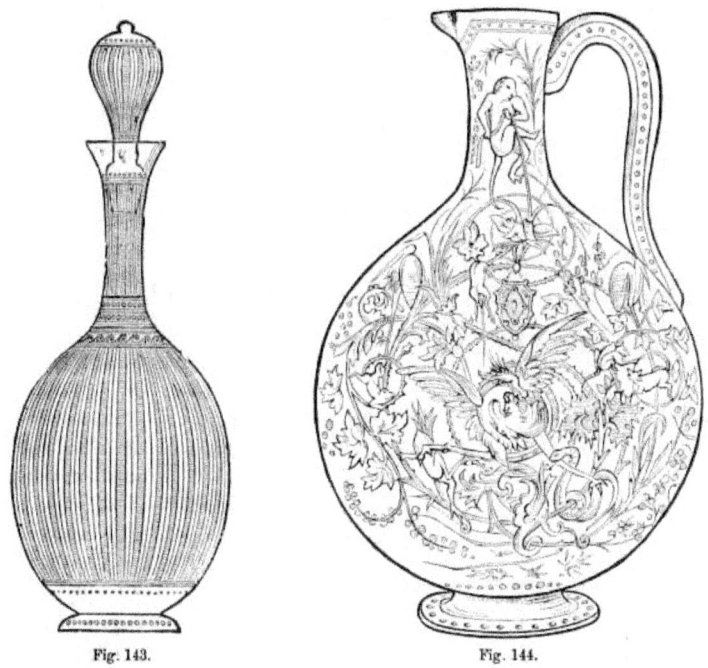

Fig. 143.   Fig. 144.

Engraving is also laborious, and while it is capable of yielding most delicate and beautiful effects, it should yet be somewhat sparingly used, for extravagance in labour is never desirable, and there is such a thing as extravagance of beauty.

However delicate ornament may be, and however well composed, yet if it covers the whole of the walls of an apartment and of the objects which it contains, it fails to please. There must be the contrast of plain surfaces with ornamented—plain for the eye to rest upon, ornament for the mind to enjoy. In the enrichment of glass these remarks fully apply. Let there be plain surfaces as well as ornamented parts, and the effect will be more satisfying than if all be covered with ornament.

All that I said respecting the decoration of damask table-linen will apply equally to glass, considering only the different way in which the effect is produced (see Chap. VI.). Thus we have ornament produced only by a variation of surface. Such simple means of producing an art-effect are capable of rendering in a satisfactory manner simple treatments only, but simple patterns are capable of yielding the highest pleasure, and such patterns can be almost perfectly rendered by engraving, as shown in Figs. 141, 142, 143.[28]

Somewhat elaborate effects can be rendered in glass by very laborious engraving, whereby different depths of cutting are attained; but such work is the result of great labour, and rarely produces an effect proportionate to the toil expended upon it; and if a bottle so engraved is filled with a coloured wine, the entire beauty of its engraving is destroyed. Fig. 144 is a drawing of a most elaborately engraved bottle, which was shown in the Exhibition of 1862. It represents, to a great extent, wasted labour.

It must be borne in mind that any ornament placed on a decanter, wine-glass, or tumbler, is to be seen almost wholly in perspective; and the remarks made respecting the effects of folded or waved surfaces on ornament (Chap. VI., page 110), and those made in reference to the application of ornament to earthen vases (Chap. VII., page 126), apply equally here.

---

[28] Fig. 143 represents a decanter made for the Prince of Wales by Messrs. Pellatt and Co., which is in good taste. Fig. 141 is a goblet from Austria: it was shown in the International Exhibition of Paris in 1867.

It is not my province to enter into the various methods of manipulating glass, nor into all the classes of art-effect which glass is capable of yielding: I can only call attention to general principles, and leave the art-student to think for himself what should be the treatment of any particular object. There is a sort of crackle glass which has come into use during the last few years, and is an imitation of old Venetian work; this is in some respects pleasant in appearance, but it is somewhat uncomfortable to handle, and difficult to keep clean; its use must therefore be limited. The Romans were in the habit of forming glass which was opaque, dark, and of many colours. Fig. 145 is an illustration of this kind of glass, the pattern being formed by portions of various coloured glass being imbedded in the substance of the vessel.

In another chapter I shall have a few remarks to make upon stained glass; but as our present remarks pertain to hollow vessels chiefly, and as general principles regulate the formation of all such, whether they are formed of earthenware, glass, or metal, I think it better to proceed to the consideration of silversmiths' ware, and thus continue a notice of hollow vessels, than to pass to glass windows, although they are formed of the material now under review. What we are specially considering at present are vessels of capacity, or hollow wares.

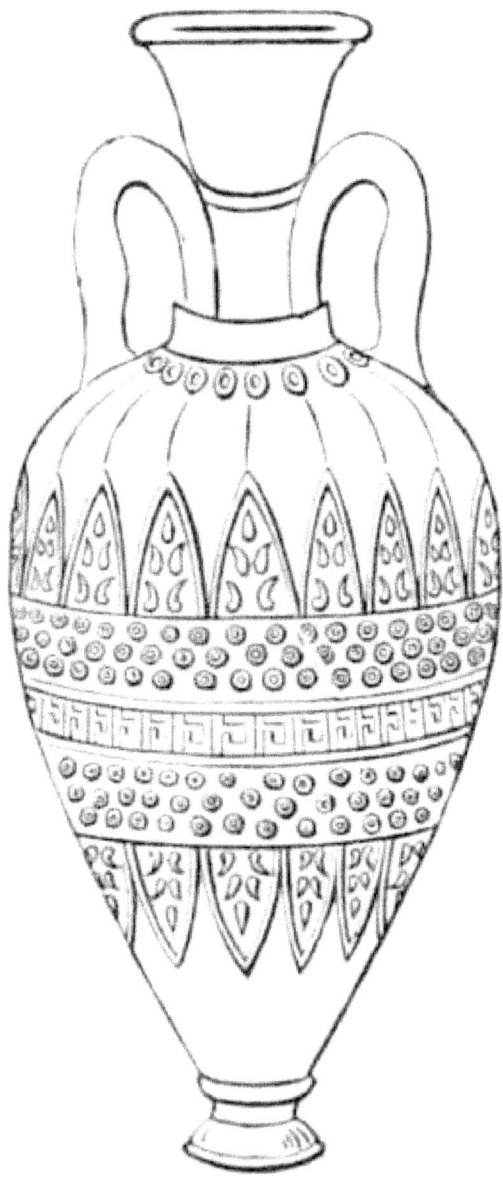

Fig. 145.

DIVISION III.

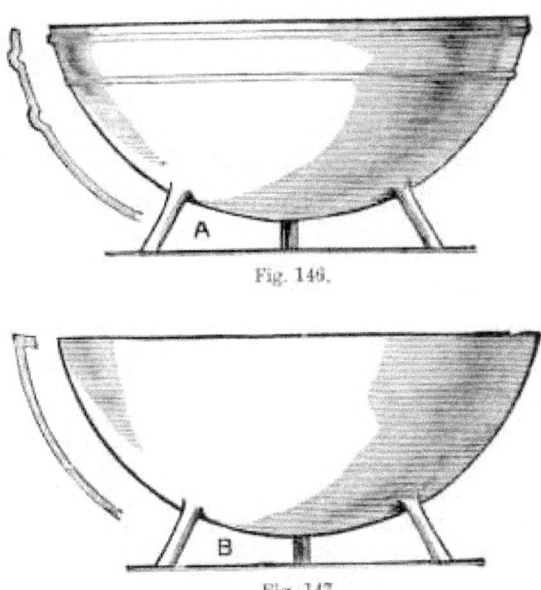

Fig. 146.

Fig. 147.

Continuing our remarks upon hollow vessels, we have now to notice silversmiths' work, and here we may observe that while the material with which we have now to deal differs in character widely from that of which those vessels already noticed have been formed, yet that many principles which have been enunciated are equally applicable to the objects now under consideration. Silver objects, like those formed of clay or glass, should perfectly serve the end for which they have been formed; also, the fact that ornament applied to rounded surfaces should be adapted for being viewed in perspective remains as binding on us as before; but herein the works of the silversmith differ from those already discussed— they are formed of a material of intrinsic value, which is not the case with articles of earthenware or glass. Silver and gold being materials of considerable worth, it is necessary that the utmost economy be observed in using them, and in order to effect this a special mode of construction must be resorted to. If we propose to ourselves the formation of a sugar-basin of semi-circular shape, of what thickness must the metal be in order that it may not bend when lifted? It is obvious that the vessel must not yield its shape to ordinary pressure, nor be subject to alterations of form when in ordinary use; but if it is to be formed throughout of metal of such thickness as will secure its retaining its shape, it will be costly and heavy, and an amount of metal will be used in its formation sufficient for the manufacture of two or three such articles.

Instead of forming the vessel throughout of thick metal, we may construct it from a thin sheet of silver; but in order that it possess sufficient strength we must indent one or more beads in its side; or we can form an angle by having a rim projecting into the basin (Fig. 147), or extending from it, and thus give strength; but the two beads are the more desirable, as the one gives strength at the top and the other at a lower portion of the vessel.

Modes of economising material, when we are forming vessels of costly substances, are of the utmost importance, and should be carefully thought out. If the designer forms works which are expensive, he places them beyond the reach of those who might otherwise enjoy them, and if heavy they appear clumsy in the hands of those accustomed to delicate and light objects.

Besides this, works in silver and in gold are always in danger of being destroyed, owing to the intrinsic value of these metals; for if stolen, the theft is promptly hidden in the melting-pot. Now if we form the vessels of thin metal, we render the money value of the material less, and thus our works are to a smaller degree tempting to the avaricious, and their chance of long existence is greater. The precious metals are at all times perilous materials for the formation of works of art; but while we use them, let us take care so to employ them as to give to our works every possible opportunity for long existence. If a work is to be so formed that it may exist for many years, it becomes of the highest importance that those objects which we create be well considered as to their utility, and at the same time be beautiful in form. Long existence is an evil in the case of an ugly object, or an ill-considered vessel; that which is not refining in its influence is better blotted out. Let that man who will not seek to embody beauty in his works make them heavy with metal, so that they may tempt the thief, and thus sooner blot out his works from existence, as they tend only to debase and degrade; but he who loves refinement, and seeks to give chasteness of character to the objects which he creates, may well strive to secure to them length of duration.

There are various modes of working metal. It may be cast, hammered, cut, engraved, and manipulated in various ways.

Little that is satisfactory can result from casting. Casting is a rough means of producing a result, and at best achieves the formation of a mass which may be less troublesome to cut into shape than a more solid piece of metal; but casting without the application of other means of working-metal achieves little of an art nature.

Some of the fine iron castings of Berlin are wonderfully good in their way, and are to an extent artistic; and certainly they contrast strangely with the cast handles and knobs which we often see applied to vegetable-dishes, and similar silver objects here in England; yet even these will not compare with works wrought by the hammer and the chisel. Thin metal hammered into form, and touched where necessary with the chisel, the graver, and the chasing-tool, is capable of the very finest effects which can be achieved in metal-work. Let the reader consider the beautiful vessels with which Arabian metal-work presents us: these are all formed by the hammer and chisel, with the assistance of the graver and chasing-tool, and how marvellously delicate and beautiful are the results! We have in these vessels beauty and dignity of form, richness of design, great intricacy and delicacy of detail, and altogether a refinement of effect which may long be considered and repeatedly enjoyed (Fig. 148).

Several, I may almost say many, of these beautiful objects are to be found in the South Kensington Museum, and it should be generally known that fac-similes of these lovely works, in the form of electrotype copies, have been prepared by Messrs. Elkington and Co., under the sanction of the authorities of the Department of Science and Art, and that these are procurable at small cost. For purposes of study these copies are of almost equal value with the originals, and for the adornment of a sideboard they are hardly inferior. I strongly advise those who can afford to purchase these beautiful copies to garnish their sideboards with plate of this description, rather than with the meretricious electro-plate which we often see in our shop-windows.

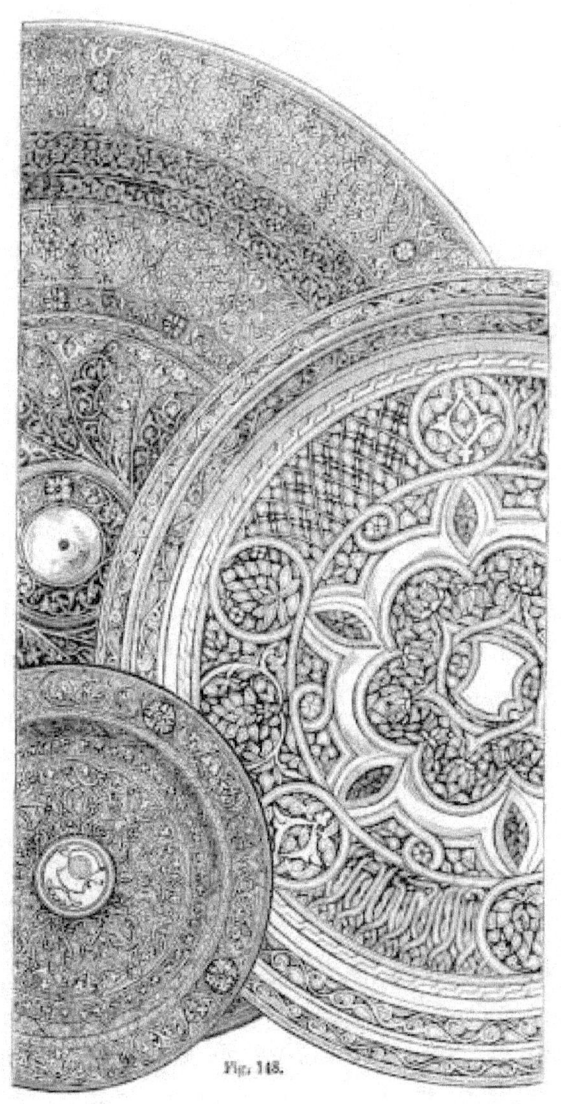

Fig. 148.

Having determined on the best mode of working the material, consider carefully the requirements which the work to be produced is intended to meet, and then strive to form the object so that it may perfectly answer the end proposed by its creation.

Let us take a sugar-basin. What form should it have? After much consideration, I have arrived at the conclusion that the two shapes engraved in Figs. 149 and 150 are those which best fulfil the requirements of such a vessel, for in them the sugar is always collected together, and the dust sugar separates itself from the lumps.

The handles of a sugar-basin are often so small as to be partially or wholly useless. It not unfrequently happens that only one or two fingers can rest on the handle, owing to its smallness, while the thumb has to be placed within the orifice of the basin when it is desired to move it. This should not be so; if a handle is to exist at all, it should be so formed as to be useful, and afford a means of moving the object with ease and comfort.

To form a handle as a mere ornament is an absurdity, for the handle is part of the vessel structurally, while the ornamentation is an after and separate consideration. In order to its existence a vessel must be constructed, but when formed it need not of necessity be ornamented; ornamentation must ever be regarded as separate from construction.

Such a sugar-basin as I have suggested would not stand without legs: it must therefore have them; but I see no reason why the legs and handles should not be combined; hence I propose three feet so formed as to serve as handles throughout their upper parts (Figs. 149, 150), they being convenient to hold.

Modern European silversmiths have fallen into the error (an error now prevailing wherever art can be applied to any object) of making their works of a pictorial, rather than an ornamental, character—an error which the Arabians, Indians, and Japanese never perpetrate, whose works in metal are unsurpassed by any, and equalled by indeed few. It is a mistake to cover an entire vase with figures in high relief; but wherever anything of the kind is attempted, care must be exercised in causing the groups to follow the line of the vase, and not to appear as irregular projections from it. As to the modes of decorating works in silver and in gold, they are many; of ornamentation by *repoussé* work we have already spoken, and of chasing and engraving. But besides these there are other methods, and some of great interest, for there is damascene work, or inlaying; and applying colour, or enamelling; and niello work; jewels may also be added.

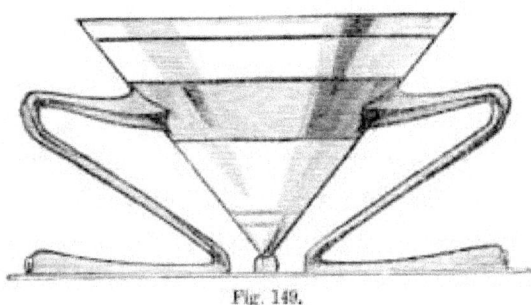

Fig. 149.

Damascene work is of great interest. Metal of one colour is inlaid into metal of another colour. India produces, perhaps, the rarest examples of this kind of work, the Indians being experts at this manufacture; but the Indian work consists chiefly of silver inlaid in iron. This mode of work seems to be capable of producing many beautiful effects, as all who have examined the large inlaid hookahs of India will admit.

Having chosen a form for a vessel, the next question with which we have to deal is, will it require a handle and spout? It is curious that while the position of a spout and handle in relation to a vessel is governed by a simple natural law, we yet rarely find them placed as they should be. This is the more curious, as a vessel may become practically of great weight, owing to the handle being misplaced.

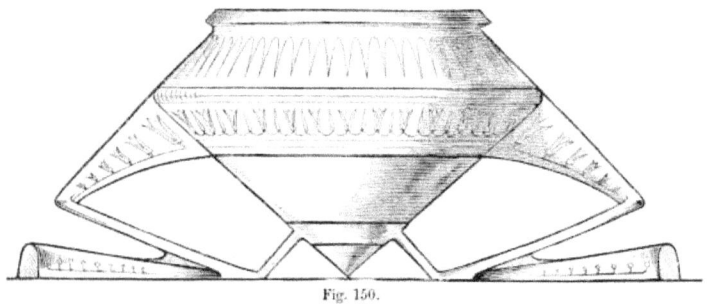
Fig. 150.

A pound weight is easily lifted, but when applied to the shorter end of the steel-yard it will balance a hundredweight. If this principle is applied to a tea-pot which actually weighs but little, it may yet be very heavy to lift. In nineteen cases out of twenty, handles are so placed on tea-pots and similar vessels that they are in use lifted only by a force capable of raising two or three such vessels, if the principle of the steel-yard was not acting against the person who uses the vessel. Take our ordinary forms of tea-pot, and see how far the centre of the weight (the centre of gravity) is from the handle in a horizontal direction, and you will be able to judge of the leverage acting disadvantageously to the person who may pour tea from such pots. Now if the part which is grasped is to the right or left of a right line passing through the centre of gravity of any vessel, there is leverage acting to the disadvantage of the person desiring to pour from that vessel, and this leverage increases just as the point held is removed from the central line spoken of.

Fig. 151 would pour when in the position shown in Fig. 152, but see how far the hand that holds it would be to the right of the centre of gravity (*a*), which distance is of great disadvantage, as it causes the vessel to appear much heavier than it actually is, and requires a much greater expenditure of force in order that the tea-pot be put to its use than is necessary were it properly formed.

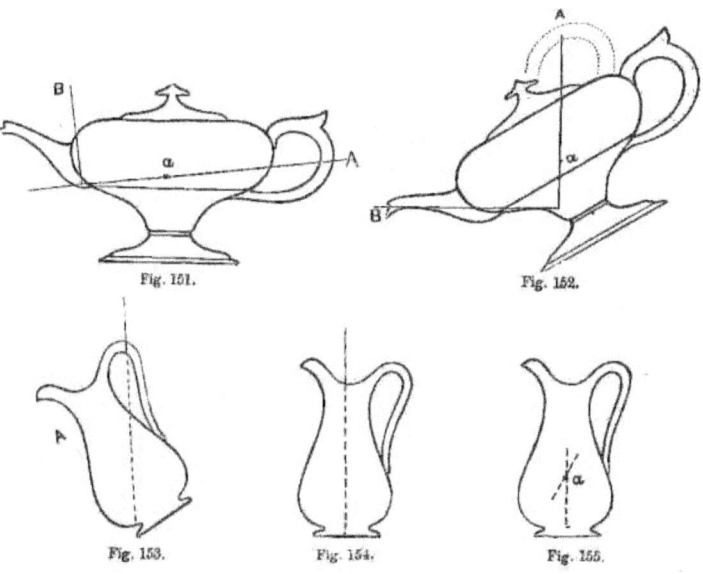

Fig. 151. Fig. 152.

Fig. 153. Fig. 154. Fig. 155.

The law governing the application of handle and spout to vessels is this, and the same principle applies whether the vessel be formed of metal, glass, or earthenware:—Find the centre of gravity of the vessel, which can easily be done by letting a vertical line drop over it when placed in two different positions, as in Figs. 153, 154, and where the two vertical lines intersect, as in *a* in Fig. 155, is the centre of gravity. The position of the handle being fixed on, draw a line through the centre of the handle, and continue it through the centre of gravity of the vessel. The spout must now be at right angles to this line. If this be the case the vessel will pour freely while the handle is just hung upon the thumb or finger of the person desiring to pour from it, as may be seen from Figs. 156, 157, in which the straight line A, passing through the centre of gravity *a*, is at right angles, as it should be, with the straight line passing through the spout.

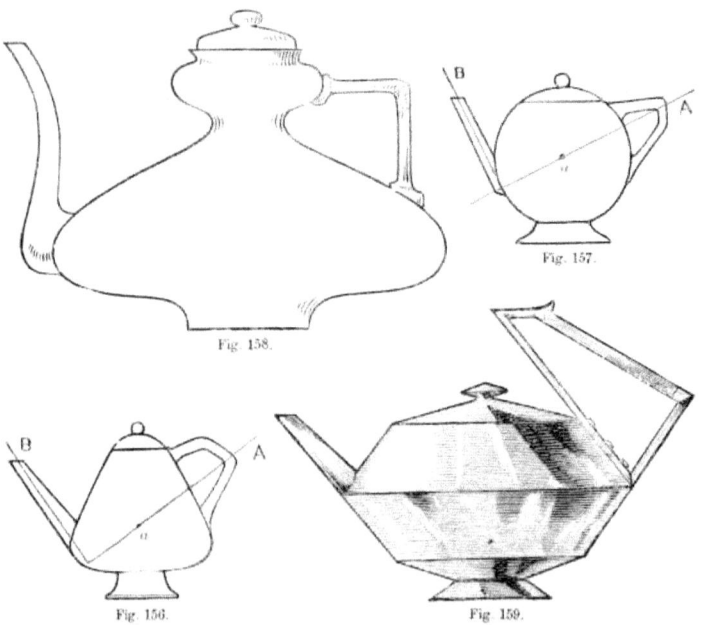

Fig. 158.

Fig. 157.

Fig. 156.

Fig 159.

234

This law, if obeyed, will always enable liquid to be poured from a vessel without its appearing heavier than it actually is, but it will be seen that the shape of the vessel must be considered so that the spout and handle can bear this relation to each other, as in Figs. 156, 157, 158, 159, and 160. Some shapes will not admit of it, so they must be avoided, as may be seen by examining Figs. 151 and 152, which show a tea-pot of faulty shape in this respect.

A consideration of this law shows that the handles of jugs—those formed of silver, of glass, and of earthenware alike—are usually placed too high; but in this respect things are much better than they were a few years back. Now we somewhat frequently see a jug with the handle in the right place, while some years back we never did. Silver jugs are now the most generally faulty in this respect, and such mistakes as the wrong placing of the handle or spout of a vessel result only from ignorance, for no man knowing the law would violate it. Fig. 161 shows a common form of jug with its handle, but the handle is too high; the position which it should occupy is shown by the dotted line. A very excellent handle is applied to many of the French water-pots, as shown in Fig. 162.

It is unnecessary that I say more respecting the shape and general construction of silver and gold vessels, except to remark that if figures or other ornaments are beaten up on their surfaces, they must not destroy or mar their general contour.

Iron is not used with us as it should be. Not only is the effect produced when it is inlaid with silver and other metals excellent, but by this mode of work our art-creations are greatly preserved, for the iron is valueless, and the labour of removing the small quantity of precious metal inlaid would be so great as to render the gain inadequate remuneration for the time consumed in collecting it.

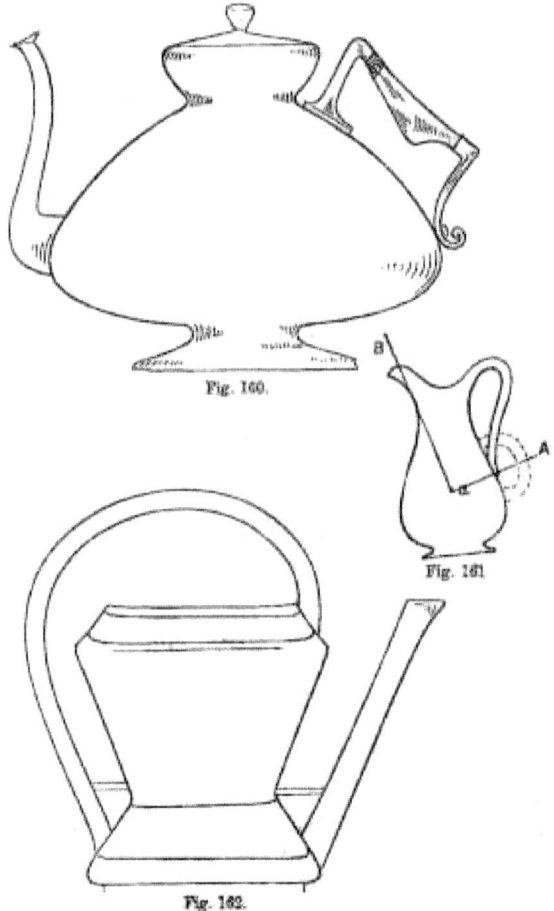

Fig. 160.

Fig. 161

Fig. 162.

M. Christophle, of Paris, and also M. Barbedien in a lesser degree, have commenced to inlay copper vessels with silver, and some of their works are very beautiful. The Japanese have from an early time inlaid silver in bronze. This inlaying of silver into copper is a step in the right direction, and should be encouraged by all lovers of art. The Indians not only inlay silver in iron, but also gold in silver and in iron; and the Italians and other peoples have inlaid metals in a similar way; and the firmness and intricacy of some specimens of this inlaying are truly marvellous.

By the process of enamelling, colour can be applied to metal, and of all arts this art of enamelling produces works which are most lovely; at least, if the best works of enamel do not surpass those produced by any other manufacture, they are equal in beauty to the works of the highest excellence. Transparent enamels are in some cases very beautiful, but they do not generally compare with the opaque enamels, such as were largely used by the Chinese about a hundred and fifty years back, and by the Japanese, or those now so skilfully produced by Barbedien, the Algerian Onyx Company, and Christophle, all of Paris.

Chinese *cloisonné* enamel vases may be seen at the South Kensington Museum, and here you may also find one or two small pieces of Japanese enamel, as well as one or two grand specimens by Barbedien, of Paris.

The Chinese enamels have most frequently a light blue (sort of turquoise) ground, but they occur with both red, white, green, and yellow grounds; while the ornament is of mixed colours, but generally with light yellow-green, deeper blue-green, or dark blue prevailing in it.

The Japanese enamels have a lower tone of colour-effect than the Chinese, and the work is finer and the colours more mingled, while the modern French enamels are full in colour, and are yet rich and subdued in general effect—some of them, indeed, are most beautiful works.

The Elkingtons, of Birmingham and London, have also produced some beautiful things in this way, but not in the quantities that Barbedien has. I most strongly advise the art-student to study these works in enamel.

Niello-work is a form of enrichment applied to metal, but is not in general use; it is a difficult process. Silver snuff-boxes and pendants for watch-chains with a niello pattern upon them are not uncommon, however, in Belgium and Russia, the niello pattern appearing as dark lead-pencil work upon the silver. Some niello-work is very quiet and beautiful, but much need not be said respecting it.

Jewels may be inserted in metal, but if this is done they should be somewhat sparingly used, even in the most costly of works, for if they are abundant they produce mere glitter, and the aim of the ornamentist must in all cases be the production of repose.

CHAPTER VIII.

HARDWARE.

Having considered metal-work in its more costly branches, we come to the consideration of hardware, and I am glad that we have now to deal with such metal-work as results from the use of inexpensive materials, for it is such that must be generally employed, while works formed of the precious metals can be used only by comparatively few persons. The object of art is the giving of pleasure; the mission of the artist is that of giving ennobling pleasure. If as an artist I give pleasure, I to an extent fulfil my mission; but I do so, perfectly, only when I give the greatest amount of the most refined pleasure by my art that it is possible for me to give. If by producing works which can be procured by many I give pleasure, it is well that I do so; but if the many fail to derive pleasure from my works, then I must address myself to the few, and be content with my lesser mission. Education appears to be necessary to the appreciation of all art; the artist, then, is a man who appeals to the educated. If some persons, by their superior education, are enabled to appreciate art more fully than those who are ignorant, and can consequently derive more pleasure from it than the less cultured person, it might then be desirable that the artist should address himself, through costly materials, to the few, for thereby he might be giving the greatest amount of pleasure. I always, however, like to produce works in cheap materials, for then I know that I form what is capable of giving pleasure to the poor man—if appreciative—who may possess it, as well as the rich.

In hardware we find two classes of work in the market which appear to have little in common—the one class being characterised by a preponderance of excellence, and the other by the dominance of what is coarse and inartistic. The first class of work is that which is produced by what are termed ecclesiastical metal-workers; the second consists of what is generally known as Birmingham ware.

It is an error to suppose that these so-called ecclesiastical—or mediæval, as they are sometimes called—metal-workers produce only ecclesiastical and mediæval work. On the contrary, some of these men—and they are now many in number—devote themselves almost exclusively to domestic work, and most of them fabricate articles in all styles of art. If I wanted an artistic set of fire-irons, I should go to one of the ecclesiastical warehouses, for there I have seen many sets that my reason commends and my judgment approves; but I never saw a set produced for the general market that I liked; and the most artistic fenders, grates, and gas-fittings, in almost any style, are to be got at these shops. I do not mean to convey the impression that all things made at these ecclesiastical warehouses are good, and that all things of Birmingham (or Sheffield) manufacture are bad, for I have seen indifferent works in these mediæval shops, and I have seen excellent things from Birmingham—especially I might mention as good certain gaseliers produced by two of the smaller Birmingham houses—but as a rule the works found in the mediæval warehouses are good, and as a rule the works in hardware produced by Birmingham and Sheffield are bad, in point of art.

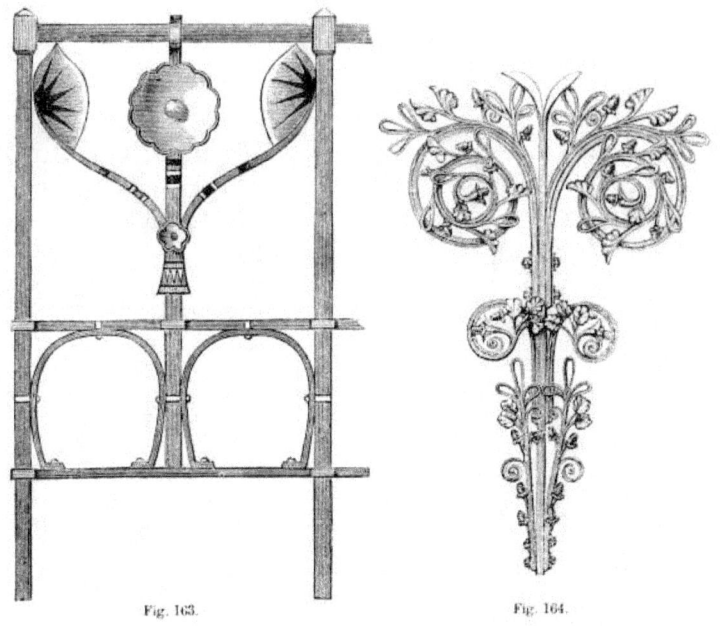

Fig. 163.   Fig. 164.

It will appear a mere repetition if I insist that the materials of which works of hardware are formed be used in the easiest manner in which they can be worked, and that every article be so formed as perfectly to answer the end of its formation. Yet I must do so. Let us look for a common set of fire-irons, and we shall find that nine pokers out of ten have a handle terminating in a pointed knob. Now, as the object of this knob is that of enabling us to exercise force wherewith to break large pieces of coal, the folly of terminating this knob with a point is obvious. A poker is, essentially, an object of utility; it should therefore be useful. It is ridiculous to talk of a poker as an ornament; yet we find it fashionable now to have a bright poker as an ornament, which is obtrusively displayed to the visitor, and a little black poker, which is carefully concealed from view, reserved for use. I cannot imagine what people will not do for show and

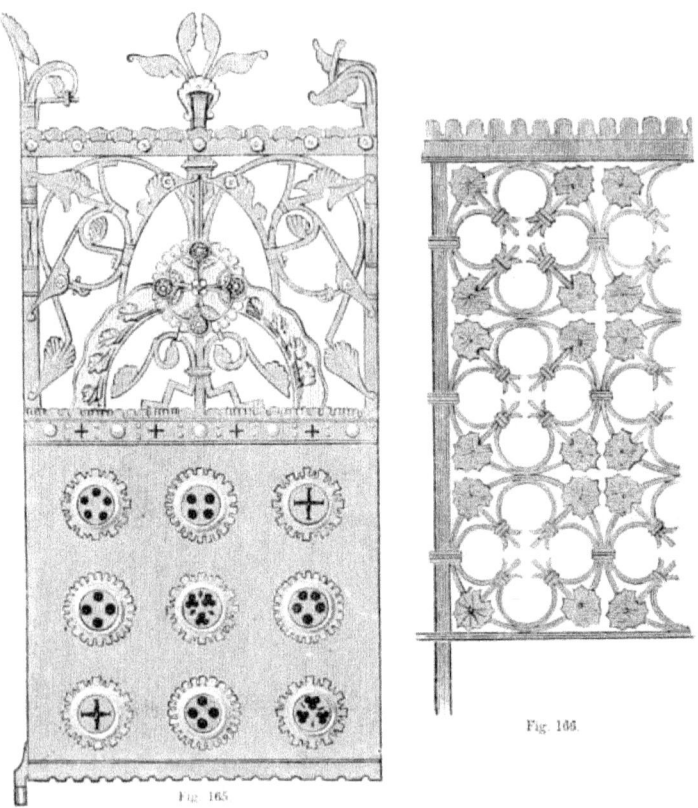

Fig. 165.

Fig. 166.

fashion, but to the thinking mind such littleness as that which induces women to keep a poker as an ornament must be distressing; and until persons who desire to be regarded as educated learn to discriminate between an ornament and an article of utility, little progress in art can be made. If a poker is simply a thing to be looked at, then it may be as inconvenient as you please, for if it has no purpose to fulfil by its creation it cannot be unfitted to its purpose. The same remarks will apply to shovel and tongs. If they are intended as works of utility, then their form must be carefully considered;

but if they are to be mere ornaments I have nothing to say respecting them.

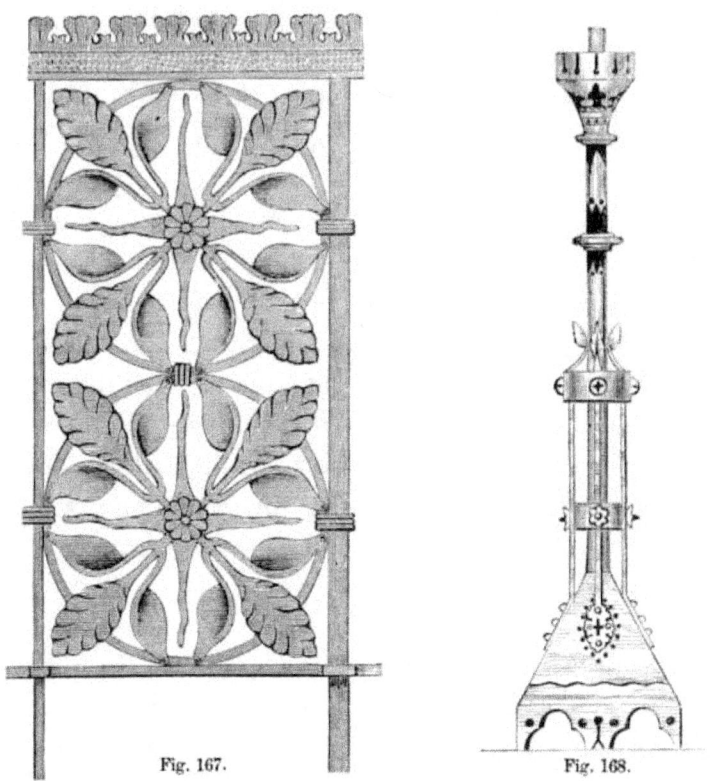

Fig. 167.

Fig. 168.

Utility and beauty are not inseparable; but if an article of any kind is intended to answer any particular end, it should be fitted to answer the end proposed by its formation; but after it is created as a work of utility, care must be exercised in order that it be also a work of beauty. With due consideration, almost every work may be rendered both useful and beautiful, and it must ever be the aim of the intelligent ornamentist to render them so.

Iron is capable of being wrought in various ways; it maybe cast, or hammered, or cut, or filed. Casting is the least artistic mode of treating iron; but if iron is to be cast, the patterns formed should be so fully adapted to this method of manufacture that the mode of working may be readily apparent. It is foolish to seek to make cast-iron appear as wrought-iron: cast-iron should appear as cast-iron, and wrought-iron as wrought-iron. Cast-iron is brittle, and must not be relied upon as of great strength; while wrought-iron is tough, and will bend under great pressure rather than break. Wrought-iron can be readily bent into scrolls, or the end of a rod of metal can be hammered flat and shaped into the form of a leaf, and parts can either be welded together or fastened by small collars, pins, or screws. One or two illustrations of good wrought-iron work by Skidmore, Benham, and Hart, are given in the engravings.

As an illustration of a simple railing, is figured one shown in the International Exhibition of 1862 (Fig. 163), which is in every respect excellent. Its strength is very great, yet it is quaint and beautiful. As it was shown it was coloured, and the colours were so applied as to increase its effect and beauty. If the student will carefully devote himself to the consideration of excellent works in metal, he will learn more than by much reading. Let him procure, if possible, the illustrated catalogues of such men as Hart of London, Hardman of Birmingham, and Dovey of Manchester, and study the sketches which he will there see, and he will certainly discover the principles of a true art, such as he must seek to apply in a manner concordant with his own original feelings.

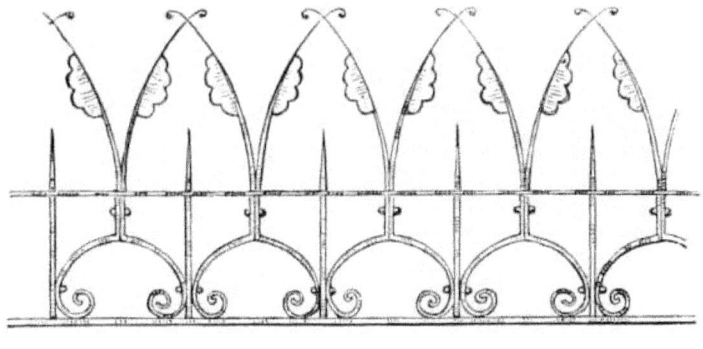

Fig. 169.

Of our illustrations, the example by Skidmore (Fig. 161) furnishes us with an excellent mode of treatment. Iron bands are readily bent into volutes, or curves of various descriptions, and the parts so formed can be united by welding, screws, or bolts. Hardman's gate (Fig. 165) is in every respect excellent; it is quaint, vigorous, and illustrative of a true mode of working metal. The two foliated railings (Figs. 166, 167) are also very meritorious. They are simple in design, and their parts are well fastened together. I advise very strongly that the student carefully consider the illustrations which accompany this chapter.

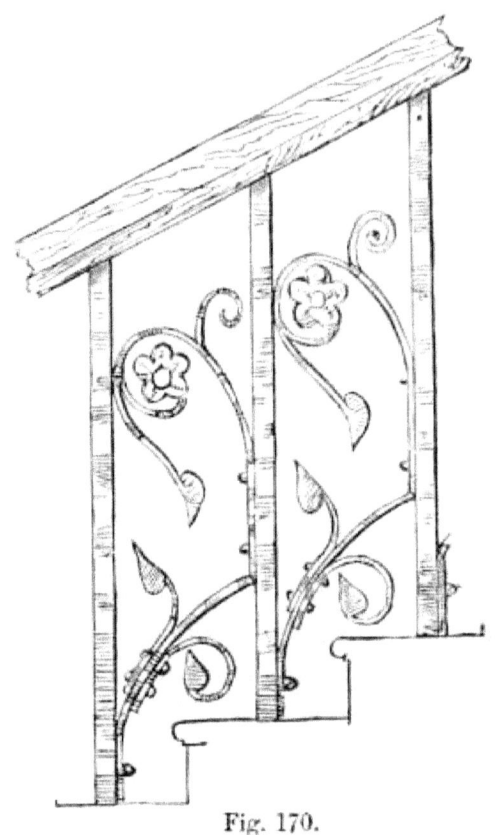

Fig. 170.

In iron-work the manifestation of a true constructive principle is beyond all things desirable. Iron, being a strong material, should not be formed into heavy masses unless immense weight has to be sustained, or very great strength is required. If we form lamps, candelabra, and such works of iron, it is obvious that the portions of metal employed in their construction may be thin, as the material is of great strength. Were we to form such works of wood, then a greatly increased thickness of material would be necessary, in order that the same strength be secured, as wood is not nearly so strong as iron.

My remarks will have special reference to wrought-iron, as cast-iron cannot so fully be said to have a constructive character. The small railing (Fig. 163) is an admirable illustration of a true constructive formation, as the parts are all held together, and strengthened to a wonderful degree, by the introduction of a horseshoe-shaped member. This railing is worthy of the most careful study, for its strength is great. Besides strength we have also beauty. The horseshoe form, especially when judiciously applied, is far from being offensive. Utility must come first, and then beauty, and so it does in this particular railing; but here we have great simplicity, and a correct structural character has been arrived at in its production rather than any elaboration of the principles of beauty.

From the catalogue of J. W. Dovey, of Manchester, I select an illustration of structure in the form of a candelabrum which is highly satisfactory in character as a simple work (Fig. 168). There is a solidly-formed heavy base, an upright stem terminating in a candle-holder. There is an arrangement for catching waste grease, and extra strength is given to the stem by four slender buttress-like brackets, which are securely and well attached to the base and to the stem above; and these are strengthened by two hoops, which prevent their bending under pressure.

Figs. 169 and 170, the former being a ridge or wall cresting, and the latter a stair railing, are each illustrations of a correct treatment, inasmuch as strength (a structural quality) and beauty (an art quality) are secured at the same time. Fig. 169

is admirably constructed, only it is a little slender above the middle horizontal line. These two illustrations are also from Mr. Dovey's catalogue.

In the catalogue just named, and in those previously named also, many good examples may be found illustrative of the successful combination of true structural qualities with a considerable amount of beauty, and also acknowledging the strength of the material by the lightness of the parts.

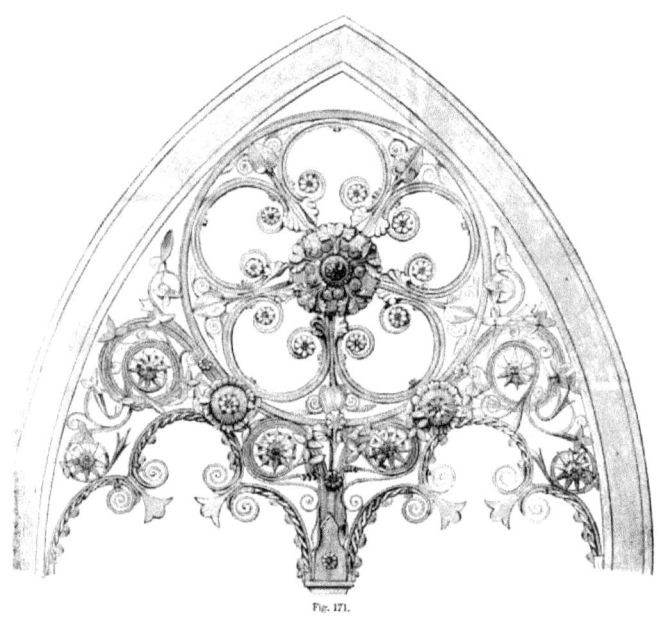

Fig. 171.

Those who reside in, or visit, London, will do well to go to the South Kensington Museum, and study a large and splendid, candelabrum of Messrs. Hurt, Son, and Peard, which is well worthy of consideration. It is rather heavy, and is of enormous strength, but in most other respects it is highly commendable. It, is beautiful, well proportioned, and illustrative of a correct treatment of metal. Besides this, it exemplifies the manner in which stones or jewels may be applied to works in hardware with advantage. As a further illustration of a correct and very beautiful treatment of metal, we give one segment of the Hereford Cathedral Screen (Fig. 171), the work of that most intelligent of metal-workers, Mr. Skidmore of Coventry. This screen was shown in the International Exhibition of 1862, in London, and was from there removed to its place in the cathedral. All who can will do well to view this beautiful work, which is one of the finest examples of artistic metal-work with which we are acquainted. Notice the ease with which iron may be treated if a correct mode of working be employed. Let a bar of iron be taken which is about half an inch in thickness, by 1¼ broad. This can be rolled into a volute (the filigree mode of treatment), or its end can be hammered out into stems and leaves, and to it can be attached other leaves by rivets, screws, or ties, or it can be bent into any structural form. To the student I say, study the shapes into which simple bars of iron can be beaten, both mentally and by observing well-formed works.

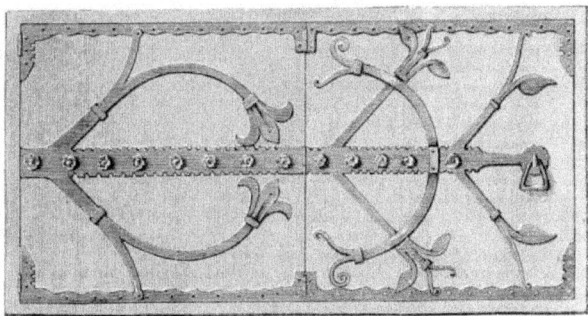

Fig. 171.

249

Brass, copper, and other metals may be associated with iron in the formation of any works. If well managed, brass and other bright metals may act as gems—that is, they may give bright spots; but where the bright metals are used with this view, care must be exercised in order that the bright spots be formed by beautiful parts, and that their distribution be just, for that which is bright will attract first attention.

Before leaving this part of our subject, I must call attention to a hinge by Hardman, of Birmingham, which was shown in the International Exhibition of 1862, as it is both quaint and beautiful (Fig. 172). The door to which this hinge was applied opened twice; the first half opened and folded back on the second half, and then the two halves opened as one door, as will be seen from the illustration. It is very desirable that we have a little novelty of arrangement in our works. We are too apt to repeat ourselves, hence it is a sort of relief to meet with a new idea.

It is impossible that I take up each article of hardware and consider it separately. All I can do is to point out principles, and leave the learner to consider and apply them for himself—principles which, once understood, may result in the construction of many excellent works, and may lead to the formation of a correct judgment respecting such objects as may be brought forward for criticism. I will, however, just call attention to gas-branches, as they are often wrongly constructed. A gas-branch is a duct through which gas is to be conveyed. It must be strong if it is to be exposed to pressure, or if it runs the chance of coming in collision with the person, as do standard lights in public buildings. The main part of a gas-branch is the tube or pipe which is to convey the gas, but this may be supported in many ways, as by such buttress-like brackets as in the candelabrum shown in Fig. 168; and if there are branch tubes for several lights, these may well be connected with the central tube, not only by their own attachment, but by brackets of some sort, or with one another by some connecting parts. Whether the gas-branch be pendent or standard, this mode of strengthening the tube-work should be employed, for the tubes themselves are but slightly held together, and by pressure being brought to bear upon them, a dangerous and expensive escape of gas may result.

In the manufacture of gaseliers one or two of the smaller Birmingham houses have certainly distinguished themselves by the production of works both beautiful and true; and these lead me to think that a better day is dawning for Birmingham, in which its art shall be exalted rather than degraded, and shall be such as will win to it the esteem of the world rather than call forth the execrations of art-loving people.

As to the colouring of iron I can say little. In my judgment the best modes of colouring metals were originated by Mr. Skidmore of Coventry, of whom I have before spoken. His theory is this, that metals are best coloured by the tints of their oxides. When a metal, especially brass, is seen in a furnace in a molten condition, the flames, where the oxygen of the atmosphere is uniting with the vapour of the metal, present the most resplendent tints. The same thing in a lesser degree occurs in the case of iron, but here the colours are less brilliant, and are more tertiary in character. Mr. Skidmore applies to a metal the colours seen in the flames of the furnace where it melts. Without attempting to limit the colourist to any theory whereby his ideas might be restricted, I must say that Skidmore's colouring of the metals is very good.

CHAPTER IX.

STAINED GLASS.

From early times it has been customary to colour glass. To the ancient Egyptians a method of forming glass of various tints was known, and by producing a mass of glass consisting of variously coloured pieces vitreously united, and cutting this into slices, they, in a costly and laborious manner, produced a sort of stained glass which might have been employed for the sides of lanterns or other purposes. The Greeks were acquainted with a similar process, and bowls formed in this manner by them are common in our museums.

Soon after the re-discovery of glass in our own country, methods of colouring it were sought, and cathedral windows were formed, which were of such beauty, and were so thoroughly fitted to answer the end of their creation, that little or no improvement upon these early works has even yet been made, and much of the decorative glass which we now produce is far inferior to them as regards design, colour, and mode of treatment.

A window must fulfil two purposes—it must keep out rain, wind, and cold, and must admit light; having fulfilled these ends, it may be beautiful.

If a window commands a lovely view let it, if possible, be formed of but few sheets (if not very large, of one sheet) of plate-glass; for the works of God are more worthy of contemplation, with their ever-changing beauty, than the works of man; but if the window commands only a mass of bricks and mortar inartistically arranged, let it, if possible, be formed of coloured glass having beauty of design manifested by the arrangement of its parts. A window should never appear as a picture with parts treated in light and shade. The foreshortening of the parts, and all perspective treatments, are best avoided, as far as possible. I do not say that the human figure, the lower animals, and plants must not be delineated upon window glass, for, on the contrary, they may be so treated as not only to be beautiful, but also to be a consistent decoration of glass; but this I do say, that many stained windows are utterly spoiled through the window being treated as a picture, and not as a protection from the weather and as a source of light.

If pictorially treated subjects are employed upon window glass, they should be treated very simply, and drawn in bold outline without shading, and the parts should be separated from each other by varying their colours. Thus, the flesh of a figure may be formed of glass having a pink tone; the robe of the figure of glass which is green, purple, or any other colour; a flower may be formed of white glass, or of glass of any colour; the leaves of green glass; and the sky background of blue glass. All the parts will thus be distinguished from each other by colour, and the distinction of part from part will be further enhanced by the strong black outline which bounds the parts and furnishes the drawing of the picture.

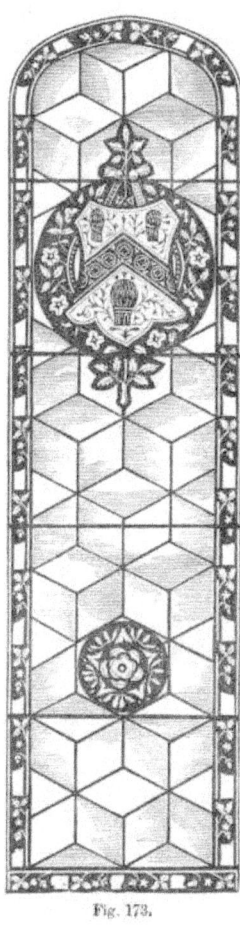

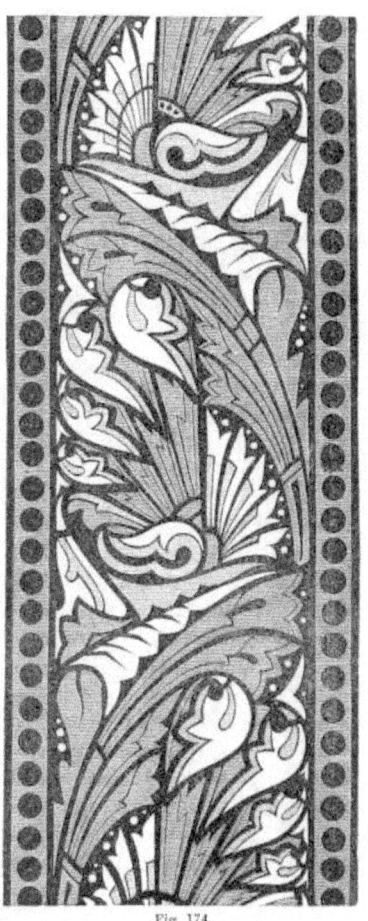

Fig. 173.   Fig. 174.

Strong colours should rarely be used in windows, as they retard the admission of light. Light is essential to our well-being; our health of body depends in a large measure upon the amount of light which falls upon the skin. Those wonderful chemical changes, in the absence of which there can be no life, in part, at least, depend upon the exposure of our bodies to light; let our windows, then, admit these life-giving rays. It must also be remembered that if light is not freely admitted to an apartment the colours of all the objects which it contains, and of its own decorations if it has any, are sacrificed, for in the absence of light there is no colour.

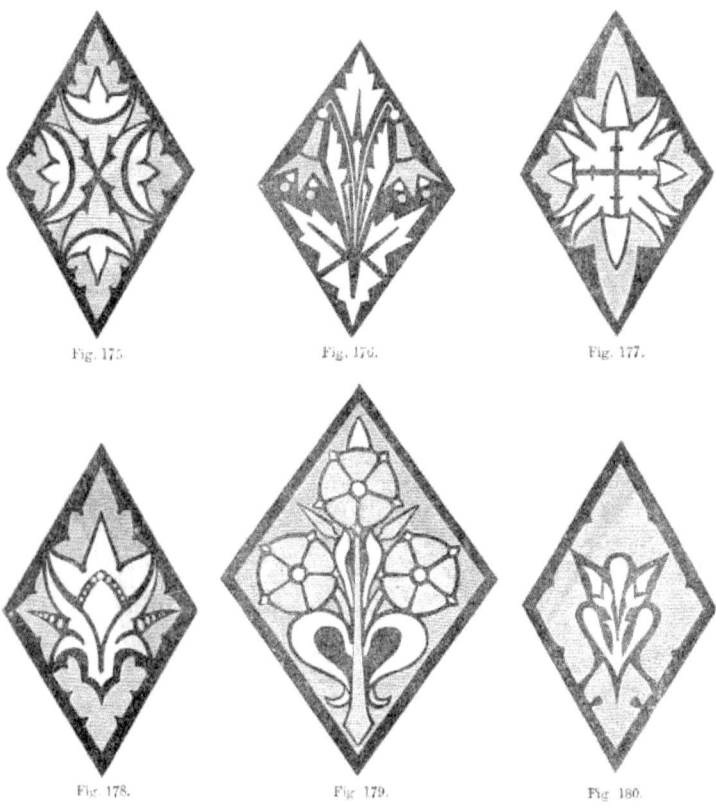

Fig. 175.   Fig. 176.   Fig. 177.

Fig. 178.   Fig. 179.   Fig. 180.

It is not necessary, in order to the production of a beautiful window, that much strong colour be used; tints of creamy yellow, pale amber, light tints of tertiary blue, blue-grey, olive, russet, and other sombre or delicate hues, if enlivened with small portions of ruby or other full colours, produce the most charming effects, and by their use we have consistent windows.

A good domestic window is often produced by armorial bearings in colour being placed on geometrically arranged tesseræ of slightly tinted glass. In some cases such an arrangement as this is highly desirable, for the room may thus get the benefit which a bit of colour will sometimes afford, and at the same time a pleasant view may be had through the uncoloured portion of the window. As an illustration of this class of window, we extract one from the catalogue of those excellent artists in stained glass, Messrs. Heaton, Butler, and Bayne, of Garrick Street (Fig. 173). A good window may also be formed by bordering a plain window with colour, (Fig. 174), or in place of the plain centre squares of glass may be used, each bearing a diaper pattern, as Figs. 175 to 182.

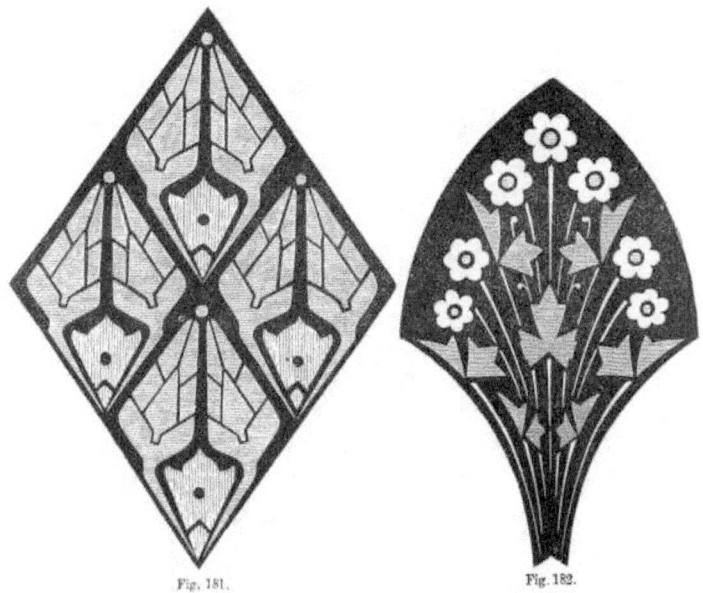

Fig. 181.   Fig. 182.

No architectural constructive feature should be introduced into a window—thus, an elaborate architectural canopy overshadowing a figure is not at all desirable. If a figure is formed of a perishable material, and stands on the outside of a building, it is well that it be protected from the rain by a canopy; but such a contrivance when introduced over a figure drawn on a flat window is absurd, being useless. Let us always consider what we have to do before we commence the formation of any ornamental article, and then seek to do it in the most simple, consistent, and beautiful manner. Figs. 183 and 184 represent my views of what stained glass may advantageously be.

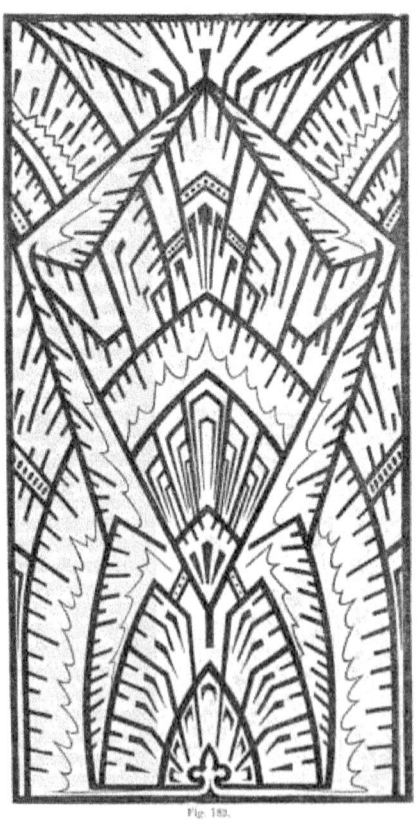

Fig. 183.

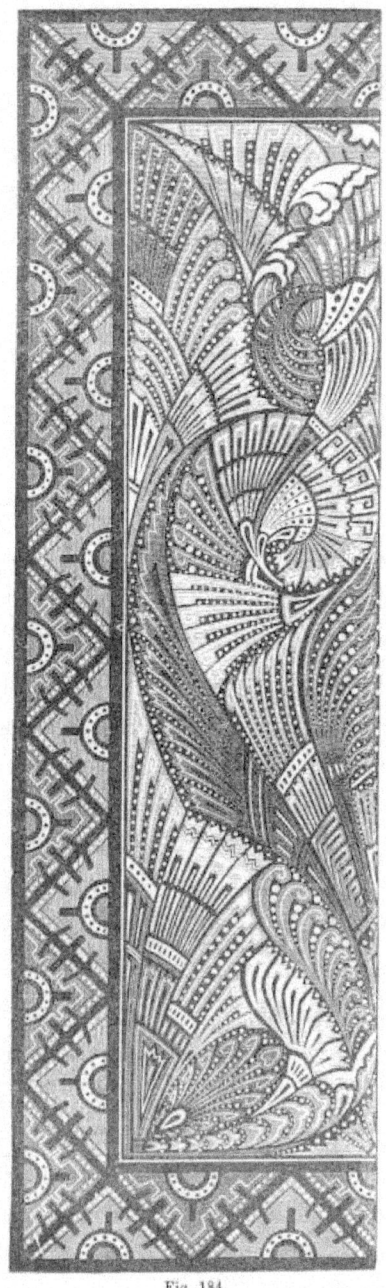

Fig. 184.

More than once in the course of these chapters I have protested in strong terms against pretence in art and art-decoration—the desire to make things appear to be made of better material or more costly substances than what they have in reality been wrought from—that leads men to paint and varnish a plain freestone mantelpiece in imitation of some expensive marble, or to make doors and window-shutters, skirting and panelling that the carpenter has fashioned out of red or yellow deal, assume the appearance of oak, or maple, or satinwood, by the deceptive skill of the grainer. In no case can the imitation ever approach a fair resemblance to the reality it is proposed to imitate. The coarse, rough grain of the soft freestone, which is incapable of receiving a polish, or rather of being polished until it becomes as smooth, and even, and lustrous as good glass, can never be made by successive coatings of paint and varnish to afford a satisfactory resemblance to the marble that it is supposed to represent, however carefully the cunning hand of the painter may have imitated the veins, and spots, and curious diversities of colour with which Nature has variegated the surface of the substance that he is endeavouring to copy. Nor, again, can a coarse-grained, soft wood, however skilled may be the hand that manipulates it, be treated so as to resemble the texture and smoothness of hard, close-grained wood, which from its very nature is capable of receiving the high polish that the softer material can never take if treated by the same process—that is, unless the expense of producing the imitation greatly exceeds the cost of the thing imitated. And what is applicable to the treatment of wood and stone is applicable also to the treatment of glass: for as a freestone mantelpiece, or deal door, however suitable and pleasing to the eye either may be when simply painted in the one case and varnished in the other to preserve the surface from the deteriorating influences of dirt of any kind, can never be made by the exercise of reasonable time and skill to present the appearance of marble or oak; so glass, by the application of colour rendered transparent by varnish, can never be brought to resemble glass stained or painted by the legitimate method, either in delicacy of tint, or depth, and richness, and brilliancy of colour. The greater part of the imitative stained glass, or "diaphanie" as it is styled, fails not only in colour, but in design; and in this indeed it may perhaps be said to be especially faulty. The designs, which are printed on paper, with the view of imitating glass patterns, err principally in being too elaborate, and in representing figures and scenery which are not in character or keeping with the designs that are usually represented in painted glass. If confined to simple diaper work, or borderings and heraldic emblems, as shown in Figs. 173 and 174, or patterns similar to that shown in Fig. 183, the artistic effect produced would be more satisfactory, although it can never equal genuine stained glass in depth of colour or purity of tone.

CHAPTER X.

CONCLUSION.

I have now treated of art as applied to our industrial manufactures, and have pointed out principles which must be recognisable in all art-works which pretend to merit. We have seen that material must in all cases be used in the simplest and most natural manner; that, wherever possible, we must avail ourselves of the friendly aid of natural forces;[29] that the most convenient shape must always be selected for a vessel or art-object of any kind; and that beauty must then be added to that which is useful. All art-objects must be useful and then beautiful; they must be utilitarian, and yet so graceful, so comely, that they shall be loved for their beauty as well as valued for their usefulness. While I have set forth those principles which must ever govern the application of ornament to useful articles, I cannot show the student any royal road to the attainment of art-knowledge. There is something in a true art-work which is too subtle for expression by words; there is a "quality" about an art-work, or the expression of an amount of "feeling," which cannot be described, yet which is so obvious as to be at once apparent to the trained eye.

The only way in which the power of appreciating art-qualities can be gained, especially if these qualities are of a subtle nature, is by the careful study of works of known excellence. Could the student visit our museums in company with a trained ornamentist, who would point out what was good and

---

[29] See chapters on glass and earthenware.

262

what was bad in art, he would soon learn, by studying the beautiful works, to perceive art-qualities; but as this is not possible to most, the learner must be content to consider each art-work with which he comes in contact in conjunction with the principles I have set forward.

Let him take a work—say a tea-pot. He will now ask himself—has the material of which it is formed been judiciously and simply used?—is the shape convenient?—is the handle properly applied, and does the spout bear a proper relation to the handle?—is the form graceful or vigorous?—is the curve which bounds the form of a subtle nature?—is the engraving applied in judicious quantities and in just proportions?—are the engraved forms beautiful, and such as do not suffer by being seen in perspective on a rounded surface? By such questions the student will inquire into the nature of whatever is presented to his consideration, and only by constantly making such inquiries, and seeking to answer them correctly, can he gain the knowledge which will enable him rightly to judge of the nature of art-works.

Some of these inquiries the young student will readily answer, with others he will have difficulty; for, his taste being yet uncultivated, he will not know whether a form is beautiful or not. Nevertheless, I say to the learner, try to answer these various inquiries as well as you can, and then note the shape of the object in a memorandum-book, and write your opinion respecting it in brief terms, and your reasons for your opinion. By thus noting your studies you gain many advantages; thus, you must frame your ideas with some degree of exactness when you have to put them into words, and exactness of idea is essential to your success. You can also refer to previous thoughts, and thus impress them upon the memory; and you can observe your progress, which is important, and should be encouraging. In order that you acquire the power of perceiving art-merit as quickly as possible, you must study those works in which examples of bad taste are rarely met with, you must at first consider art-objects from India, Persia, China, and Japan, as well as examples of ancient art from Egypt and Greece. But in selecting modern works from the East, choose those which are not altogether new if possible.

During the last ten years the art-works of Japan have deteriorated to a lamentable extent. Contact with Europeans unfortunately brings about the deterioration of Eastern art: in order that the European demand be met, quantity is produced and quality disregarded, for we cavil respecting price, and yet by thus creating a demand for inferior work we raise the price even of that which is comparatively bad, and soon have to pay for the coarser wares a price for which superior articles could at first be procured.

But this should be noted: that the commonest wares which we receive from Japan and India are never utterly bad in art. Inharmonious colouring does not appear to be produced by these nations, and the same may be said of Persia and China, and, to an extent, of Morocco and Algeria, the only exceptions being where European influence has been long continued. In selecting examples for study you may almost rely upon the beauty of all works from China, Japan, Persia, and India, which have not been produced under European influence.

A notable example of the deteriorating influence of European taste (perhaps chiefly English taste) upon Eastern art is apparent if we examine old carved sandalwood boxes from India, and those which are now sent to us from the same country; the quiet, unobtrusive consistency of the ornament by which it was sought only to enrich a properly constructed box was not sufficiently attractive to suit European (or English?) taste. The ornament must be more pronounced and in higher relief, and the entire work must be more attractive—more vulgarly attractive I might say, and thus the exquisite refinement of the older works is sacrificed to the wants of a rich but vulgar people, whose taste for art is infinitely below that of their conquered brethren, from whom they learn the principles of a beautiful art but slowly, while they do much to destroy the refinement of art-taste which the workmen of our Eastern empire appear to inherit. Study the works of the Eastern nations in conjunction with the remarks which I made in my first chapter , and then consider the numerous objects left to us by the early Egyptians and Greeks, and bear in mind while viewing them what we have said on Egyptian and Greek art, and after having learned to understand the merits of Persian, Japanese, Indian, and Chinese art, and of that of the ancient Egyptians and Greeks, you may commence to consider other styles, taking up the study of Italian and Renaissance art in its various forms last of all; for in these styles, or dialects of a style if I may thus speak, there is so much that is false in structure, false in representation, untruthful in expression, and pictorial rather than ornamental in effect, that a very complete acquaintance with ornamental art is necessary in order that all the defects of these styles be apparent, and in order that the student avoid falling into the error of regarding a pictorial effect as the result of a true style of ornamental art.

Study, when accompanied by individual thought, is the means whereby art-knowledge will be gained. No mere looking at works which are beautiful and true will make a great ornamentist. He who would attain to great knowledge must *study* whatever commends itself to him as worthy of his attention, and, above all, must think much upon the works which he contemplates; it is the evidence of mind—not of degraded but of noble mind, of refined mind, of cultivated mind, of well-informed mind, of mind which has knowledge, of mind which has vigour, of mind which is fresh and new— that we find impressed upon a work and giving to it value. While we, as art-students, have, above all things, to attain to cultivation of the mind, we cannot give expression to refined feelings manifested in form unless we can draw, and draw almost faultlessly; and the ability to draw with accuracy, power, and feeling can only result from much practice.

Let every spare moment, then, find the sketch-book in your hand, and be constantly trying to draw both carefully, neatly, and with exactness and finish, such objects as you see around you, even if examples of good art-works are not at hand; for by constant and careful practice you can alone acquire the necessary power of expressing refined thought in refined form. Avoid making hasty sketches. When a finished artist, you can afford to make sketch memoranda; but till you can draw with great power, energy, truthfulness, and refinement, let your every drawing be as careful and as finished in character, however simple the object portrayed, as though your welfare in life depended upon its character, for upon every sketch your future position does, to a great extent, depend. The habit of careful painstaking should sedulously be cultivated; and with every drawing thus made an amount of power is gained which the making of a hundred careless sketches would not afford. Let painstaking, then, be characteristic of your working.

Ornament of some kind is applied to almost every article that we see around us. The papers on our walls, the carpets on our floors, the hangings at our windows, the plates from which we eat, are all covered by patterns of some kind; yet it is rare, even now when ornamentation has become general, to find anything original in ornament; and if we do meet with something new in kind it is often feeble or timid-looking, if it does not altogether fail to impress us with the idea that the producer was a man of knowledge. Let the reader be assured that if the designer is a man of knowledge, his ornamental compositions will never fail to reveal his learning; that if he is a man of power, his works will reveal his strength of character; if he is a man of refined feelings, that his designs will manifest his tenderness of perception. In like manner, if a man is ignorant he cannot withhold from his patterns the manifestation of his ignorance. Did not the Egyptians express their power of character in their ornaments? did not the Greeks manifest their refinement in the forms which they drew? do we not even find an expression of religious feeling strongly, yea, impressively, set forth by some art-works, as by the illuminated manuscripts of the early Middle Ages? and do we not every day see the impress of the ignorant upon certain wall-papers, carpets, and other things? It is a fact, and it is necessary that we fully recognise it, that the knowledge of the producer is manifested by his works; and that the ignorance of the ignorant is also manifested in his works.

If ornament is produced having new characters, it is often feeble, and is generally without grace; while power is the expression of manliness, and grace of refinement. Without claiming to have made a successful effort, I put forth, in the frontispiece to this volume (Plate I.), four of my studies in original ornament, all of which are to me more or less satisfactory as studies in composition. I have endeavoured to secure in each an amount of energy, vigour—the power of life, yet at the same time to avoid coarseness, or any glaring want of refinement. I have sought to combine right lines, which are expressive of power, with such curved shapes as shall, with them, produce a pleasing contrast of form, and express a certain amount of grace. In the light ornament on the citrine ground (that at the lower left-hand corner of our plate) I have endeavoured especially to secure an expression of grace in combination with that amount of energy which avoids any expression of feebleness.

In the border ornament I have introduced the arch form, as it hints at a structural "setting out" which is pleasant; and I have endeavoured to cause the composition to appear as though it rested on the lower dotted band, as this gives a feeling of security. I do not say that it is necessary that this be so: all I assert is that in some cases it gives a feeling of satisfaction.

So far as I know, the colouring is also original. The colours employed are chiefly of a tertiary character, but small masses of primary or secondary colours are employed in order to impart "life" to the composition.

I do not set these studies before my readers with the idea of showing them what original ornament should be: I only set them forth as examples of new compositions, and must leave each to clothe his own thoughts with a befitting expression of his individual original ideas.

As I am writing for the working man, as well as for others, will he pardon me reminding him that we are called to exercise an art, yet at the same time our art is associated with the scientific professions—a knowledge of natural sciences, of botany, zoology, natural philosophy, and chemistry can be very fully utilised in our art—and that we should, therefore, act as professional men and as artists of the highest rank; for thereby only can we hope to place our calling in that position of esteem in which it should be held, and must be held, by the people at large, if we are to administer to their pleasure as we ought.

In taking leave of my reader, let me say that if I personally can aid him in any way, I shall be glad to do so. If any who really seek knowledge of decorative design, and are hard workers, choose to send me designs for criticism or comment, or desire any other aid that I can give them, I shall be happy to do what little I can for them. My address will be found at the end of the Preface.

www.ingramcontent.com/pod-product-compliance
Lightning Source LLC
Chambersburg PA
CBHW051446170526
45166CB00001B/136